The Politics of Radioactive Waste Management

Environmental concerns have pushed the decarbonisation of the European economy high on the EU political agenda. This has renewed old debates about the role of nuclear energy in the European economy and society that gravitate around the issues of nuclear safety and radioactive waste management (RWM). RWM carries many elements of technical complexity, scientific uncertainty and social value, which makes policy decisions highly controversial. Public participation is usually believed to improve these decisions, ease their implementation by solving substantial conflicts, and enhance trust and social acceptance.

Drawing upon sources including Euratom and the OECD Nuclear Energy Agency, the author offers a detailed overview of public involvement in RWM in the EU, analysing the implementation of national policies through official programmes and the views of stakeholders from all Member States. This book highlights the key successes and challenges in the quest for greater participation in RWM, and extrapolates insights for other contested energy infrastructures and controversies in land use.

This book will be of great relevance to students, scholars and practitioners with an interest in radioactive waste management, energy policy, and EU environmental politics and policy.

Gianluca Ferraro is a policy analyst. He has worked for the European Commission and the University of Leuven, Belgium

Routledge Studies in Waste Management and Policy

Waste Prevention Policy and Behaviour
New approaches to reducing waste generation and its environmental impacts
Ana Paula Bortoleto

Decision-making and Radioactive Waste Disposal
Andrew Newman and Gerry Nagtzaam

Nuclear Waste Politics
An Incrementalist Perspective
Matthew Cotton

The Politics of Radioactive Waste Management
Public Involvement and Policy-Making in the European Union
Gianluca Ferraro

For more information about this series, please visit: https://www.routledge.com/Routledge-Studies-in-Waste-Management-and-Policy/book-series/RSWMP

The Politics of Radioactive Waste Management

Public Involvement and Policy-Making in the European Union

Gianluca Ferraro

LONDON AND NEW YORK

First published 2019
by Routledge
2 Park Square, Milton Park, Abingdon, Oxon OX14 4RN

and by Routledge
52 Vanderbilt Avenue, New York, NY 10017

First issued in paperback 2020

Routledge is an imprint of the Taylor & Francis Group, an informa business

British Library Cataloguing in Publication Data
A catalogue record for this book is available from the British Library

Library of Congress Cataloging in Publication Data
Names: Ferraro, Gianluca, 1975- author.
Title: The politics of radioactive waste management : public involvement and policy-making in the European Union / Gianluca Ferraro.
Description: Abingdon, Oxon ; New York, NY : Routledge is an imprint of the Taylor & Francis Group, an Informa Business, 2019. |
Series: Routledge studies in waste management and policy |
Includes bibliographical references and index.
Identifiers: LCCN 2018029139 (print) | LCCN 2018033864 (ebook) |
ISBN 9781315452937 (Master) | ISBN 9781315452920 (Adobe Reader) |
ISBN 9781315452913 (ePub) | ISBN 9781315452906 (Mobipocket unencrypted) |
ISBN 9781138211483 (hbk) | ISBN 9781315452937 (ebk)
Subjects: LCSH: Radioactive wastes–Government policy–European Union countries. | Radioactive wastes–Management–Political aspects–European Union countries.
Classification: LCC TD898.14.G68 (ebook) | LCC TD898.14.G68 F47 2019 (print) | DDC 363.17/996094–dc23LC record available at https://lccn.loc.gov/2018029139

ISBN 13: 978-0-367-58334-7 (pbk)
ISBN 13: 978-1-138-21148-3 (hbk)

Typeset in Sabon
by Taylor & Francis Books

Contents

List of illustrations vi
Foreword vii
Preface ix
Abbreviations xi

Introduction 1

1 Nuclear energy and the management of radioactive waste 18

2 Public involvement in policy-making 39

3 The institutional challenge, key issues and stakeholders' needs 59

4 General principles for public involvement 77

5 National practices of public involvement 98

6 The involvement of local stakeholders 118

7 Public involvement, trust and social acceptance 137

8 Public involvement in RWM: answers and implications 153

Conclusions 173

Index 180

Illustrations

Figures

1.1 Nuclear energy: major trends and events 19
2.1 Objectives of public involvement in policy-making 43
2.2 Analytical framework 49
3.1 Distribution of responses per category of stakeholders 61
3.2 Emergent themes 65
5.1 Instruments for public involvement in RWM across the EU 102
6.1 Actors involved in the implementation process 119
7.1 Public involvement, trust and social acceptance 138
8.1 Public involvement: instruments, resources and objectives 160

Tables

0.1 Research questions 10
2.1 Citizens, public and stakeholders 41
2.2 Benefits and costs of public involvement 44
4.1 Euratom projects on public involvement in RWM 79
4.2 General principles for public involvement in RWM 81
4.3 Combined table 92
5.1 The right of public information and participation in national legislations 99
5.2 Summary table 114
6.1 Summary table (central and local perspectives) 132
7.1 RWM and trust: confidence factors 141

Foreword

I am delighted that Gianluca Ferraro has asked me to provide a few words of introduction to this interesting and timely book. I got to know Gianluca while he was still working at the Joint Research Centre of the European Commission, when we collaborated on a review of the issues of social acceptance facing the wind energy sector in Europe. This highlighted that, although there is an abundance of wind resource in Europe and highly successful technical expertise and economically supportive financial regimes, wind energy is still not contributing to the European energy mix as much as it could. Although there are complex drivers to this, it highlights that the adoption of any innovation, be it technical, social or even financial, relies ultimately on its acceptance by society.

In the case of wind energy, deep and sometimes unfounded concerns by potential host communities act as factors in delaying projects, increasing costs and introducing an element of risk that some developers would prefer to avoid, despite the dire need for us to expand our renewable base as soon as possible to respond to the potential calamities of climate change. In this context, and in many countries, the level of social acceptance has perhaps become the limiting factor in the expansion of wind energy. Developers, governments and regulators appear poorly equipped to respond, and instead often resort to suggestions that these unhelpful communities are irrational, selfish and somehow "deviant" – exemplified by using the NIMBY (Not In My Backyard) label – which then just entrenches more distrust and makes the context for future developments even more adversarial.

Clearly this poses a very real danger for how we deal with the focus of this book, radioactive waste management (RWM), where the risks are potentially many more times significant for health, stigma and long-term prospects for a host community.

Gianluca provides a stimulating and valuable guide to how the public are involved in RWM, which is one of the most challenging, wicked and unresolved public policy problems we face in the field of energy management. We are in desperate need of low carbon generating capacity and many countries have looked to the nuclear industry to provide this. While it appears to be a functionally attractive form of energy, the issue of radioactive waste (and of course, siting of new projects) has created a situation that many European countries continue to struggle with. As Gianluca notes, a commonly deployed strategy has often been to "Decide Announce Defend" when it comes to dealing with RWM, but this rarely results in an effective solution and tends to exacerbate the tensions around this sensitive issue.

He also makes clear that there is no technical fix that can resolve the issues of RWM, which ultimately rests on issues of trust and values. As such, as a public policy problem, it challenges us to find novel ways of framing, new forms of knowledge and deliberation, and even innovative approaches to governance in order to explore potential solutions. This all aligns with the broader paradigm of post-normative forms of investigation that appear better equipped to unlocking wicked problems than more conventional approaches to policy-making and demands effective engagement with the public.

Gianluca describes and provides a rich guide to the various methods that have been deployed across Europe to ensure public involvement with RWM decisions, in an attempt to nurture trust and unlock innovative solutions. From this, he is able to establish key principles for public engagement, make far-reaching recommendations for policy at international, national and sub-national levels, as well as setting out an agenda for future research.

However, this book does have much greater salience than just for providing a space to discuss RWM in the EU, as its insights can justifiably apply to many challenging issues of environmental governance, in many parts of the world. In so doing, it highlights that the broader project of sustainable development should be as much about creating new forms of governance and knowledge as ensuring we respect local and global environmental limits. Indeed, the two aspects are intrinsically linked, and Gianluca provides many valuable insights in to how this can be achieved.

Geraint Ellis
School of Natural and Built Environment,
Queen's University, Belfast

Preface

Radioactive materials are used in many activities of our modern societies, from the production of electricity through nuclear power to multiple applications in research, medicine and industry. The radioactive waste (RW) generated by these activities constitutes an important public problem that governments need to manage with political caution as well as technical accuracy. The management of RW constitutes a highly political item on many national agendas. In Europe, the salience of radioactive waste management (RWM) has been fully acknowledged by the European Union (EU) and a Directive was adopted in 2011 for the management of RW and spent fuel (SF) (i.e. Council Directive 2011/70/Euratom). The Directive also stresses the involvement of the public as key in the development and execution of national policies for RWM.

Public opposition has often slowed down or blocked national programmes for the storage and disposal of RW. In particular, attempts to develop solutions for the deep geological disposal (DGD) of high-level waste (HLW) have met strong public reactions mainly in the localities directly (or potentially) impacted by the siting of these facilities. Public involvement has, thus, been assumed as a fundamental condition for a less conflictual management of RW, although it is not often clear to all actors involved from the national to the local level what it means in practice. The use of public involvement varies according to the context where it is applied; the same understanding of the concept largely depends on national cultural and institutional traditions.

However, several European initiatives have produced an important amount of knowledge on the topic of public involvement in RWM. These initiatives include projects of social research funded by the European Commission (EC) under the Euratom Framework Programmes (FPs) and the multiple debates hosted within the EU, for instance through the European Nuclear Energy Forum (ENEF). With a broader geographical scope, the Nuclear Energy Agency (NEA) of the OECD has also hosted important discussions in the framework of the work conducted by its Forum on Stakeholder Confidence (FSC).

Coming from the Social Sciences and, more precisely, from the academic discipline of Public Policy, I was exposed to this fascinating topic during my work as a European civil servant at the Joint Research Centre (JRC) of the EC. The book does not have the ambition of covering all that is known about public involvement in RWM and it aims at providing an insight on the subject from the specific perspective of the policy science. The interpretations and opinions contained in the book are solely those of the author.

The time spent at the JRC was a unique experience due to the people I was privileged to work with. I am grateful to the colleagues that I met at one moment or another of my experience at the EC, particularly those with whom I worked on a daily basis; Ulrik von Estorff, César Chenel Ramos and Maria Stergiopoulou, thank you.

Many more people – within and outside the JRC – have provided me with important inputs during my work on public involvement in RWM. I am very thankful to Samuel Young and Robert Langmuir for their help during data collection and perseverance in the contact with stakeholders across the EU; to Annabarbara Friedrich and Meritxell Martell for their useful contribution at different points of the data analysis; to Marleen Brans and Jan Van Damme for their support in the re-organisation of some material.

Finally, I would like to thank Michele Altomonte, Flavia Gangale, Eleonora Guidi and Elena Lai for their comments on earlier versions of the various chapters. Tim Gillmair, thank you for your support in the last stage of the preparation of this book.

The book is dedicated to these people, to those who inspired it and to the many social scientists who adventure in technical territories. The political and social sciences must help in reframing the technological and environmental challenges of our era from technical and physical into socio-political problems.

Abbreviations

DG	Directorate-General
DGD	Deep Geological Disposal
DG ENER	Directorate-General for Energy
DG RTD	Directorate-General for Research and Innovation
EC	European Commission
EIA	Environmental Impact Assessment
ENEF	European Nuclear Energy Forum
EU	European Union
Euratom	European Atomic Energy Community
FP	Framework Programme
FSC	Forum on Stakeholder Confidence
GHG	Greenhouse Gas
GMF	Group of European Municipalities with Nuclear Facilities
HLW	High-Level Waste
IAEA	International Atomic Energy Agency
ILW	Intermediate-Level Waste
IPCC	Intergovernmental Panel on Climate Change
LLW	Low-Level Waste
LULUs	Locally Unwanted Land Uses
JRC	Joint Research Centre
MS	Member State
NEA	Nuclear Energy Agency
NGO	Non-Governmental Organisation
NIMBY	Not In My Back Yard
NP	National Programme
NPP	Nuclear Power Plant
NSA	National Safety Authority
OECD	Organisation for Economic Co-operation and Development
RW	Radioactive Waste
RWM	Radioactive Waste Management
SEA	Strategic Environmental Assessment

SF	Spent Fuel
UNECE	United Nations Economic Commission for Europe
WMO	Waste Management Organisation
WNA	World Nuclear Association

Introduction

Public policies have traditionally been the responsibility of public authorities. In those policy areas where public problems have presented high levels of scientific or technical complexity, public authorities have also relied on the additional inputs of scientific and technical experts (Dietz & Stern 2008). This has happened, for instance, for environmental policies; the environmental field is notoriously affected by the complexity of natural phenomena and knowledge gaps due to insufficient or inadequate data (Dietz & Stern 2008). In Western representative democracies, citizens have usually influenced public policies through the electoral vote: they choose, through elections, which political parties will have a parliamentary majority and govern a country[1] (Beierle & Cayford 2002; Creighton 2005; Thomas 2012).

However, during the last decades, citizens have gained more direct influence on collective decisions affecting their lives through public involvement in policy-making (Michels & De Graaf 2010). In many areas of governmental action, public policies have ceased to be decided and executed by national governments and legislatures only and become the product of interactions among a multitude of actors that includes economic and social actors as well state organisations. In the context of this radical change from government to governance, forms of participative democracy have developed across many policy areas. The involvement of multiple societal interests in policy-making has been particularly strong in the environmental field.

Public involvement can occur in several moments of policy-making: citizens can take part in the formulation, enactment and implementation of public policies (Parry *et al.* 1992). The academic political and policy literature has dedicated great attention to public involvement during the legislative process with many studies investigating the lobbying activities of interest groups aimed at influencing elected officials in the formulation of national policies[2] (Beierle & Cayford 2002; Creighton 2005; Thomas 2012; West 2005). Public involvement during policy implementation has been less studied, although it has been acknowledged as critical for the success of public policies. Indeed, opposition to many policies tends to increase at this stage, during the execution of policy objectives, when decisions contained in national laws are implemented through rules, regulations, programmes, plans, projects and other activities (Lee *et al.* 2013).

The book looks at public involvement in policy-making by focusing on policy implementation and the opportunities that citizens and other stakeholders have to influence administrative decision-making and the executive functions that are delegated by governments to public agencies. Public administrations do not simply execute decisions taken by elected representatives; they play a key role in the success or failure of public policies through the issuing of delegated legislation, the management of governmental programmes and the delivery of services (Kerwin & Furlong 2011; Thomas 1995). Public involvement is crucial for environmental policies particularly during policy implementation when diverging views among the actors involved become manifest (Beierle & Cayford 2002).

Within the broad area of environmental policy, the book investigates public involvement in the specific domain of radioactive waste management (RWM). The topic of RWM spans across two policy areas: energy and environment. RWM deals with the final part of the cycle of fuel used to produce nuclear energy – indeed, its waste – but has a considerable environmental component since it can have serious environmental, as well social, impacts. The primary objective of RWM is, thus, the protection of human health and the environment.

RWM is a relevant topic because of its centrality in the whole debate about the nuclear option to produce energy for a low-carbon society. Indeed, environmental concerns have pushed the decarbonisation of the European economy high on the political agenda of the European Union (EU). This has renewed an old debate about the role of nuclear energy in European economy and society that gravitates around the issues of nuclear safety and RWM. Furthermore, RWM brings with itself elements of technical complexity, scientific uncertainty and emotive nature, which converge all together in policy-making and make it highly controversial and politically relevant.

Public involvement is generally expected to improve public decisions, solve substantial conflicts and, ultimately, benefit the development of new policies by easing their implementation. Therefore, reliance on more participatory practices might deflate the tensions around RWM policies. Understanding the salience of public involvement in RWM in the EU has great importance especially now that a Directive (i.e. Directive Euratom/2011/70 or "Waste Directive" of 2011) has established a community framework for the responsible and safe management of spent fuel (SF) and radioactive waste (RW) generated by civilian activities. The Waste Directive recommends that national policies for RWM have to be based on public information and participation. All Member States (MSs) are expected to comply with the Directive, whether they produce nuclear energy or not. Although an important source of RW is the SF originating from power production, RW is also generated by many industrial, medical and research activities, and the decommissioning of nuclear facilities.

The chapter introduces the topic of public involvement in RWM and frames it in the broader context of environmental governance. It does so by briefly explaining the relevance of the topic for controversial hazardous facilities, contested infrastructures and, more generally, (unwanted) land uses. The chapter also presents the legal framework that governs public information and participation in environmental matters internationally and in the EU. The clarification of the purpose of the book and the presentation of its structure conclude this introductory chapter.

Public involvement in environmental matters

Environmental policy-making is populated by disputes of facts and values. Disputes of facts are the direct consequence of the scientific uncertainties and technical complexity that affect this policy area. Disputes of values originate from the diverse belief systems of the actors involved. Environmental decisions are not only scientific and technical, but also political, social, cultural and economic (Dietz & Stern 2008). Therefore, environmental policy-makers must combine science and public involvement so that public decisions are informed by the best available scientific knowledge and take into account the preferences of the affected parties. The traditional way of making policies – based on pure technical arguments with only minimal public involvement – can lead to societal opposition and the failure of governmental policies and initiatives (Dietz & Stern 2008).

Public involvement in environmental policy-making has become particularly relevant in the second half of the twentieth century under the pressure of a growing societal awareness, the environmental movement and the development of international policy initiatives (Aldrich 2005; Beierle & Cayford 2002; Mann & Jeanneaux 2009). National governments have, indeed, adopted various instruments at the international level – such as agreements, conventions, protocols, declarations, etc. – to promote environmental governance (Blomgren Bingham *et al.* 2005). An increasing number of governments in the Western world have also committed to (more) public involvement in national public policies. However, the rhetorical call for more public participation in environmental policy-making has not always been followed by the practice. Despite formal commitments, national institutions and public officials from many countries do not always allow citizens adequate engagement and influence in policy choices (Depoe & Delicath 2004).

Environmental policy stretches over a broad spectrum of topics and issues that go from the management of natural resources to climate change, from pollution to the use of public land for multiple purposes. The result is that a variety of environmental policy-making contexts exist (Depoe & Delicath 2004). The book focuses on the strand of environmental policy that has to do with land use, particularly for the purpose of siting and developing contested infrastructures and controversial hazardous facilities such as the ones developed and operated for the management of RW.

Land use and locally unwanted land uses

Within the environmental policy field, land use represents a dominant topic in the literature addressing public involvement (Mann & Jeanneaux 2009). Public involvement in land use has been studied for specific economic activities, such as the mining industry (e.g., Hilson 2002), and a wide range of infrastructures[3] and facilities. Examples span from urban planning to transport and energy, and include a very long list of projects: social housing, hospitals, prisons, motorways, bridges, ports, tunnels, railways, rapid transit lines, power transmission lines, hydro-electric dams, wind farms, oil refineries, pipelines, nuclear power plants (NPPs), etc. (Boholm & Löfstedt 2004; Bollens 1993; Huizar 2011).

These projects are usually meant to drive societal and territorial change, and their execution has generally improved the life of many people. However, many of these infrastructures and facilities have also had important side effects (i.e. externalities) for the quality of life, particularly of local residents, in terms of smell, noise, ugliness, pollution, hazard and risks[4] for human health and the environment (Armour 1991; Boholm & Löfstedt 2004).

While the benefits generated by these infrastructures and facilities are usually broadly distributed, their costs are concentrated locally (Aldrich 2005). Often, externalities like environmental impact and risk are disproportionately concentrated on local communities that are already disadvantaged such as poor communities or racial minorities (Weingart 2007). The uneven distribution of benefits and costs creates a feeling of injustice; this has caused such a strong local opposition to many of these facilities and infrastructures that they have been named "locally unwanted land uses" (LULUs) (Armour 1991; Bollens 1993; Popper 1981). The strong local conflicts accompanying LULUs have often resulted in delays and the halting of many national public projects (Aldrich 2005; Armour 1991).

As a direct consequence of the conflictual nature of LULUs, it has become clear that greater attention has to be given to their social aspect (Armour 1991). In particular, public involvement of local communities and the general public in the decision-making around specific projects has emerged as an important mechanism for conflict resolution and social acceptance (Breukers & Wolsink 2007; Hilson 2002; Jobert *et al.* 2007; Walker *et al.* 2011; Wolsink 2000). Participative approaches have, thus, become an important strategy for land use decision-making (Mann & Jeanneaux 2009). As explained by Armour,

> people who feel that they have not been given the opportunity to become fully informed, to have their concerns listened to, and to exercise what they feel to be their basic democratic rights are not very likely to accept siting recommendations and decisions regardless of how substantively-sound such decisions may be.
>
> (Armour 1991: 24)

Hazardous facilities

Relevant cases of LULUs are hazardous facilities such as those used for the treatment of waste (e.g., incinerators) or the disposal of potentially noxious waste (e.g., chemicals and RW). Like all LULUs, hazardous (or noxious) facilities imply externalities that are concentrated locally. In addition, they bring with themselves an element of risk that is disproportionately born by a local community compared to the national territory.

Because of the hazard and risk that they entail, these facilities have attracted even stronger opposition than non-hazardous LULUs from the local communities designated to host them (Hayden Lesbirel 2005; Kasperson 2005; Kuhn & Ballard 1998; Shaw 2005). Despite the fact that the community of experts (or epistemic community) may agree that a given well-designed and well-managed facility poses limited risks, host communities and publics may have a different risk perception (Armour 1991).

Kuhn and Ballard (1998) notice that hostility often amplifies under the perception of risk rather than the real risk itself. In particular, certain types of facilities, such as those used for chemicals and RW, are commonly associated with high risk in public perception. The resulting public opposition to hazardous facilities has often caused policy impasses in many countries, with disagreements, conflicts and delays surrounding their siting and development. The social resistance has obvious political repercussions and stands as a major policy challenge in all democratic nations.

In this context, new approaches for general land uses, and LULUs and hazardous facilities, in particular, must be explored (Hayden Lesbirel 2005; Kasperson 2005). The traditional hierarchical approach based on "decide, announce and defend" (also shortened as DAD) was a top-down process where sites were selected on the basis of sound and unbiased technical criteria of safety and health protection. It resulted in an imposed decision on the prospective host community accompanied by a process of defence of the project aimed at demonstrating the environmental and technical credibility of the decision (Kasperson 2005; Kuhn & Ballard 1998). In the light of general social distrust and specific local opposition resulting from the top-down (DAD) approach, an open and voluntary approach has become the new paradigm because of its capacity to ease potential and actual socio-political conflicts around the siting of a facility. Key components of this approach are: transparency, information, consultation, communities' referenda, participation, partnership and right of withdrawal from a project at any time (Kasperson 2005; Kuhn & Ballard 1998).

Radioactive waste management

The general trend of moving from a coercive to a more collaborative institutional approach is evident also in RWM in many Western countries. RWM has always been considered as a highly technical domain. Its social and political implications have been neglected for long time despite their importance (Kraft 2000; NEA 2012d). However, over the last decades, public involvement has emerged as a necessary component of RWM and many initiatives have been taken to develop, implement and evaluate participatory practices.

Public resistance against RWM projects has grown over the last decades and has concerned any type of RW – with low, intermediate or high levels of radioactivity. Delays and stalls in several RWM projects due to public (mainly local) opposition have been common feature for many MSs of the EU since the 1980s. (Similar developments can be seen also outside the EU, in countries that fall, though, outside the scope of the book.) The technocratic and elitist approach where policy-makers and experts decide, announce and defend has revealed its weakness. Faced with recurrent policy failures, many MSs have started to adopt a more participatory approach to RWM. The same EU has established a new legal framework with the adoption of Council's Directive 2011/70/Euratom that is expected to mark a participatory turn in the way RWM is dealt with in the EU.

The international and EU legal framework for public involvement in environmental matters

The attention on public involvement that has characterised the environmental debate in recent years has determined important legal developments internationally, at both global and EU level (Lee *et al.* 2013; Luyet *et al.* 2012). This section does not attempt to cover all agreements, conventions and legislative acts that deal with public involvement and the environmental field. It briefly presents the major international instruments that have promoted the principle of public involvement in environmental matters and have relevance for nuclear energy and RWM. Environmental law has, indeed, expanded in recent years and included a growing number of areas including nuclear energy. This was mainly due to the environmental impact that nuclear activities may have. The overlap between environmental law and nuclear energy has, thus, resulted in developments in environmental policy that are also important for the nuclear field (NEA 2012d).

An interesting example is the application of two environmental conventions (i.e. Aarhus and Espoo Convention) and two EU Directives on environmental impact to nuclear activities, including RWM; these documents are:

- Convention on Access to Information, Public Participation in Decision-Making and Access to Justice in Environmental Matters (or "Aarhus Convention");
- Convention on Environmental Impact Assessment in a Transboundary Context (or "Espoo Convention");
- Directive 2001/42/EC on the assessment of the effects of certain plans and programmes on the environment (or Strategic Environmental Assessment Directive);
- Directive 2014/52/EU amending Directive 2011/92/EU on the assessment of the effects of certain public and private projects on the environment (or Environmental Impact Assessment Directive).

The international legal framework

Environmental governance has been promoted internationally since the UN Rio Declaration on Environment and Development of 1992. In particular, Principle 10 of the Declaration states:

> Environmental issues are best handled with participation of all concerned citizens, at the relevant level. At the national level, each individual shall have appropriate access to information concerning the environment that is held by public authorities, including information on hazardous materials and activities in their communities, and the opportunity to participate in decision-making processes. States shall facilitate and encourage public awareness and participation by making information widely available. Effective access to judicial and administrative proceedings, including redress and remedy, shall be provided.
>
> (Rio Declaration, Principle 10)

In the wake of the Rio Declaration and its Principle 10, the United Nations Economic Commission for Europe (UNECE) adopted the Aarhus Convention in 1998; it entered into force in 2001.[5] The Convention is a regional environmental agreement that commits national states to guarantee 'the rights of access to information, public participation in decision-making, and access to justice in environmental matters' (art. 1). These environmental matters include RWM as specified in Annex I of the Convention. According to the Aarhus Convention, public information and participation should be promoted during both the development of a policy and its implementation (i.e. in the preparation of rules and regulations, programmes and plans, and decisions on specific activities). The public entitled to participate is identified by the relevant public authority or the applicants/developers.

In the case of specific activities and projects that have transboundary environmental impact, the Espoo Convention calls for the consultation of other affected states. Because environmental threats transcend national borders, the contracting parties have decided to consult each other on major projects that can cause environmental externalities across borders. The Convention was adopted in 1991 and entered into force in 1997 (Lee *et al.* 2013). In 2003, a Protocol on Strategic Environmental Assessment was added to the Espoo Convention; it entered into force in 2010. The Protocol calls for an environmental assessment also on plans and programmes, and requests cross-country public consultation in case of transboundary environmental effect of national plans/programmes.[6].

The EU legal framework

Two EU Directives rule the Strategic Environmental Assessment (SEA) of plans and programmes and the Environmental Impact Assessment (EIA) of projects.

The SEA Directive calls for MSs to integrate environmental considerations in the preparation and adoption of *plans* and *programmes* for the management of natural resources, land use and other sectors, including energy, that may have significant effects on the environment (art. 1). The draft plan or programme (together with a report on its environmental effects) has to be made available to the authorities and the public indicated by the MS for public consultation before it is adopted (Lee *et al.* 2013). The Directive leaves freedom to the MSs to determine the arrangements for the information and consultation of the authorities and the public. In line with the Protocol of the Espoo Convention (see above), the SEA Directive calls for transboundary consultations in case a national plan or programme is likely to have significant effects on the environment of another MS (art. 7).

The EIA Directive applies 'to the assessment of the environmental effects of those public and private *projects* which are likely to have significant effects on the environment' (art. 1); most RWM installations fall in this definition (see Annex I of the Directive). During the EIA, the project developer[7] provides information on the environmental effects of a project and allows for public consultation before the project is authorised (Lee *et al.* 2013). The MS decides on the information and consultation arrangements that will be used to reach out to the public and concerned local and regional authorities designated by the MS.

Purpose of the book

In the field of environmental policy, public involvement has become crucial for multiple land uses such as the siting and development of contested infrastructures, particularly when they imply hazard for the hosting communities. This is the case for the facilities aimed at the management of RW, which constitutes the focus of the book. RWM is a relevant case in environmental, as well as energy, governance because it constitutes one of the most debated aspects in the use of the land and peaceful use of nuclear energy.

More precisely, the book is about public involvement in RWM in the EU. The topic is particularly relevant at this moment, since a few years have passed from the adoption of Directive Euratom/2011/70 that establishes a common framework for a responsible, safe and transparent RWM. We know that a longer time perspective (between 10 and 15 years) should be preferred for a correct implementation assessment (Sabatier 1986) and the book does not aim at any evaluation of national implementation. It is, indeed, too early to evaluate the actual impact of the Directive on national RWM programmes, with many MSs still trying to determine how they can comply. However, Europe as a *region* is advancing further in RWM (e.g., with the siting of HLW disposal facilities) and its participatory component; hence, the book wants to develop insights and offer valuable recommendations based on this regional experience. Together with this broad objective, the book also serves five more specific purposes as I detail here.

Looking at the institutional challenge

RWM faces three major challenges that are technical, social and institutional. The technical challenge has to do with the technological aspects of how we manage RW in our societies. The social challenge consists of the ways in which we respond to citizens' concerns. The institutional challenge relates to the integration of both technical knowledge and social concerns in the process of collective decisions, and how such a process mediates the technical and social aspects of the problem (on this point, see also Bergmans *et al.* 2015). The institutional challenge has somehow been neglected even in the social sciences to the benefit of research on citizens' attitude towards nuclear energy (Rosa & Short 2004). According to Rosa and Short (2004) the institutional process of formation and implementation of nuclear energy policies and its specific facets, such as RWM, deserves more attention. More attention should also be paid to the possible influencing factors (or independent variables) such as (state and non-state) organisations' interactions.

The book takes this approach and focuses on the institutional challenge faced by RWM. It is concerned with the 'institutions, rules, procedures of the political system[,] organisational structures and relationships between different arms of government as well as the impact of policy networks on politics and policy outcomes' (Hayden Lesbirel 2007: 6).

The book looks at the process of policy-making and, more precisely, policy implementation from a political perspective that is informed by the academic field of policy science. It investigates the processes rather than results: it looks, indeed, at the way public decisions are taken and policy actions conducted, rather than the nature and effects of such decisions and actions. Reed (2008) argues that few studies of public involvement have focused on the process; more have looked at the results. Yet, it is the focus on the process that allows a better understanding of the delicate relationship between citizens and public administration (Napolitano 2007).

Answering fundamental questions

In the early 2000s, Blomgren Bingham *et al.* (2005) noticed that not much attention had been devoted by the academic field of public administration to the processes of inclusion of the civil society in decision-making processes. Several points remain insufficiently explored in a systematic way and multiple questions are still completely or partially unanswered by research on public administration and policy: At which point in the policy process can citizens be involved? What forms can public participation take? How can horizontal networks be built or facilitated by policy makers and public managers? How can public administrators manage complex networks? Which tools, practices and processes are most effective? Are there best practices of public participation processes and mechanisms? etc.

Therefore, the study of the relationship between citizens (or, more broadly, stakeholders) and governmental administration in RWM calls for the investigation and clarification of several aspects of public involvement (Table 0.1). First, we need to understand the rationale of public involvement in RWM and *why* participation initiatives are needed in the field. In other words, it is important to understand the reasons that motivate the need for more participatory approaches and what these approaches want to achieve. Second, it has to be clear *when* public involvement can (or should) take place. Public

Table 0.1 Research questions

1) Why do we need public involvement in RWM?
2) When can public involvement in RWM take place?
3) How can the public be involved in RWM?
4) Who should be involved in RWM?

involvement is possible in different moments of policy-making, namely in the stage of development of national policies or during their execution. We will look mainly at policy implementation. Third, we need to understand *how* public involvement happens. Not many systematic efforts have been made in the literature to study the practices of public involvement – that we will call procedural implementation instruments. The book tries to fill this gap while looking at RWM across the EU. Fourth, we need to understand the nature of *who* participates, which interests they represent, the reasons behind their involvement and the criteria according to which certain participants are involved. The role of local communities will be given careful consideration in the book.

Ensuring a plurality of views

Van der Hel and Biermann (2017) claim that knowledge relevant for decision-makers can be found also outside established peer-reviewed academic journals. This calls for research to look beyond scientific literature and draw on a more diverse knowledge base. In particular, a rich amount of both academic and practitioner literatures has been produced on public involvement (Duffield Hamilton 2004). In the domain of RWM, important insights have been developed by scholars involved in academic research and published in scientific journals and by several organisations of practitioners (e.g., European Repository Development Organisation and World Nuclear Association).

However, the study of public involvement in RWM lacks a clear and structured organisation of the many insights developed on the topic from scholars and practitioners. We need a better connection between theories of the policy process and national practical experiences: '[t]he academy can inform work on the ground, and practice can ground the work of the academy' (Blomgren Bingham *et al.* 2005: 555). We also need a clearer organisation of the knowledge cumulated from many sources so that such knowledge can be more easily communicated to a broad audience. Therefore, the book compiles and synthesises a large amount of both academic and grey literature. It brings together several threads of academic research on the subject of public involvement in RWM and, more broadly, (energy) contested infrastructures and controversial technologies. It uses theoretical insights from the field of policy science and analytical tools from the study of policy implementation to support the structured organisation of the studies produced by numerous initiatives promoted and conducted by researchers and practitioners.

In particular, the book gathers insights on the topic of public involvement in RWM from five different sources of high relevance: two decades of social and political research funded by the European Commission (EC) through Euratom funding schemes (i.e. Framework Programmes FP5, FP6 and FP7); two decades of insights developed by the OECD, in the framework of the Forum on Stakeholder Confidence of the Nuclear Energy Agency (NEA); a survey that has targeted all organisations involved in RWM in the 28 MSs of the EU; the National Programmes of the 28 MSs of the EU issued in compliance with Directive Euratom/2011/70; a workshop with mayors of localities with RWM facilities.

Therefore, data sources have included academic research, institutional debates, stakeholders' responses, national official positions and local informal opinions. This ensures a multi-actor perspective on the topic, which is fundamental in the polarised field of RWM. Data have been collected through multiple research methods: document analysis, survey, interviewing and focus groups. In particular, documentary sources have included journal articles, books, websites, newspapers and magazines, government reports, statistical archives, position papers, etc. This "hybrid methodological approach" (Aldrich 2005) was important in order to capture a clearer picture of state–society interaction in the domain of RWM.

Covering a region of 28 countries

The book has a regional focus on the EU. It looks at the EU as a region and does not analyse individual national cases. The objective of the analysis was not to compare and assess experiences of different MSs, but rather to collate, arrange and synthesise existing knowledge on RWM in the EU, across its 28 MSs. The national diversities that are present in the EU are extremely useful to understand public involvement in RWM and allow generalisations.

Indeed, the different national experiences provide a relevant pool of empirical material. The United Kingdom (UK) is still included in the EU at the time of writing for two main reasons. First, the book analyses a period of time that precedes Brexit (planned for end March 2019). Second, the UK is part of the primary and secondary sources used for data collection (i.e. scientific literature, policy reports, survey on stakeholders, Euratom social research, National Programmes for RWM and NEA studies). In addition, relevant analytical insights have also been borrowed from studies on non-EU cases (e.g., from the North American literature).

Serving the theory and the practice

The book addresses both practitioners and scholars. The regional scope also allows for an international audience, both inside the EU and out of Europe.

The book targets policy-makers in national and subnational governments, and public administrators in regulatory and implementing agencies. Moreover, its findings constitute a useful instrument for organisations such as the EU, the International Atomic Energy Agency (IAEA), the Nuclear Energy Agency (NEA) and the World Nuclear Association (WNA). The book also targets practitioners in the private and non-profit sectors (e.g., industrial organisations, NGOs and citizens associations) who are involved in RWM and nuclear energy. More broadly, the analysis of public involvement in one of the wicked problems faced by our societies might elicit the interest of government officials at any level of governance (international, national and subnational) as well as from industry, NGOs and all citizens interested in the value of public involvement in contested (energy) infrastructure and, more in general, environmental policy-making. For this purpose, its synthesising effort seems particularly important: 'policy makers and practitioners often say that the sheer volume of research that exists is a barrier to using it' (Nutley *et al.* 2007: 72).

With its anchoring in policy science, the book is also likely to attract the attention of scholars from the field of public administration, energy policy, European politics, environmental politics, environmental sciences, political science and other social sciences (e.g., sociology, human geography, urban planning, etc.).

Plan of the book

This introduction has served the purpose of presenting the topic of public involvement and providing useful background information. It has stated the scope – i.e. public involvement in RWM in the EU – and framed it in its broader context, i.e. environmental governance. It has introduced the emergence of public involvement in policy-making, and briefly shown its development in the international environmental debate and legal framework. The chapter has also narrowed down the focus to land use – particularly for contested and hazardous infrastructures such as RWM facilities – and stated the objectives of the book.

The book wants to analyse the institutional challenge of RWM (see above). However, Weingart (2007) points out that the study of public involvement in RWM intertwines with two other important topics: the future (as well as the past) of nuclear power in the national choices of energy mix and the role of the public in governmental policy-making in general. These topics are dealt with by the first two chapters.

Chapter 1 introduces the topic of RWM. It offers a brief historical overview on the major developments of nuclear energy and touches upon the concerns that this form of energy has raised over time. The chapter discusses, then, the role of nuclear energy in a low-carbon economy and society, and its current challenges in terms of safety and, more extensively, RWM. The chapter also explains the distinction between low-, intermediate- and high-level radioactive waste, and touches upon deep geological disposal as the ultimate solution for high-level waste. Finally, the chapter presents Directive 2011/70/Euratom and its call for transparency in RWM in the EU.

Chapter 2 presents the theoretical background of the study and defines its analytical framework. It explains the concept and rationale of public involvement, and clarifies its salience for policy implementation. The chapter also stresses the focus of the study on the implementation process and its linkage with policy design. In doing so, it introduces the topic of policy networks and relates this subject to the research conducted on procedural implementation instruments and their effect on inter-organisational relations. The chapter concludes with some considerations on the political nature of policy implementation.

The following four chapters (3, 4, 5 and 6) discuss public involvement in RWM by relying on four different types of data sources: a survey targeting all stakeholders to unveil *issues* and *needs*; a synthesis of research projects in the Euratom framework to extract *general principles*; a review of official national programmes for RWM that describe *national practices*; and a direct input from municipalities about their *local perspective* on public involvement in RWM.

Chapter 3 analyses the data collected through a survey conducted across the EU on a wide range of stakeholders involved in national RWM systems: national policy-makers and governmental departments, municipalities and local authorities, national regulatory bodies and implementing agencies, industrial organisations, advisory and consultative bodies, scientific research institutes, civil society associations and NGOs, and other organisations (e.g., sectoral and professional associations, and consultancies). The survey was designed to explore the major issues and needs perceived by these different categories of actors with regard to public involvement in RWM. The survey results indicate several important themes, thus suggesting relevant directions for investigation.

Chapter 4 extracts the knowledge about public involvement in RWM developed by the Euratom research programmes over the last twenty years and synthesises the major lessons learnt. Several research projects have investigated the social dimension of RWM and produced useful insights on matters of participation. The findings of these projects are analysed and systematised in the chapter and used to define a list of general principles for public involvement. Such principles are meant to work as indications for promoting and enhancing public involvement in the formulation, design and implementation of RWM policies.

Chapter 5 analyses national practices of public involvement in RWM across the EU. It focuses on policy implementation, investigates the use of procedural implementation instruments and develops an inventory of how MSs pursue and realise information, consultation and active participation in the management of RW. The chapter also assesses whether and to what extent national experiences align with general principles for public involvement in relation to emergent themes. Before looking into national practices, the chapter provides an overview on the enactment of the principle of transparency in national legal frameworks.

Chapter 6 explores to what extent local communities have found their way into national decision-making on RWM, whether the instruments reported by Member States in their National Programmes have created actual opportunities of involvement and how interactions among actors at different levels of governance take place. Procedural implementation instruments are, indeed, aimed at opening policy networks to invite more and new participants into policy-making. The chapter discusses the relevance of the local dimension in the implementation process and adds insights on public involvement in RWM from the perspective of local communities.

Public involvement intertwines strictly with matters of trust and social acceptance. Chapter 7 clarifies the link between public involvement and trust. After defining trust in general, the chapter takes a closer look at trust in the domain of RWM and reviews the major works issued by the OECD's Nuclear Energy Agency on the topic. It explains which factors influence citizens' trust in the process of decision-making, the structure of roles and responsibilities, the actors and key organisations, and the facilities that all together constitute a national RWM system. Finally, the chapter touches upon the relationship between public involvement, trust and social acceptance, and its relevance for the nuclear energy field.

Chapter 8 draws conclusions about public involvement in RWM in the EU. It starts by reflecting upon the findings of this research and answers the questions from where we started our investigation, i.e. the "why", "when", "how" and "who" of public involvement in RWM. It discusses the main achievements and open issues analysed in the previous chapters along these questions. Later, the chapter builds on these answers to indicate major implications for policy practice and policy research. It proposes policy recommendations for political actions by international, national and subnational institutions, and suggests indications for theoretical investigation by the academic world.

The conclusive chapter generalises insights on public involvement derived from the field of RWM to other land uses and, more broadly, environmental matters. It takes a final look at public involvement and emphasises its strong ties with politics, particularly when it takes place during policy implementation. Public involvement interrelates, indeed, with elements that are at the core of politics: the resolution of conflicts; the distribution of power; and democracy.

Notes

1 In the Western world, citizens can also participate to democratic life through forms of *direct* democracy such as referenda.

2 Channels of public involvement such as electoral vote, national referenda and lobbying are not the focus of the book. Likewise, forms of public involvement that are often conducted on an individual and non-organised basis (e.g., letters, phone calls, face-to-face meetings), or are the expression of overt opposition and protest (e.g., strikes, picketing and violent demonstrations) are not covered by the book.

3 A recent part of this literature has started to refer to very large infrastructures as "megaprojects" (e.g., Lamari & Prévost 2014; Lehtonen 2014). As we will see in chapter 1, Deep Geological Disposal (DGD) constitutes a nuclear megaproject (Lehtonen 2015).

4 It is worth stressing here that hazard and risk are different concepts. Hazard indicates the intrinsic *ability* of a substance, human activity or natural event to potentially cause harm. This harm (or damage) can consist of death, injuries, disease and environmental damages. Risk consists of the *probability* that such substance, activity or

event will actually cause harm as a consequence (mainly) of exposure (Kasperson *et al.* 1988; Lofstedt 2011; Renn 1998).

5 The European Commission signed the Convention in 1998.

6 See http://www.unece.org/env/eia/sea_protocol.html (last access: 05.12.2016).

7 The project developer is 'the applicant for authorisation for a private project or the public authority which initiates a project' (art. 1).

References

Aldrich, D. P. (2005) "Controversial Project Siting. State Policy Instruments and Flexibility", in *Comparative Politics*, Vol. 38, No. 1, pp. 103–123.

Armour, A. M. (1991) *The Siting of Locally Unwanted Land Uses: Towards a Cooperative Approach*, Pergamon Press, Oxford.

Bardach, E. (2012) *A Practical Guide for Policy Analysis. The Eightfold Path to More Effective Problem Solving*, SAGE, London.

Beierle, T. C., and Cayford, J. (2002) *Democracy in Practice. Public Participation in Environmental Decisions*, Resources for the Future, Washington DC.

Bergmans, A., Sundqvist, G., Kos, D. and Simmons, P. (2015) "The Participatory Turn in Radioactive Waste Management: Deliberation and the Social–Technical Divide", in *Journal of Risk Research*, Vol. 18, No. 3, pp. 347–363.

Blomgren Bingham, L., Nabatchi. T. and O'Leary, R. (2005) "The New Governance: Practices and Processes for Stakeholder and Citizen Participation in the Work of Government", in *Public Administration Review*, Vol. 65, No. 5, pp. 547–558.

Boholm, A. and Löfstedt, R. E. (2004) "Introduction", in Boholm, A. and Löfstedt, R. E. (Eds) *Facility Siting. Risk, Power and Identity in Land Use Planning*, Earthscan, London.

Bollens, S. A. (1993) "Restructuring Land Use Governance", in *Journal of Planning Literature*, Vol. 7, No. 3, pp. 211–226.

Breukers, S. and Wolsink, M. (2007) "Wind Power Implementation in Changing Institutional Landscapes: An International Comparison", in *Energy Policy*, Vol. 35, pp. 2737–2750.

Council Directive 2011/70/Euratom establishing a community framework for the responsible and safe management of spent fuel and radioactive waste.

Creighton, J. L. (2005) *The Public Participation Handbook. Making Better Decisions Through Citizen Involvement*, Jossey-Bass, San Francisco.

Depoe, S. P. and Delicath, J. W. (2004) "Introduction", in Depoe, S. P., Delicath, J. W. and Aepli Elsenbeer, M.-F. (Eds) *Communication and Public Participation in Environmental Decision-Making*, State University of New York Press, New York.

Dietz, T. and Stern, P. C. (2008) *Public Participation in Environmental Assessment and Decision Making*, The National Academy Press, Washington DC.

Directive 2001/42/EC of the European Parliament and of the Council on the assessment of the effects of certain plans and programmes on the environment.

Directive 2011/92/EU of the European Parliament and of the Council on the assessment of the effects of certain public and private projects on the environment.

Directive 2014/52/EU of the European Parliament and of the Council amending Directive 2011/92/EU on the assessment of the effects of certain public and private projects on the environment.

Duffield Hamilton, J. (2004) "Competing and Converging Values of Public Participation: A Case Study of Participant Views in Department of Energy Nuclear Weapons

Cleanup", in Depoe, S. P., Delicath, J. W. and Aepli Elsenbeer, M.-F. (Eds) *Communication and Public Participation in Environmental Decision-Making*, State University of New York Press, New York.
Hayden Lesbirel, S. (2005) "Transaction Costs and Institutional Change", in Hayden Lesbirel, S. and Shaw, D. (Eds) *Managing Conflict in Facility Siting*, Edward Elgar, Cheltenham and Northampton.
Hayden Lesbirel, S. (2007) "Facility Siting: The Theory-Practice Nexus", in the Proceedings of the International Conference on Siting of Locally Unwanted Facilities: Challenges and Issues, 12–14 December, Hong Kong.
Hilson, G. (2002) "An Overview of Land Use Conflicts in Mining Communities", in *Land Use Policy*, Vol. 19, pp. 65–73.
Huizar, L. (2011) "Meaningful Community Participation in Land Use Decision Making Through Ad Hoc Procedures in New Haven, Connecticut", in *Student Legal History Papers*, Papers 14.
Jobert, A., Laborgne, P. and Mimler, S. (2007) "Local Acceptance of Wind Energy: Factors of Success Identified in French and German Case Studies", in *Energy Policy*, Vol. 35, pp. 2751–2760.
Kasperson, R. E. (2005) "Siting Hazardous Facilities: Searching for Effective Institutions and Processes", in Hayden Lesbirel, S. and Shaw, D. (Eds) *Managing Conflict in Facility Siting*, Edward Elgar, Cheltenham and Northampton.
Kasperson, R. E., Renn, O., Slovic, P., Brown, H. S., Emel, J., Goble, R., Kasperson, J. X. and Ratick, S. (1988) "The Social Amplification of Risk: A Conceptual Framework", in *Risk Analysis*, Vol. 8, No. 2, pp. 177–187.
Kerwin, C. M. and Furlong, S. R. (2011) *Rulemaking: How Government Agencies Write Law and Make Policy*, Congressional Quarterly, Inc., Washington DC.
Kraft, M. E. (2000) "Policy Design and the Acceptability of Environmental Risks: Nuclear Waste Disposal in Canada and the United States", in *Policy Studies Journal*, Vol. 28, No. 1, pp. 206–218.
Kuhn, R. G. and Ballard, K. (1998) "Canadian Innovations in Siting Hazardous Waste Management Facilities", in *Environmental Management*, Vol. 22, No. 4, pp. 533–545.
Lamari, M. and Prévost, J.-R. (2014) *Ex Ante Evaluation of Mega-projects in a Time of Uncertainty: What Counts and What is Countable in the Canadian Context?* Paper of the Evaluation Research Center, National School of Public Management, University of Quebec.
Lee, M., Armeni, C., de Cendra, J., Chaytor, S., Lock, S., Maslin, M., Redgwell, C. and Rydin, Y. (2013) "Public Participation and Climate Change Infrastructure", in *Journal of Environmental Law*, Vol. 25, No. 1, pp. 33–62.
Lehtonen, M. (2014) "Evaluating Megaprojects: From the 'Iron Triangle' to Network Mapping", in *Evaluation*, Vol. 20, No. 3, pp. 278–295.
Lehtonen, M. (2015), "Megaproject Underway. Governance of Nuclear Waste Management in France", in Brunnengräber, A., Di Nucci, M. R., Isidoro Losada, A. M., Mez, L. and Schreurs, M. (Eds) *Nuclear Waste Governance – An International Comparison*, Springer.
Lofstedt, R. E. (2011) "Risk versus Hazard – How to Regulate in the 21st Century", in *European Journal of Risk Regulation*, Vol. 2, pp. 149–168.
Luyet, V., Schlaepfer, R., Parlange, M. B. and Buttler, A. (2012) "A Framework to Implement Stakeholder Participation in Environmental Projects", in *Journal of Environmental Management*, Vol. 111, pp. 213–219.
Mann, C. and Jeanneaux, P. (2009) "Two Approaches for Understanding Land-Use Conflict to Improve Rural Planning and Management", in *Journal of Rural and Community Development*, Vol. 4, No. 1, pp. 118–141.

Michels, A. and De Graaf, L. (2010) "Examining Citizen Participation: Local Participatory Policy Making and Democracy", in *Local Government Studies*, Vol. 36, No. 4, pp. 477–491.

Napolitano, G. (2007) (Ed.) *Diritto amministrativo comparato*, Giuffré, Milan.

NEA (2012d) *Nuclear Energy Today*, OECD, Paris.

Nutley, S. M., Walter, I. and Davies, H. T. O. (2007) *Using Evidence. How Research Can Inform Public Services*, Policy Press, University of Bristol, Bristol.

Parry, G., Moyser, G. and Day, N. (1992) *Political Participation and Democracy in Britain*, Cambridge University Press, Cambridge.

Popper, F. J. (1981) "Siting LULUs", in *Planning*, Vol. 47, No. 4, pp. 12–15.

Reed, M. S. (2008) "Stakeholder Participation for Environmental Management: A Literature Review", in *Biological Conservation*, Vol. 141, pp. 2417–2431.

Renn, O. (1998) "Three Decades of Risk Research: Accomplishments and New Challenges", in *Journal of Risk Research*, Vol. 1, No. 1, pp. 49–71.

Rosa, E. A. and Short, J. F. (2004) "The Importance of Context in Siting Controversies: The Case of High-Level Nuclear Waste Disposal in the US", in Boholm, A. and Löfstedt, R. E. (Eds) *Facility Siting. Risk, Power and Identity in Land Use Planning*, Earthscan, London.

Sabatier, P. A. (1986) "What Can We Learn from Implementation Research?", in Kaufmann, F. X., Majone, G. and Ostrom, V. (Eds) *Guidance, Control and Evaluation in the Public Sector*, de Gruyter, Berlin and New York.

Shaw, D. (2005) "Visions of the Future for Facility Siting", in Hayden Lesbirel, S. and Shaw, D. (Eds) *Managing Conflict in Facility Siting*, Edward Elgar, Cheltenham and Northampton.

Thomas, J. C. (1995) *Public Participation in Public Decisions: New Skills and Strategies for Public Managers*, Jossey-Bass, San Francisco.

Thomas, J. C. (2012) *Citizen, Customer, Partner: Engaging the Public in Public Management*, Routledge, Abingdon and New York.

UN (1992) *Rio Declaration on Environment and Development*.

UNECE (1991) *Convention on Environmental Impact Assessment in a Transboundary Context*, United Nations Economic Commission for Europe, Geneva.

UNECE (1998) *Convention on Access to Information, Public Participation in Decision-Making and Access to Justice in Environmental Matters*, Aarhus

UNECE (2003) *Protocol on Strategic Environmental Assessment to the Convention on Environmental Impact Assessment in a Transboundary Context*, United Nations Economic Commission for Europe, Geneva.

van der Hel, S. and Biermann, F. (2017) "The Authority of Science in Sustainability Governance: A Structured Comparison of Six Science Institutions Engaged with the Sustainable Development Goals", in *Environmental Science and Policy*, Vol. 77, pp. 211–220.

Walker, G., Devine-Wright, P., Barnett, J., Burningham, K., Cass, N., Devine-Wright, H., Speller, G., Barton, J., Evans, B., Heath, Y., Infield, D., Parks, J. and Theobald, K. (2011) "Symmetries, Expectations, Dynamics and Contexts: A Framework for Understanding Public Engagement with Renewable Energy Projects", in Devine-Wright, P. (Ed.) *Renewable Energy and the Public – From NIMBY to Participation*, Earthscan, London and Washington DC.

Weingart, J. (2007) *Waste Is A Terrible Thing To Mind*, Rivergate Books, New Brunswick (NJ).

West, W. (2005) "Administrative Rulemaking: An Old and Emerging Literature", in *Public Administration Review*, Vol. 65, No. 6, pp. 655–668.

Wolsink, M. (2000) "Wind Power and the NIMBY-Myth: Institutional Capacity and the Limited Significance of Public Support", in *Renewable Energy*, Vol. 21, pp. 49–64.

1 Nuclear energy and the management of radioactive waste

Nuclear energy is a major source of energy. It supplies about 14% of electricity in the world, more than 18% in OECD countries and approximately 30% in the European Union (EU) (Garwin 2013; NEA 2017). The nuclear energy currently produced is released by a process of nuclear fission that involves the splitting of atoms using uranium (NEA 2012d). In 2017, about 450 nuclear reactors were in operation in 30 countries.[1]

Nuclear energy has had a difficult history, more than any other technology of the 20th century. Mixed feelings accompanied the discovery of radiation and fear followed the use of the atomic bomb in World War II. Nevertheless, the peaceful application of nuclear energy that started in the 1950s was met with initial enthusiasm. Only through the decades, particularly after the 1970s, the general support for this source of energy has faded as a result of major accidents, safety issues and the problematic management of its waste.

This chapter introduces the topic of radioactive waste management (RWM). It offers a brief historical overview on the major developments of nuclear energy[2] and touches upon the concerns that this form of energy has raised over time. The chapter discusses, then, the role of nuclear energy in a low-carbon economy and society, and its current challenges in terms of safety and, more extensively, RWM. The chapter also explains the distinction between low-, intermediate- and high-level radioactive waste, and touches upon deep geological disposal as the ultimate solution for high-level waste. Finally, the chapter presents Directive 2011/70/Euratom and its call for transparency in RWM in the EU.

Looking backward: a brief history of nuclear energy

Nuclear science is a relatively recent discipline that has developed over the last century. Its origin can be traced back to the late 1800s when the phenomenon of radioactivity was discovered (U.S. Department of Energy 2011; Weingart 2007). Radioactivity consists of a process by which the nucleus of an unstable atom loses energy by emitting electromagnetic waves or sub-atomic particles. This energy is called radiation (NEA 2012d). We know, now, that a specific type of radiation, i.e. *ionising* radiation, is capable of causing damage to living cells. In particular, the radiation generated during the production of nuclear energy has the potential to harm people and the environment if it is released accidentally (NEA 2012d). Exposure to high doses of radiation increases the chance of developing cancer; very high doses can cause immediate death (Weingart 2007). For this reason, high levels of safety are considered essential for the use of nuclear energy (NEA 2012d).

Studies and discoveries on radioactivity and radiation continued in the early 1900s. It became clear that atoms are divisible, unlike what had always been believed; they can divide and transform (or "decay") into other elements. In particular, when uranium was bombarded with neutrons, lighter elements were produced; the missing mass had transformed into energy on the basis of Einstein's equation ($E=mc^2$). Nuclear fission was, thus, discovered: a neutron can cause an atomic nucleus to split and release more neutrons that cause other atoms to split in a chain reaction that generates energy in the form of heat (NEA 2012d). Atoms of many elements can be split to obtain small amounts of energy, but only uranium and plutonium can produce the neutrons needed for a self-sustained nuclear fission reaction (Garwin 2013). The nuclear age started in 1942, when Fermi conducted the first human-controlled self-sustaining nuclear fission reaction (Brook *et al.* 2014; U.S. Department of Energy 2011).

The demonstration by Fermi was immediately exploited for military application during World War II, in the framework of the "Manhattan Project". Two atomic bombs were, later, launched in Japan in 1945 on the cities of Hiroshima and Nagasaki, marking nuclear energy's destructive debut (Figure 1.1). In the wake of the tragic demonstration of the great atomic power released during the bombing, the international community realised the importance of harnessing such power and decided to commit to the peaceful use of nuclear energy for the benefit of mankind. As a result, the International Atomic Energy Agency (IAEA) was founded in 1957 with the purpose of promoting nuclear cooperation at a global scale (Brook *et al.* 2014; Brunnengräber & Schreurs 2015; Garwin 2013; U.S. Department of Energy 2011).

The use of nuclear energy was, thus, diverted to the production of electricity, which started in the 1950s in several countries outside Europe (i.e. US and the

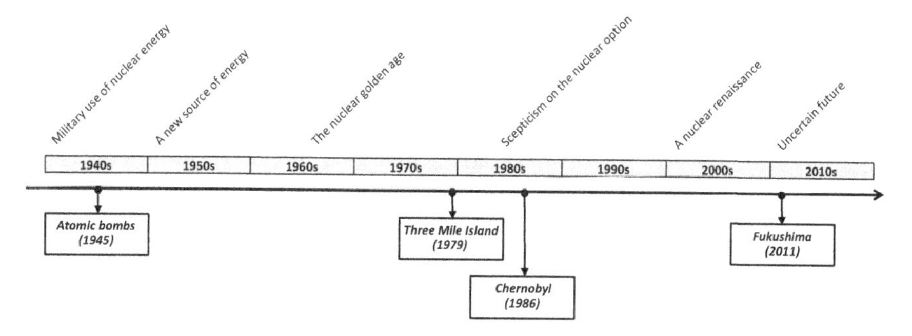

Figure 1.1 Nuclear energy: major trends and events
Source: Personal elaboration

ex-USSR) as well as inside (i.e. UK and France) (NEA 2012d). The nuclear power industry grew rapidly in the 1960s in many other countries around the world (e.g., Belgium, Germany, Italy, Sweden, Canada and Japan) (Chater 2005; Lester & Rosner 2009). At that time, nuclear energy was portrayed as a "miraculous and limitless form of energy" (Brunnengräber & Schreurs 2015; see also Garwin 2013) and a "glittering technological panacea" (Pasqualetti & Pijawka 1996).

Nuclear power generation intensified during the oil crisis of the 1970s. This period marked, nonetheless, a turning point in the history of nuclear energy (Figure 1.1). The positive attitude around nuclear power started to decrease mainly because of the economic costs of building nuclear power plants (NPPs) and the growth of anti-nuclear environmentalist movements concerned with safety issues and radioactive waste (RW) (Chater 2005; Pasqualetti & Pijawka 1996; U.S. Department of Energy 2011). At the end of the 1970s, the first major nuclear accident of Three Mile Island (1979) heavily struck the popularity of nuclear energy[3] (Kasperson *et al.* 1988).

While public confidence in nuclear energy was still low, a second major accident occurred in Chernobyl in 1986 (Brunnengräber & Schreurs 2015; Chater 2005). Confidence in scientific knowledge and expertise in the field decreased. The events of Three Mile Island and Chernobyl brought the fear of atomic energy from its military application and the memories of World War II to its civilian employment (2007). As a consequence, nuclear power generation faced a period of stagnation and decline, particularly in the Western world (NEA 2012d).

In the late 1990s an apparent revival of nuclear energy – a so-called "nuclear renaissance" (NEA 2012d) – was on its way, mainly as a response to the difficulty of meeting energy demands with renewable energy sources alone, the increasing cost of fossil fuel, the dependence on foreign oil and the necessity of reducing CO2 emissions (Lester & Rosner 2009; Sundqvist & Elam 2010; Weingart 2007). The chance of a nuclear renaissance was, though, shattered by the Fukushima accident of 2011 which brought many national governments and public opinion to question the safety and use of nuclear energy (Brunnengräber & Schreurs 2015).

Following the third major nuclear accident of Fukushima-Daiichi, some countries have decided to freeze any nuclear development, close existing plants over the following years and turn away from nuclear energy (notably Germany and, outside the EU, Switzerland) (Brunnengräber & Schreurs 2015; NEA 2012d). However, several other countries are embarking on a new expansion of nuclear energy or have confirmed previous programmes of investment (e.g., UK). National policies towards nuclear energy vary across the EU depending on the national political priorities, the resources available and the technology possessed by each Member State (MS). In a world facing rising electricity demands under the need of lowering CO2 emissions through the decarbonisation of energy supplies, the nuclear option still remains attractive in terms of competitiveness of electricity production, security of supply and reduction of greenhouse gas emissions (NEA 2012d).

If we move from the political orientations of national governments to public opinion across the EU, we see that more than 40% of European citizens are in favour of nuclear power generation according to the last Eurobarometer on the topic (Eurobarometer 2008). Finland and Sweden score at the top of pro-nuclear countries, with (respectively) 61% and 62% of the population in favour of nuclear energy. Public opposition to nuclear energy is commonly due to people's concerns about safety issues, radioactive waste (RW) and nuclear weapons proliferation[4] (Brunnengräber & Schreurs 2015; Eurobarometer 2008; IAEA 2014).

In particular, the management of RW affects public acceptance of nuclear energy so strongly that it has been defined as the "Achilles' heel" of nuclear power generation (Brunnengräber & Schreurs 2015). According to some studies (e.g., Di Nucci *et al.* 2015; Sundqvist & Elam 2010), a large portion of people's opposition to nuclear power would disappear if citizens perceived that a permanent and safe solution for RW exists. Instead, a general sense of distrust populates the whole nuclear field, including RWM. The reasons for this lack – or, rather, loss – of trust must be found in the nuclear history itself.

The loss of trust

Nuclear energy has experienced a considerable loss of public trust over the decades (Brunnengräber & Schreurs 2015; NRC 2003). Public fear surrounds both operating nuclear installations, and facilities for the storage and disposal of RW (NEA 2003). This low level of trust can be explained as the sum of two processes, i.e. the general erosion of public trust in government and historical developments specific to the nuclear field.

As a general trend, public trust in government and public agencies has declined across all developed countries and in many policy areas (Armour 1991; Pharr & Putnam 2000; Tuler & Kasperson 2014). The unquestioning trust in authorities typical of the 1940s and 1950s has been substituted by growing citizens' awareness, activism and scepticism since the1960s and 1970s. We live today in 'an era of general public distrust of government' (Weingart 2007: vii; see also OECD 2017). Several factors are responsible for this "alienation from government" (Weingart 2007): the recent prolonged economic crisis; poor performance of national administrations; episodes of dishonesty and corruption in governments; and the political inability to address current crises such as large-scale migration. This goes well beyond the nuclear field and relates to a broader political and social debate that falls outside the scope of the book.

In the nuclear field, distrust for government – and industry – is well acknowledged (Pasqualetti & Pijawka 1996). According to the Nuclear Energy Agency of the OECD (NEA 2003: 17), this lack of credibility reflects the general trend explained above. Undoubtedly, though, something specific to the nuclear field makes it highly distrusted by the general public. Multiple elements in the history of nuclear energy explain such strong distrust: the role of images; the military legacy; the production of RW; mistakes in (crisis) communication; major accidents; popular ignorance; and media intensification.

First, popular concerns about nuclear energy and RW are rooted in images of danger that predated the very discovery of nuclear power. Even before nuclear weapons and nuclear energy became a reality, the discovery of radiation was surrounded by a belief of extreme powers in the public imagery. Radiation was believed to be capable of (almost) magical effects that would go from medical miracles to destruction and horrific mutations induced in living beings (Weart 1991; 2013; Weingart 2007).

Second, the use of atomic bombs confirmed the massive destructive nature of nuclear energy. Public opposition to nuclear energy is still partly due to the fear of radiation perpetuated by memories of the nuclear weapons used during World War II and their effects. Prejudices in popular culture about radiological safety are, indeed, still very strong. The secrecy that surrounded the military use of nuclear energy before it became a source of electricity for civilian purposes contributed to these prejudices in public imagery (Brook *et al.* 2014; Weingart 2007).

Third, RW started to solicit greater anxieties than other types of industrial waste (Weart 1991). In the 1950s, the peaceful use of nuclear energy was still accompanied by the expectation (or hope) of a utopian future steered by nuclear innovative devices (Garwin 2013). It is in the 1970s that Weart (1991; 2013) identifies an important turning point. The fear of radiation dating back to the atomic bombs was revamped by more recent concerns for the fallouts from bomb tests. Such fear broadened, then, also to the civilian use of nuclear energy and its related waste (Weart 1991, 2013; Weingart 2007).

Fourth, feelings of fear and distrust escalated in a context of "arrogance, indifference to the public, and secrecy" shown by responsible governmental agencies and the nuclear industry (Weart 1991; 2013). The nuclear sector (both governmental and commercial organisations) can be blamed for mistakes of communication, particularly miscommunication and delayed disclosure of information during nuclear accidents (Shrader-Frechette 2015).

Fifth, three nuclear accidents – i.e. Three Mile Island, Chernobyl and Fukushima – have marked a clear decrease in public trust: '[a]fter each major accident, the industry has suffered major setbacks with loss of public confidence' (Brunnengräber & Schreurs 2015: 55).

Sixth, nuclear energy implies risks but the field is so highly technical and its technology still relatively unknown to laymen that the degree of such risks is often misunderstood. Ignorance creates fear, independently from facts. The perception of danger in the public imagery, memories of past events and miscommunication (particularly during crises) have hampered the development of correct awareness and understanding of actual risks among people (Kuhn & Ballard 1998; Renn 1998; Weingart 2007).

Seventh, media have often exploited this popular ignorance and used people's fear to make news more spectacular. According to Brook *et al.* (2014), the sensationalised coverage of nuclear incidents by news media has amplified distrust for the nuclear field. Likewise, media attention on RW has somehow fomented public concerns about RWM; these concerns have been used by anti-nuclear activists to build up opposition against nuclear energy (Pasqualetti & Pijawka 1996).

To sum up, the images of the severe harm that may be caused by radiation and RW, a nuclear war escalating to planetary destruction, the aversion for the behaviour of distant institutions and organisations particularly during accidents, and the strong (often distorted) messages coming from media in a technical and complex domain have all contributed to create suspicion around nuclear energy far more than it has ever happened for any other technological development.

Despite social concerns, most experts agree that nuclear energy may tackle several problems faced by contemporary societies, namely a growth in energy demand, matters of energy security and concerns for climate change (NEA 2012d).

Looking forward: nuclear energy in a low-carbon society

The energy field faces several challenges in the current time, namely the growth of energy demand, the security of energy provision and environmental alarm.

First, population is growing on the planet, mainly in developing countries. This trend will continue in the coming years and will determine a higher demand of energy on a global scale. Such demand is expected to grow by about one third by 2040, under the energy demand of China, India and the Middle East. This will very likely imply higher energy prices (Brunnengräber & Schreurs 2015; European Commission 2012; IEA 2016; Lester & Rosner 2009; NEA 2012d).

Second, several energy sources, particularly oil and gas, are characterised by a heavy dependency on imports from foreign countries that have high political instability. This poses serious problems for assuring future supplies and suggests that the dependence of the EU on imported oil and gas should be decreased (Brunnengräber & Schreurs 2015; European Commission 2012; IEA 2016; Lester & Rosner 2009; NEA 2012d).

Third, in the light of evident signs of climate change on a planetary scale, the emission of greenhouse gases (GHGs) has become a serious problem (Brunnengräber & Schreurs 2015; European Commission 2012; IEA 2016; Lester & Rosner 2009; NEA 2012d). Particularly, emissions of CO2 are a recurrent item in public debates, national political agendas and specialised international *fora* such as the Intergovernmental Panel on Climate Change (IPCC). In 2015, the Paris Agreement was adopted[5] as a global response to the threat of climate change through the pursuit of a low-carbon society (Eurobarometer 2008; IEA 2016; NEA 2012c).

In this context, nuclear energy can be crucial to ensure power generation while decreasing dependence on foreign supplies of energy. More importantly, NPPs do not emit CO2 (Brook *et al.* 2014; Lester & Rosner 2009); hence, nuclear energy occupies an important place in the debate over climate change. According to the NEA (2012d), nuclear energy and hydropower are the two main sources of significant amounts of low-carbon energy. More recently, the IPCC has formally recognised that 'nuclear energy is one way to reduce GHG emissions and to protect the climate' (Brunnengräber & Schreurs 2015: 58).

The EU has committed to reduce its GHG emissions by 80–95% when compared to 1990 levels by 2050 ("decarbonisation objective") as it is reported in the Energy Roadmap 2050 (European Commission 2012). This strategy for energy policy in the EU explores the transition of the EU's energy system in ways that are compatible with the target of GHG reduction as well as increased competitiveness and security of supply. The EC identifies its route towards a competitive, secure and decarbonised energy system through several possible options: energy efficiency and savings, renewable energy sources, carbon capture and storage, and nuclear energy (European Commission 2012[6]). According to the European Commission,[7] nuclear energy generates about 30% of the electricity produced in the EU, although each MS is free to decide whether to include nuclear power in its energy mix or not. In the EU-28, 14 MSs[8] currently operate NPPs, with a total number of 128 nuclear reactors.[9]

If the nuclear option is likely to remain in the energy mix of the EU, then this will pose serious problems of social acceptance as acknowledged in the same Energy Roadmap 2050. As pointed out earlier in the chapter, two aspects of nuclear energy mostly worry the general public: the safety of nuclear operations and the management of RW (Eurobarometer 2008; European Commission 2012). The EU has committed to rule on both aspects and has recently adopted important legal instruments, namely the Safety Directive[10] and the Waste Directive.[11] In particular, the management of RW represents an important component of the overall debate about nuclear energy (Anshelm & Galis 2009; Garwin 2013).

The salience of radioactive waste

In the EU, each MS is free to define its own national energy mix.[12] While some MSs have for a long time included nuclear power generation in their energy mix (e.g., France), others have decided for future exploitation only recently (e.g., Poland[13]). Some other MSs have, instead, opted for the termination of their nuclear energy policy after the Fukushima-Daiichi accident (2011) and started decommissioning their NPPs (e.g., Germany) (European Commission 2011). No matter which strategic vision MSs pursue for their national nuclear energy policy (continuation, expansion or phase-out), they all generate RW from several sources; 21 MSs among them also manage spent fuel (SF) from power production and research reactors (European Commission 2010).

SF is the fuel used for power generation or research and permanently removed from a reactor. The operation of any nuclear reactor generates SF; it can, then, be partially reprocessed and reused[14] or directly classified as RW. With or without reprocessing, the SF coming from the operation of nuclear reactors constitutes an important source of RW in the EU (see p. 25-6). RW is radioactive material (in solid, liquid or gaseous form) that derives from the operation of NPPs and research reactors for which no further use is foreseen (IAEA 2011a). Amounts of RW are also produced by other uses of radioactive material such as its applications in industrial and medical activities[15] (European Commission 2009).

In addition, the decommissioning of NPPs generates a large amount of RW. Decommissioning refers to the set of administrative procedures and technical actions that follow the final closure of a nuclear installation. It includes removal of all radioactive material, dismantling and demolition of the facility, and site clearance with the aim of making the site available for other uses (NEA 2012d). The decommissioning of existing NPPs will become more important in the coming years due to the aging of the nuclear fleet. This activity will generate more RW and will require increasing storage and disposal capacity (European Commission 2017). The same MSs that decide to phase out nuclear energy will have to manage the RW produced by decommissioning (European Commission 2009). As clearly stated by Brunnengräber and Schreurs (2015: 48), '[f]or countries that are planning to phase out nuclear energy, the nuclear energy "problem" cannot be considered solved until the nuclear waste challenge has been addressed in a satisfactory manner'.

RW is usually classified into three types of waste according to its radiological characteristics (i.e. the doses of ionising radiation emitted) and potential hazard: Low-Level Waste (LLW), Intermediate-Level Waste (ILW) and High-Level Waste (HLW) (NEA 2012d). LLW consists of materials that may contain small amounts of mainly short-lived radioactivity, such as paper and plastic, tools and laboratory equipment, clothing and gloves, etc. It constitutes the majority of the waste produced in the nuclear fuel cycle and during decommissioning. ILW comprises resins, chemical sludges, metal fuel cladding and contaminated materials from the decommissioning of reactors. It contains higher amounts of radioactivity and requires shielding. HLW contains highly radioactive and very hot products generated in the reactor core. It needs to be heavily shielded. The SF unloaded from a nuclear reactor that will not be reprocessed is included in this category. HLW remains hazardous for tens of thousands of years, but the actual amount of material is very low (Brunnengräber & Schreurs 2015; European Commission 2009; NEA 2012d; Weingart 2007). As it has been recently reported by the European Commission (2017), less than 1% of the RW generated in the EU is HLW.

Because of its ionising radiation and the resulting potential hazard, RW needs to be isolated from the biosphere and managed in a way that is harmless for human health and safety as well as for the environment (Saling & Fentiman 2001; Weingart 2007). Current feasible options available for the management of RW are storage and disposal. Storage is intended to be temporary. Disposal, instead, refers to the emplacement of RW in an authorised facility with no intention of retrieval[16] (EU & EASAC 2014). Disposal of LLW and ILW is a mature practice; LLW and ILW are already disposed in repositories in many European countries (NEA 2012d). Instead, disposal of HLW still poses several problems. Due to the longevity of HLW, the international scientific community has analysed different options for its safe and final disposal since the 1970s. Most options have been rejected because they are too risky or inadequate: disposal in space, under the seabed or continental glaciers; ocean dumping; and long-term supervised storage.

The permanent disposal of HLW in deep geological repositories, also called deep geological disposal (DGD), is a solution almost universally accepted by the scientific and technical community. However, this option is strongly opposed by civil society in many countries (European Commission 2009; Kraft 2000; Mays 2004; NEA 2012d; Saling & Fentiman 2002; Stanič 2011). The result is that there is still not a single country in the entire world that has an operating repository for the final disposal of HLW (Brunnengräber & Schreurs 2015; Di Nucci *et al.* 2015; NEA 2012d). The very nature of DGD and the multiple issues that it implies have resulted in delays in several DGD programmes (NRC 2003). DGD facilities are planned to be built and operating in the next 10–20 years in three countries of the EU: Finland (2020), France (2025) and Sweden (2023). Other countries are expected to follow in the subsequent decades (Di Nucci *et al.* 2015; European Commission 2009).

Deep geological disposal

DGD involves placing HLW in a carefully selected repository deep below the Earth's surface in a stable geological formation. This is important in order to isolate HLW from humans and the environment for very long periods of time until the waste no longer represents any hazard for humans and the environment. DGD is recognised by the international scientific community as the most adequate long-term management option for HLW.[17] It ensures the highest levels of safety and security with a passively safe system that does not place burden of care on future generations (Di Nucci et al. 2015; IAEA 2011a; NEA 2012d; NRC 2003).

Because of its features, DGD constitutes a nuclear "megaproject" (Lehtonen 2015). Compared to LULUs (see Introduction), megaprojects – or large infrastructures – present further challenges. They have ambitious objectives often in the absence of previous experiences of similar projects. They present scientific uncertainties and a high level of technical complexity. They demand large budgets (for their high costs and frequent cost overruns), imply large temporal scales (due to their long-life cycle and possible time delays) and need large spaces (because of their colossal size). They also have important impacts on individuals, communities and the social structure. Therefore, they are characterised by social and political uncertainties, for instance in terms of fluctuating social acceptance and political support (Lamari & Prévost 2014; Lehtonen 2014).

Compared to other large engineering projects, DGD has even more scientific, technical, institutional and societal challenges (European Commission 2009). The longevity of HLW (over 100,000 years) implies a time frame for DGD that is beyond human comprehension. Not only are there scientific and technical uncertainties due to gaps in knowledge about geological formations, chemical effects, corrosion and containment over such a long period of time, but DGD also demands stable social institutions and no human civilisation has ever endured for so long (Brunnengräber & Schreurs 2015; Di Nucci *et al.* 2015;

Hamilton 2013). In addition, HLW repositories are perceived as posing serious risks. In a field like nuclear energy populated by distrust and fear, the risk (and risk perception) linked to the hazardous nature of HLW has put DGD at the centre of strong disagreements over its safety (Lehtonen 2014; NRC 2003).

In particular, the geological, economic and social prerequisites needed for the development and execution of DGD programmes represent important obstacles. Not all countries have the appropriate geological conditions for a DGD and, in countries with small nuclear programmes, the financial resources required for DGD are excessive. Social acceptance of DGD has also proven to be difficult to achieve (Brunnengräber & Schreurs 2015; Di Nucci *et al.* 2015). Although technical experts have confidence in DGD as the solution for HLW, many people do not share this confidence (NEA 2012d). As put by Lehtonen,

> [...] one single and generic solution – deep geological disposal – has been widely accepted by governments and key international organizations as the "best" solution for the problem, whereas public opposition, potential changes in nuclear energy policies, and persisting local opposition represent "external risks" that push for "opening up" of the governance situation.
>
> (Lehtonen 2014: 285).

In this context, transparency and a "stepwise approach" have been recommended internationally (European Commission 2009; NEA 2004a). This means that small incremental steps are taken in the process of repository decision-making and development. Along these steps, clear points of entrance for public inputs are ensured in order to make the whole regulatory and implementation process of DGD programmes more transparent (see chapter 4). Although DGD programmes vary across countries, they present a common set of stages: siting, construction, operation, closure and post-closure (IAEA 2011a; 2014; NRC 2003).

The siting stage includes planning, identification, characterisation and confirmation of a site. At first, the project implementer plans deadlines, funding, resources and regulatory constraints. Then, major areas for hosting a DGD are screened on the basis of maps and geological criteria and some potential sites are identified. Later, the project implementer investigates one or more sites, conducts a safety assessment and underground exploration (through underground laboratories).[18] Finally, the suitability of one site is confirmed. During this stage, the implementer prepares an Environmental Impact Assessment (EIA), a preliminary design and safety case to justify and support a license application. The application is reviewed by the regulator for the purpose of checking whether the proposed repository meets the health and safety standards. In case of a positive result of the review, the regulatory authority issues the licence[19] for construction (IAEA 2011a; 2014; NRC 2003).

At this point, the construction of surface and subsurface facilities can begin. In some countries, a licence is required for each step of the facility development. Licences must also be obtained during the subsequent stages, for operation and closure. Once a licence for operation is issued by the regulator, the implementer can receive HLW from generators (i.e., typically NPPs and research reactors) or centralised interim storage facilities. This stage consists of the receipt, handling, conditioning and emplacement of RW. Closure concludes the operational stage of a repository; during the post-closure stage an institutional control is maintained. This is done actively – e.g., by employing guards – or passively – by identifying the controlled areas through signs and markers and distributing information to the responsible government institutions (IAEA 2011a; 2014; NRC 2003).

At present, only three countries in Europe have selected a site for DGD: Finland, France and Sweden. Siting has started in the UK. No MS is in the construction stage.[20]

Radioactive waste management and public involvement

RWM is a multifaceted problem with technical, environmental, economic, societal, political and institutional implications. It brings with itself elements of technical complexity, scientific uncertainty and emotive nature due to potentially associated risks and a polarised socio-political context. All these elements make RWM a "wicked problem" (Bergmans *et al.* 2008). New approaches to policy-making are, thus, needed in order to allow the involvement of all affected interests.

Radioactive waste management as a wicked problem

Policy-makers and public administrators face a large amount of public problems with varying degrees of complexity during their daily work. According to Roberts (2000), public problems can be simple, i.e. with a clear definition and a clear solution, or complex, when the issue is clearly defined but disagreement and conflicts exist about possible solutions. A third category of public problems are "wicked". Their level of complexity is very high: they are imperfectly understood, have no straightforward definitions and imply no easy solution (Beierle & Cayford 2002). This type of public problem generates disagreement and conflicts around both their definition (or issue-framing) and possible solution (or problem-solving) (Roberts 2000): 'actors perceive the problems that are being discussed differently, have different opinions about the desirable solutions and make different interpretations of available information or research that is being done' (Klijn 2007: 257).

Rittel and Webber (1973) explain in detail the reasons why wicked problems are so difficult (and sometimes impossible) to solve. They are usually technology-driven, affected by cognitive uncertainties – because of incomplete information and contradictory understanding – and characterised by a high-risk dimension and a long time-scale. They are also embedded in often radically different belief systems or world views. In a few words, wicked problems are characterised by the combination of intellectual complexity due to the tractability of the problem – i.e. some issues are difficult to understand and solve – and political malignancy, understood as the amount of conflict that a problem can generate among stakeholders (Sabatier 1980; Underdal 2000; 2002; Victor *et al.* 1998).

RWM involves a variety of interests that are environmental, economic, social and political. Strong disagreement exists among the multiple actors involved about the facts and values that surround both the definition of the issue and the solution of the problem. (Kraft 2000). RWM facilities can be thought of as LULUs needed to manage the hazardous waste of a contested activity such as nuclear energy production. This has important consequences.

First, as for all LULUs (see Introduction), those who are asked to bear the impact of RWM facilities (i.e. the local communities hosting the facility) are often not the only ones who have benefited from nuclear energy (Brunnengräber & Schreurs 2015).

Second, such cost-benefit unbalance is made even more controversial by the fact that RWM deals with a special type of waste; it is radioactive and can, thus, cause potential harm to human health and the environment (Di Nucci *et al.* 2015). Scientific uncertainties over the risk of leakage and contamination pervade the debate about RW storage and disposal (Sarewitz 2004). The time-scale during which some RW remains radioactive is too long for any risk assessment willing to provide definitive answers. As mentioned above, the management of HLW overpasses a real-life setting (Kraft 2000). In any case, the risk perception of ionising radiation makes RWM a subject of public concern, regardless of the level of radioactive intensity and time of decay to safe level. In the eyes of laymen there is no distinction in low-level, medium-level and high-level waste (Pasqualetti & Pijawka 1996). Social and local opposition have been strong against facility projects for the management of RW irrespective of the type of waste (Bergmans *et al.* 2015).[21]

Third, RW is the product of a contested activity, i.e. the production of electricity through the generation of nuclear power. RWM intertwines, thus, with a broader disputed issue, namely whether nuclear is a legitimate source of energy (Dietz & Stern 2008; NEA 2003). Therefore, RWM elicits social mobilisation according to the preferences, values and beliefs of stakeholders about nuclear energy (Di Nucci *et al.* 2015). Some people consider nuclear power as an attractive source of energy because it does not produce CO2 emissions and, consequently, does not impact on climate change. Others, instead, stress that nuclear energy produces RW and is, thus, unacceptable as a sustainable energy source (Kraft 2000). For the former, the disposal of RW is meant to be the solution to the use of radioactive materials and nuclear energy since it ensures environmental protection and human safety. For the latter, such disposal constitutes the environmental problem rather than a solution. Accepting the manageability of RW implicitly would mean accepting its solvability and, thus, turn nuclear power generation into an industrial activity like any other. NPPs are, instead, what anti-nuclear activists oppose (O'Connor & van den Hove 2001; Weingart 2007).

Wicked problems and collaborative strategies

Wicked problems are the direct consequence of the complexity of the contemporary world where a plurality of polarised actors lives together without a shared set of values and views. The definition and solution of problems are shaped by each one of us on the basis of our personal beliefs. In this context of multiple belief systems, it is impossible to frame unilaterally many public problems and their solutions. The problem-solving process that follows is inevitably fluid, ambiguous and highly political (Roberts 2000).

Different strategies can be adopted to manage wicked problems, with two major alternatives: authoritative or collaborative strategies. In an authoritative strategy, the problem solving of a wicked problem is put in the hands of a few actors who will define the problem and opt for a given solution; all other actors will accept and comply with this decision. This is the case when policy problems are given to experts in order to reduce the number of stakeholders involved and (hopefully) the complexity of the problem-solving process. Collaborative strategies, instead, pursue and promote alliances, partnerships and joint initiatives (Roberts 2000).

In RWM, the authoritative strategy constitutes the typical approach that has been used to deal with problem-solving. RWM has for long time been considered as a purely technical topic and dealt with along a "technocratic and expert driven route" which heavily relied on the contribution of national authorities and scientific experts (Bergmans & Barbier 2012; O'Connor & van den Hove 2001). The domain has been dominated by a "nucleocracy" (Lehtonen 2015), i.e. a technocracy of the nuclear energy establishment that includes the closed community of (nuclear) public administrators and nuclear experts. As stated by Lehtonen (2014: 293), '[u]ntil the early 1990s radioactive waste management policy was a typical example of a "policy silo", with technical engineering considerations given exclusive emphasis'. The emphasis was mostly on technical solutions capable of ensuring safety.

The importance of collaborative strategies and public involvement in RWM has been underestimated for long time. Policy-making in RWM has, indeed, been often characterised by *fait accompli* politics, experts' dominance and social distrust (Andersson 2008; Brunnengräber & Schreurs 2015). The lack of communication from the side of national policy-makers and implementing agencies towards the public and the targeted local communities has determined a strong opposition from localities to national RWM plans and projects (Brunnengräber & Schreurs 2015). This has resulted in the failures of many policy initiatives. As stressed by the NEA (2012a: 10), '[h]ost communities have proved capable of *de facto* veto power in many instances, across a wide array of countries'. The evident policy failure has pushed many national governments in the EU to embrace a new, more participatory approach to policy-making, understood as the opening of RWM agencies and the related decision-making process to non-state actors (Bergmans *et al.* 2015).

As with many other wicked problems (e.g., sustainable development, climate change and poverty), the issue-framing and problem-solving related to RW cannot be addressed from a mere techno-scientific perspective. Because of their complexity, wicked problems can only be tackled through the involvement of all interested actors from both the public and private sector and from different levels of governance (Bergmans *et al.* 2008; Bergmans & Barbier 2012; Lehtonen 2014; Thomas 2012). Traditional vertical structures of governance are inappropriate. Therefore, collaborations have attracted a remarkable interest in the last decade across several policy fields where wicked problems are involved.

Today, the state maintains a crucial role (as legislator, regulator and financer) in RWM but with an important change. The management of RW in the EU has, indeed, slowly shifted from a purely technical framing to a *socio*-technical framing (Bergmans 2006). As a consequence, it is currently commonly acknowledged that public and local involvement is pivotal for any RWM policy, programme and project (from laboratories to storage and disposal), for all types of RW (high-, medium- and low-level RW) (Saling & Fentiman 2002). Since the 1990s, the awareness of the necessity for RWM programmes to become more inclusive has increased worldwide (NEA 2003). This is particularly true for the EU (see Bergmans *et al.* 2015) where a new Directive was adopted in 2011 with the purpose, among other objectives, of enhancing transparency, public information and participation.

Directive 2011/70/Euratom and the quest for transparency

RWM has been regulated through the years at several politico-administrative levels, from global to state level, through international conventions, regional legal instruments and national legislations (Di Nucci *et al.* 2015).

The Joint Convention on the Safety of Spent Fuel Management and on the Safety of the Radioactive Waste Management (the "Joint Convention") constitutes 'the most significant international agreement in the nuclear waste management policy field' (Di Nucci & Isidoro Losada 2015: 80). The Joint Convention was developed by the IAEA in the late 1990s and entered into force in 2001. The document pursues high levels of safety in SF and RW management as its primary objective. It applies to SF and RW generated by civilian and military programmes. High levels of safety should be achieved through the enhancement of national measures and international cooperation. The Joint Convention is a binding agreement although it is not accompanied by sanctions for non-compliance and has no mechanism of enforcement. Its principles and requirements are nonetheless recognised internationally and incorporated by countries on a voluntary basis. Most MSs of the EU are contracting parties to the Joint Convention.[22] The agreement calls for its contracting parties to make information on the safety of SF and RW management facilities available to the public (art. 6); yet, it does not contain any provision on public involvement (Blohm-Hieber 2012; Di Nucci *et al.* 2015; European Commission 2010; Stanič 2011).

The management of SF and RW is also regulated at the EU level (Di Nucci & Isidoro Losada 2015). All aspects related to nuclear energy are governed by the Treaty establishing the European Atomic Energy Community (Euratom Treaty) (Di Nucci *et al.* 2015). The Euratom Treaty promotes the formation and development of a European nuclear industry, guarantees high safety standards and ensures the peaceful use of nuclear energy (Di Nucci & Isidoro Losada 2015). It is, nonetheless, rather weak in terms of requirements for public involvement. Article 37 simply requires MSs to 'provide the Commission with [...] general data relating to any plan for the disposal of radioactive waste'. On the basis of these data the Commission would deliver an opinion, which is not legally binding, on whether or not 'the implementation of such plan is liable to result in the radioactive contamination of the water, soil or airspace of another Member State' (Euratom Treaty, article 37).

In addition to the Treaty, several parts of the EU legislation have for long time covered aspects of RWM (e.g., Directive 89/618/Euratom and Directive 96/29/Euratom, now repealed by Directive 2013/59/Euratom). However, a complete legal and regulatory framework for the management of SF and RW at the EU level did not exist before 2011 (European Commission 2010; Stanič 2011). The Commission had proposed a Directive on RWM since the early 2000s with the aim of harmonising national regulations and practices for RWM through a Community framework. After two proposals were rejected in 2003 and 2004, the Commission submitted a revised text for a directive on RWM in 2010. The new proposal was adopted in 2011 as Directive 2011/70/Euratom (Di Nucci & Isidoro Losada 2015; Stanič 2011).

Directive 2011/70/Euratom, or the Waste Directive, represents the most important document ruling RWM in the EU. It establishes a Community framework for the responsible and safe management of SF and RW that is generated by civilian activities. This framework has three main objectives (see art. 1): long-term safe management, high-level of safety, and public information and participation (Blohm-Hieber 2012). The Waste Directive called for its national transposition[23] into national legislations by August 2013. In order to achieve its objectives, the Directive requires MSs to establish a dedicated national policy on SF and RW management, including the implementation of a national programme to run the national policy through practical actions for the management of SF and RW. MSs are also expected to bring into force all the necessary laws, regulations and administrative provisions. Finally, they are requested to submit a report to the Commission on the implementation of the Waste Directive every three years since 2015 (see chapter 5).

With regard to public information and participation, article 10 disciplines "transparency" in compliance with the Aarhus Convention (see Introduction); it states the following:

> 1. Member States shall ensure that necessary information on the management of spent fuel and radioactive waste be made available to workers and the general public. This obligation includes ensuring that the competent

> regulatory authority informs the public in the fields of its competence. Information shall be made available to the public in accordance with national legislation and international obligations, provided that this does not jeopardise other interests such as, inter alia, security, recognised in national legislation or international obligations.
> 2. Member States shall ensure that the public be given the necessary opportunities to participate effectively in the decision- making process regarding spent fuel and radioactive waste management in accordance with national legislation and international obligations.
>
> (Directive 2011/70/Euratom, article 10)

National arrangements and instruments to guarantee and promote more transparency in policy-making should be specified in the national programme. Nonetheless, there is no indication in the Directive concerning what types of instruments could be used for public involvement. This missing aspect is in line with the nature of EU Directives: these legal documents are, on purpose, binding with regard to the results that MSs must achieve, not to the means used for achieving them. This lack, though, makes it even more important for practitioners to have a better overview on which instruments of public involvement are used in RWM across the EU (see chapter 5).

Concluding remarks

Economic and political considerations on the costs and security of energy supplies, and environmental concerns for the emission of CO2 from fossil fuels represent important arguments in favour of the use of nuclear energy. Nuclear energy has advantages in terms of competitive production of electricity, security of energy supply and low CO2 emissions. However, it is the object of a lively political and public debate about safety issues and the management of RW.[24] These aspects remain at the core of the opposition to the employment of nuclear energy (NEA 2012d). Particularly, RWM constitutes a wicked problem of very difficult solution, unless efforts are made by policy-makers and public administrators to increase the opportunities for collaborative arrangements with citizens and other stakeholders. The complex nature of RWM calls for public involvement, as it has recently been acknowledged by the EU with the adoption of Directive 2011/70/Euratom. Public involvement is discussed in detail in the next chapter that clarifies the concept and presents analytical tools for its study.

Notes

1 Source: https://www.nei.org/Knowledge-Center/Nuclear-Statistics/World-Statistics (last access: 30.09.2017).

2 Many developments are not covered in this condensed overview. This section also relies on information coming from internet sources, such as the World Nuclear

Association (www.world-nuclear.org) and What Is Nuclear? (www.whatsinuclear.com).

3 Perception about the accident was certainly influenced by *The China Syndrome*, a movie about an accident at a nuclear power plant that was released few days before the accident (Weart 2013).

4 Political attention to nuclear security has also increased in the EU after the terrorist attacks of recent years.

5 The Paris Agreement entered into force in 2016 (IEA 2016).

6 See also https://ec.europa.eu/energy/en/topics/energy-strategy/2050-energy-strategy (last access: 07.04.2016).

7 Source: http://ec.europa.eu/energy/en/funding-and-contracts (last access: 01.02.2016).

8 Belgium, Bulgaria, Czech Republic, Finland, France, Germany, Hungary, Netherlands, Romania, Slovakia, Slovenia, Spain, Sweden and UK (see http://www.world-nuclear.org/information-library/country-profiles/others/european-union.aspx; last access 27.09.2017).

9 This is the number of reactors operable at March 2017 (see http://www.world-nuclear.org/information-library/country-profiles/others/european-union.aspx; last access 27.09.2017).

10 Council Directive 2014/87/Euratom of 8 July 2014 amending Directive 2009/71/Euratom establishing a Community framework for the nuclear safety of nuclear installations.

11 Council Directive 2011/70/Euratom of 19 July 2011 establishing a Community framework for the responsible and safe management of spent fuel and radioactive waste.

12 See art. 194 of the Consolidated Version of the Treaty on the Functioning of the European Union.

13 See http://www.world-nuclear.org/information-library/country-profiles/countries-o-s/poland.aspx (last access: 19.01.2018).

14 Some countries (e.g., France) reprocess (or recycle) their SF, which is then considered as a resource – and not as (radioactive) waste – and reused in a so-called "closed" fuel cycle (Kraft 2000; NEA 2012d).

15 Industrial uses of radioactivity include measurements of densities and thicknesses, tests on welds and employment in agriculture among many others. In the medical and pharmaceutical domain, radiation is used for scanning human organs, treating cancer, developing new medications, sterilising instruments, etc. (Weingart 2007).

16 In some repository concepts, the retrieval of waste is made possible in case more advanced technologies for RW treatment are developed in the future or a decision is taken to recycle SF in future reactors (NEA 2012d).

17 Di Nucci *et al.* (2015: 27) stress, nonetheless, that '[t]he paradigm of DGD as the sole solution started eroding in the last decade'. Some countries (e.g. the Netherlands) are storing their HLW in interim storage facilities before committing to DGD. Long-term storage above ground is motivated by the expectation that safer technological solutions may be found in the future or that RW could even become a resource (Di Nucci *et al.* 2015). By contrast, the NEA (2012d) argues that long-term storage is a less preferable solution for several reasons. For instance, it requires maintaining security and environmental surveillance of a site and this increases management costs. In addition, the long-term deterioration of waste packages and storage facilities will imply costs and risks for future generations.

18 Under a participatory approach, local communities from the screened areas would be invited to volunteer if they feel willing to host a repository and, subsequently, examined to determine whether they are suitable (see chapter 5).

19 A licence is a legal document that grants authorisation to perform specified activities.

20 Source: http://www.world-nuclear.org/information-library/nuclear-fuel-cycle/nuclear-wastes/storage-and-disposal-of-radioactive-waste.aspx (last access: 22.01.2018).

21 This is why the book investigates public involvement in RWM with no distinction among types of RW. It is true that each category of RW poses different technical challenges in terms of volume and costs, but the distinction in low-, medium-, high-level waste does not make much difference in the eyes of the general public. It could even be argued that the uninformed and indistinct public image of RW makes debate about any level of waste highly conflictual. The same survey presented in chapter 3 has revealed no distinction in the public perception of RW: as soon as it is radioactive, waste generates public concern. In terms of instruments used by governmental and regulatory authorities and agencies to pursue public involvement, it could be useful to distinguish cases of DGD but there are very few in progress; hence, policy instruments are treated with no distinction across types of waste (chapter 5). Finally, the Waste Directive calls for transparency for all RWM, not only for the development of DGD.

22 Cyprus, Malta and Portugal are not parties to the Joint Convention (see http://www-ns.iaea.org/conventions/waste-jointconvention.asp; last access: 25.12.2017).

23 'The obligations for transposition and implementation of provisions related to spent fuel of this Directive shall not apply to Cyprus, Denmark, Estonia, Ireland, Latvia, Luxembourg and Malta for as long as they decide not to develop any activity related to nuclear fuel' (Directive 2011/70/Euratom, article 15).

24 For practical reasons, the term radioactive waste management as used in the book includes the management of both RW and SF.

References

Andersson, K. (2008) *Transparency and Accountability in Science and Politics. The Awareness Principle*, Palgrave MacMillan, Basingstoke and New York.

Anshelm, J. and Galis, V. (2009) "The Politics of High-Level Nuclear Waste Management in Sweden: Confined Research versus Research in the Wild", in *Environmental Policy and Governance*, Vol. 19, pp. 269–280.

Armour, A. M. (1991) *The Siting of Locally Unwanted Land Uses: Towards a Cooperative Approach*, Pergamon Press, Oxford.

Beierle, T. C., and Cayford, J. (2002) *Democracy in Practice. Public Participation in Environmental Decisions*, Resources for the Future, Washington DC.

Bergmans, A. (2006) (Ed.) *CARL – First Comparative Report: Towards a Typology of 'Stakeholders' in RWM*, University of Antwerp.

Bergmans, A. and Barbier, J.-W. (2012) "From Stakeholders to Shareholder: a Partnership Approach to Siting and Designing a Radioactive Waste Repository", Paper presented at the Third Berlin Forum 'Innovation in Governance', 31 May – 1 June, Berlin.

BergmansA., Elam, M., Kos, D., Polič, M., Simmons, P., Sundqvist, G. and Walls, J. (2008), *Wanting the Unwanted: Effects of Public and Stakeholder Involvement in the Long-Term Management of Radioactive Waste and the Siting of Repository Facilities*, Final Report Carl Project.

Bergmans, A., Sundqvist, G., Kos, D. and Simmons, P. (2015) "The Participatory Turn in Radioactive Waste Management: Deliberation and the Social–Technical Divide", in *Journal of Risk Research*, Vol. 18, No. 3, pp. 347–363.

Blohm-Hieber, U. (2012) "The Radioactive Waste Directive: A Necessary Step in the Management of Spent Fuel and Radioactive Waste in the European Union", in *Nuclear Law Bulletin*, Vol. 2, pp. 21–35.

Brook, B. W., Alonso, A., Meneley, D. A., Misak, J., Blees, T. and van Erp, J. B. (2014), "Why Nuclear Energy is Sustainable and Has to be Part of the Energy Mix", in *Sustainable Materials and Technologies*, Vol. 1–2, pp. 8–16.

Brunnengräber, A. and Schreurs, M. (2015) "Nuclear Energy and Nuclear Waste Governance. Perspectives after the Fukushima Nuclear Disaster", in Brunnengräber, A., Di Nucci, M. R., Isidoro Losada, A. M., Mez, L. and Schreurs, M. (Eds) *Nuclear Waste Governance – An International Comparison*, Springer, Berlin.

Chater, J. (2005) "A History of Nuclear Power", in *Nuclear Exchange*, August, pp. 28–37.

Consolidated Version of the Treaty Establishing the European Atomic Energy Community.

Consolidated Version of the Treaty on the Functioning of the European Union.

Council Directive 89/618/Euratom on informing the general public about health protection measures to be applied and steps to be taken in the event of radiological emergency.

Council Directive 96/29/Euratom laying down basic safety standards for the protection of the health of workers and the general public against the dangers arising from ionizing radiation.

Council Directive 2011/70/Euratom of 19 July 2011 establishing a community framework for the responsible and safe management of spent fuel and radioactive waste.

Dietz, T. and Stern, P. C. (2008) *Public Participation in Environmental Assessment and Decision Making*, The National Academy Press, Washington DC.

Di Nucci, M. R. and Isidoro Losada, A. M. (2015) "An Open Door for Spent Fuel and Radioactive Waste Export? The International and EU Framework", in Brunnengräber, A., Di Nucci, M. R., Isidoro Losada, A. M., Mez, L. and Schreurs, M. (Eds) *Nuclear Waste Governance – An International Comparison*, Springer, Berlin.

Di Nucci, M. R., Brunnengräber, A., Mez, L. and Schreurs, M. (2015) "Comparative Perspective on Nuclear Waste Governance", in Brunnengräber, A., Di Nucci, M. R., Isidoro Losada, A. M., Mez, L. and Schreurs, M. (Eds) *Nuclear Waste Governance – An International Comparison*, Springer, Berlin.

EU & EASAC (2014) *Management of Spent Nuclear Fuel and Its Waste*, Report issued by the European Union and European Academies' Science Advisory Council, Publications Office of the European Union, Luxembourg.

Eurobarometer (2008) *Attitudes Towards Radioactive Waste*, Special Eurobarometer 297, European Commission, Luxembourg.

European Commission (2009) *Implementing Geological Disposal of Radioactive Waste Technology Platform*, European Commission, Luxembourg.

European Commission (2010) *Impact Assessment. Accompanying Document to the Revised Proposal for a Council Directive (EURATOM) on the Management of Spent Fuel and Radioactive Waste*, Commission Staff Working Document, European Commission, Brussels.

European Commission (2011) *Seventh Situation Report Radioactive Waste and Spent Fuel Management in the European Union*, Commission Staff Working Paper, European Commission, Brussels.

European Commission (2012) *Energy Roadmap 2050*, Publications Office of the European Union, Luxembourg.

European Commission (2017) *Report from the Commission to the Council and the European Parliament on Progress of Implementation of Council Directive 2011/70/Euratom and An Inventory of Radioactive Waste and Spent Fuel Present in the Community's Territory and the Future Prospects*, European Commission, Brussels.

Garwin, R. (2013) "Nuclear Energy: Splitting the Atom", in *New Scientist*, May.

Hamilton, M. S. (2013) *Energy Policy Analysis – A Conceptual Framework*, Routledge, London and New York.

IAEA (1997) *Joint Convention on the Safety of Spent Fuel Management and on the Safety of Radioactive Waste Management.*

IAEA (2011a) *Geological Disposal Facilities for Radioactive Waste*, Specific Safety Guide No. SSG-14, IAEA, Vienna.

IAEA (2014) *Planning and Design Considerations for Geological Repository Programmes of Radioactive Waste*, TECDOC-1755, IAEA, Vienna.

IEA (2016) *World Energy Outlook 2016*, IEA, Paris.

Kasperson, R. E., Renn, O., Slovic, P., Brown, H. S., Emel, J., Goble, R., Kasperson, J. X. and Ratick, S. (1988) "The Social Amplification of Risk: A Conceptual Framework", in *Risk Analysis*, Vol. 8, No. 2, pp. 177–187.

Klijn, E.-H. (2007) "Managing Complexity: Achieving the Impossible? Management between Complexity and Stability: A Network Perspective", in *Critical Policy Analysis*, Vol. 1, No. 3, pp. 252–277.

Kraft, M. E. (2000) "Policy Design and the Acceptability of Environmental Risks: Nuclear Waste Disposal in Canada and the United States", in *Policy Studies Journal*, Vol. 28, No. 1, pp. 206–218.

Kuhn, R. G. and Ballard, K. (1998) "Canadian Innovations in Siting Hazardous Waste Management Facilities", in *Environmental Management*, Vol. 22, No. 4, pp. 533–545.

Lamari, M. and Prévost, J.-R. (2014) *Ex Ante Evaluation of Mega-Projects in a Time of Uncertainty: What Counts and What is Countable in the Canadian Context?*International Political Science Association.

Lehtonen, M. (2014) "Evaluating Megaprojects: From the 'Iron Triangle' to Network Mapping", in *Evaluation*, Vol. 20, No. 3, pp. 278–295.

Lehtonen, M. (2015), "Megaproject Underway. Governance of Nuclear Waste Management in France", in Brunnengräber, A., Di Nucci, M. R., Isidoro Losada, A. M., Mez, L. and Schreurs, M. (Eds) *Nuclear Waste Governance – An International Comparison*, Springer.

Lester, R. K. and Rosner, R. (2009) *The Growth of Nuclear Power: Drivers and Constraints*, MI-IPC Energy Innovation Working Paper09–002, Cambridge (MA).

Mays, C. (2004) "Where Does It Go? Siting Methods and Social Representations of Radioactive Waste Management in France", in Boholm, A. and Löfstedt, R. E. (Eds) *Facility Siting. Risk, Power and Identity in Land Use Planning*, Earthscan, London.

NEA (2003) *Public Information, Consultation and Involvement in Radioactive Waste Management. An International Overview of Approaches and Experiences*, OECD, Paris.

NEA (2004a) *Learning and Adapting to Societal Requirements for Radioactive Waste Management. Key findings and Experience of the Forum on Stakeholder Confidence*, OECD, Paris.

NEA (2012a) *Reflections on Siting Approaches for Radioactive Waste Facilities: Synthesising Principles Based on International Learning*, OECD, Paris.

NEA (2012c), *The Role of Nuclear Energy in a Low-carbon Energy Future*, OECD, Paris.

NEA (2012d) *Nuclear Energy Today*, OECD, Paris.

NEA (2017) *Nuclear Energy Data*, OECD, Paris.

NRC (2003) *One Step at a Time: The Staged Development of Geologic Repositories for High-Level Radioactive Waste*, The National Academic Press, Washington D.C.

O'Connor, M. and van den Hove, S. (2001) "Prospects for Public Participation on Nuclear Risks and Policy Options: Innovations in Governance Practices for Sustainable Development in the European Union", in *Journal of Hazardous Materials*, Vol. 86, pp. 77–99.

OECD (2017) *Trust and Public Policy – How Better Governance Can Help Rebuild Public Trust*, OECD, Paris.

Pasqualetti, M. J. and Pijawka, K. D. (1996) "Unsiting Nuclear Power Plants: Decommissioning Risks and Their Land Use Context", in *Professional Geographer*, Vol. 48, No. 1, pp. 57–69.

Pharr, S. J. and Putnam, R. D. (2000) (Eds) *Disaffected Democracies: What's Troubling the Trilateral Countries?*Princeton University Press, Princeton.

Renn, O. (1998) "Three Decades of Risk Research: Accomplishments and New Challenges", in *Journal of Risk Research*, Vol. 1, No. 1, pp. 49–71.

Rittel, H. W. J. and Webber, M. M. (1973) "Dilemmas in a General Theory of Planning", *Policy Sciences*, Vol. 4, pp. 155–169.

Roberts, N. (2000) "Wicked Problems and Network Approaches to Resolution", in *Public Management Review*, Vol. 1, No. 1, pp. 1–19.

Sabatier, P. A. (1980) "The Implementation of Public Policy: A Framework of Analysis", in *Policy Studies Journal*, Vol. 8, No. 2, pp. 538–560.

Saling, J. H. and Fentiman, A. W. (2002) *Radioactive Waste Management*, Taylor & Francis, New York and London.

Sarewitz, D. (2004) "How Science Makes Environmental Controversies Worse", in *Environmental Science and Policy*, Vol. 7, pp. 385–403.

Shrader-Frechette, K. (2015) "Rights to Know and the Fukushima, Chernobyl, and Three Mile Island Accidents", in Taebi, B. and Roeser, S. (Eds) *The Ethics of Nuclear Energy: Risk, Justice, and Democracy in the Post-Fukushima Era*, Cambridge University Press, Cambridge.

Stanič, A. (2011) "A Step Closer to EU Law on the Management of Radioactive Waste and Spent Fuel", in *Journal of Energy and Natural Resources Law*, Vol. 29, No. 1, pp. 117–150.

Sundqvist, G. and Elam, M. (2010) "Public Involvement Designed to Circumvent Public Concern? The 'Participatory Turn' in European Nuclear Activities", in *Risk, Hazards & Crisis in Public Policy*, Vol. 1, No. 4, pp. 203–229.

Thomas, J. C. (2012) *Citizen, Customer, Partner: Engaging the Public in Public Management*, Routledge, Abingdon and New York.

Tuler, S. P. and Kasperson, R. E. (2014) "Social Distrust and Its Implications for Risk Communication: An Example of High Level Radioactive Waste Management", in Arvai, J. and Rivers, L. III (Eds) *Effective Risk Communication*, Earthscan, London.

Underdal, A. (2000) "Science and Politics: the Anatomy of an Uneasy Partnership", in Andresen, S., Skodvin, T., Underdal, A. and Wettestad, J. (Eds) *Science and Politics in International Environmental Regimes – Between Integrity and Involvement*, Manchester University Press, Manchester and New York.

Underdal, A. (2002) "One Question, Two Answers", in Miles, E. L., Underdal, A., Andresen, S., Wettestad, J., Skjaerseth, J. B. and Carlin, E. M. (Eds) *Environmental Regime Effectiveness – Confronting Theory with Evidence*, The MIT Press, Cambridge and London.

U.S. Department of Energy (2011), *The History of Nuclear Energy*, U.S. Department of Energy, Washington D.C.

Victor, D. G., Raustiala, K. and Skolnikoff, E. B. (1998) "Introduction and Overview", in Victor, D. G., Raustiala, K. and Skolnikoff, E. B. (Eds) *International Environmental Commitments – Theory and Practice*, The MIT Press, Cambridge and London.

Weart, S. R. (1991) "Images of Nuclear Energy: Why People Feel the Way They Do – Emotions and Ideas are More Deeply Rooted than Realized", in *IAEA Bulletin*, 3/1991.

Weart, S. R. (2013) *The Rise of Nuclear Fear*, Harvard University Press, Cambridge, MA.

Weingart, J. (2007) *Waste Is a Terrible Thing to Mind*, Rivergate Books, New Brunswick, NJ.

2 Public involvement in policy-making

The management of radioactive waste (RW) is regulated by national policies that are defined in national legislations and executed through rules (or regulations), national programmes (or plans) and specific projects. Formal policy-making responsibilities for radioactive waste management (RWM) are shared among legislators, ministries and public agencies (e.g., nuclear regulatory authorities, implementing and environmental protection agencies). In addition, RWM has called for the increasing involvement of all concerned actors in the definition of possible solutions (chapter 1).

A general theory of public involvement does not exist (Michels & De Graaf 2010; Rakar & Tičar 2015). Research on the topic is sparse, unsystematic and scattered across several areas, from political science and public administration to administrative law and communication science. Because of its institutional angle, the book tries to integrate these contributions and anchor them in the disciplinary field of policy science. The interdependency between public agencies, private organisations and civil society is at the core of the policy literature dealing with public participation, policy networks and governance. Governance takes place through networks of state and non-state actors participating to policy-making (Klijn 2006; 2008). I will borrow from these theoretical strands with a focus on the execution of national policies.

The chapter presents the theoretical background of the study and defines its analytical framework. It explains the concept and rationale of public involvement, and clarifies its salience for policy implementation. The chapter also stresses the focus of the study on the implementation process and its linkage with policy design. In doing so, it introduces the topic of policy networks and relates this subject to the research conducted on procedural implementation instruments and their effect on inter-organisational relations. The chapter concludes with some considerations on the political nature of policy implementation.

What is public involvement?

Modern societies are characterised by a variety of complex public problems, such as financial turbulences, migration crises, environmental emergencies, etc. (chapter 1). The way national governments decide to respond to a specific collective problem constitutes a public policy (Dye 1972). More precisely, public policies are government decisions and efforts to either change the *status quo* of social and administrative behaviours through a course of action (i.e. "positive decisions") or leave it unaltered through non-decision and inaction (i.e. "negative decisions") (Howlett 2011).

Public policies have traditionally been the responsibility of institutions invested with formal authority and legal power. For decades, national governments have adopted decisions and national bureaucracies have executed them (Blomgren Bingham *et al.* 2005; Stoker 1998). In the second half of the twentieth century, though, unilateral actions from the government and public agencies became insufficient to address new collective problems embedded in a complex network of conflicting interests, beliefs and values among a variety of actors (Ulibarri 2015).

Because of the complexity of contemporary challenges, the inclusion of a broad range of actors in the development and execution of national policies has become pivotal for the definition and solution of public problems (Hanf & O'Toole 1992; Klijn 2006; 2008). The engagement of both state and non-state actors in policy-making has grown over the years and policy-making has turned into an open process. Public policies have, thus, ceased to be the exclusive responsibility of public authorities and started to be the product of their interaction with private and non-governmental organisations (NGOs) (Geurts & Joldersma 2001; Börzel 1997; Peterson 2003; Thomas 1995). Public involvement is now crucial for policy-making at all levels of government in most Western countries and across many policy areas (science, technology, health, environment, etc.) (Irvin & Stansbury 2004; Lee *et al.* 2013; Rowe & Frewer 2000).

This change in the policy practice has attracted scholarly attention and public involvement has emerged as a popular topic in the academic literature. Nevertheless, the study of the topic has generated little consensus about what public involvement really means (Thurston *et al.* 2005). Bishop and Davis (2002) argue that the concept brings with itself "symbolic potency" and "semantic hollowness". Indeed, public involvement has gained a general positive connotation that has made it a "magic concept" (Pollitt & Hupe 2011): 'it confers a stamp of approval to whatever it names' (Munro-Clark 1992: 13). Particularly fashionable in current political and policy debates, its use is nonetheless so broad across a wide range of domains that the definition of public involvement – like many other magic concepts – often results into ambiguity and confusion (Pollitt & Hupe 2011).

In order to avoid confusion, the book defines public involvement as an organised process adopted by elected officials, government agencies or other public-sector organisations to engage citizens and other stakeholders in the formulation, adoption and implementation of public policies[1] (Joss 1999; Wilson 1999). Through public involvement, not only are public concerns, needs and values incorporated into policy-making (Creighton 2005), but policy-making powers and responsibilities are actually shared between government and the public (Bishop & Davis 2002). Ultimately, public involvement consists of the opening of the policy process which, thus, becomes more transparent (O'Connor & van den Hove 2001). For this reason, the concept of public involvement will be used as a synonym of openness and transparency in the book, although some literature highlights differences among these concepts[2] (OECD 2017a).

Terminologies often intersect and confuse: different terms can refer to the same concept and the same term can have different meanings. The same use of a concept evolves over time. Public involvement started to be conceptualised as participation of the citizens to policy-making, but the concept has gradually widened to include all stakeholders (Thomas 2012).

Citizens (often referred to as the *general* public) are members of the society (Thomas 1995; Ulibarri 2015); together with other non-state actors (e.g., industries, interest groups and NGOs) interested in or affected by a collective decision, they constitute the "public" (Dietz & Stern 2008). The public is never monolithic: strong disagreements in terms of interests and values exist among citizens, trade associations, unions, environmental groups, etc. (Kerwin & Furlong 2011). Therefore, some authors (e.g., Creighton 2005; Lee *et al.* 2013) argue that we should more correctly speak of a diverse set of *publics* (or audiences) as plural in order to better reflect their heterogeneity. The publics and governmental organisations (such as elected representatives, national agencies and subnational governments) constitute the "stakeholders" (Table 2.1). A stakeholder is any party (individual, group or organisation) who has an interest (or "stake") or is affected by a policy issue and the related public decision(s) (NRC 2003).

Table 2.1 Citizens, public and stakeholders

	Citizens	*Public*	*Stakeholders*
Non-state actors	• Citizens • Local population • Community groups • Other volunteer groups	• Citizens • Local population • Community groups • Other volunteer groups	• Citizens • Local population • Community groups • Other volunteer groups
		• Industry • Interest groups • NGOs	• Industry • Interest groups • NGOs
State actors			• Elected representatives • National agencies • Subnational governments

Source: Adaptation from Thomas (2012: 123).

The book has a preference for the use of the more comprehensive term of public involvement rather than public participation, although this does not always correspond to authors' original. The two terms are often used interchangeably in popular talk and most academic literature. However, some references used in the book, namely the Aarhus Convention and Directive 2011/70/Euratom, distinguish between public information and public participation, and indicate with the latter only higher degrees of public involvement such as consultation and active participation. The book will specify when public participation is used as synonym of public involvement or to indicate only forms of engagement that are more than simple public information (i.e. consultation and active participation).

Information, consultation and active participation

When policy-makers and public administrators decide to involve the public in policy-making, they may aim at different objectives that go from informing and listening to the public, to engaging it in problem-solving and the co-production of public decisions. Several degrees of public involvement are, indeed, possible depending on the amount of decision-making authority that policy-makers and public administrators share with their publics (Arnstein 1969; Creighton 2005; Rowe & Frewer 2000; Thomas 2012). A wide variety of typologies has been developed by the scientific literature to define degrees of public involvement in policy-making (Reed 2008). Academic taxonomies go from Arnstein's (1969) "participation ladder" to more recent attempts (e.g., Luyet *et al.* 2012). With a more pragmatic focus on the practice rather than on analytical nuances, the OECD (2001a; 2001b; 2017a) distinguishes three objectives/degrees of public involvement: information, consultation and active participation (Figure 2.1).

In their relations with the public, governments and their administrations may aim at the simple provision of information about a public issue, possible solutions, new policy initiatives or the process of a decision. This is the least interactive level of involvement. It consists of one-way relation where communication flows from state actors to the public (Figure 2.1). Governmental agencies produce and deliver information to citizens and societal actors (or allow them to access governmental documents), but there is neither a channel for feedback from the public to government, nor power for negotiation. The public plays a passive role as simple consumer of government information (André 2006; Arnstein 1969; Bishop & Davis 2002; Rowe & Frewer 2000; OECD 2001a; 2001b).

Policy-makers and public administrators can also decide to seek and listen to the opinion of interested and affected groups, for instance on the proposal of a specific policy initiative. Consultation brings into the policy process people's ideas and concerns on public problems, solutions or decisions (Figure 2.1). The result is an overview available to state actors on the wide spectrum of existing perceptions, perspectives and arguments of the public. In this two-way relationship, information flows between government and interested societal groups in both directions. The public is not directly

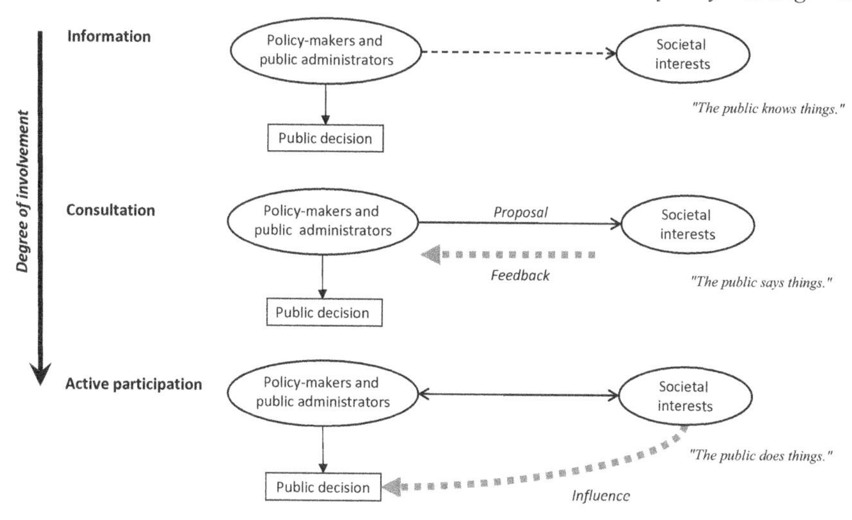

Figure 2.1 Objectives of public involvement in policy-making
Source: Adaptation from OECD (2001b: 2)

involved in shaping policy options, but the public input is taken into account for final policy or administrative decisions (André 2006; Bishop & Davis 2002; Rowe & Frewer 2000; OECD 2001a; 2001b).

Finally, the public (as individuals or groups, at national or local level) can take part to the preparation and execution of public decisions through active participation (Figure 2.1). Through active participation, public organisations aim at sharing decision-making powers with the public (Thomas 2012; Ulibarri 2015). Collaboration between governmental organisations and societal actors becomes stronger: the latter can formulate recommendations, develop alternatives and identify more acceptable solutions (André 2006; Arnstein 1969; Bishop & Davis 2002; Rowe & Frewer 2000; OECD 2001a; 2001b). The public becomes, thus, a partner of the government and public agencies in the formulation and execution of public policies (Thomas 2012); active participation is, indeed, based on the principle of partnering (see chapter 4). The final responsibility for (policy or administrative) decisions can remain in the responsible political/operating organisation or be shared with non-state actors through forms of joint decision-making.

To sum up, policy-makers and governmental agencies can involve societal interests (i.e. citizens, industries, interest groups, NGOs, etc.) in their action with different objectives in mind, according to the degree of engagement that they pursue. The result is that "the public knows things" (information), "the public says things" (consultation) or "the public does things" (active participation) (adapted from OECD 2005). Each level builds on the precedent, so that there can be no consultation and active participation without previously informing the public.

Although the degree of public involvement pursued under the three objectives increases while we move from information to consultation and active participation, this does not imply that there is a *best* level of involvement. It is important to acknowledge that public involvement is not limited to simply providing information. Citizens and any societal actor must be able to influence public decisions by having their concerns, needs and values included in policy-making (Creighton 2005; Ulibarri 2015). However, active participation does not always have to be the ultimate goal (Reed 2008). As pointed out by Thomas (2012), in some cases consultation can be sufficient; other times, the simple information solves a problem. The pursuit of public involvement should take into account the specific context of a public policy and the costs as well as the benefits of public involvement (Beierle & Cayford 2002).

Reasons for public involvement: benefits vs. costs

Public involvement in policy-making is expected to improve public decisions and the way they are taken. However, it can also cause unintended consequences to the policy process and public policies that it is supposed to improve. Both benefits and costs are discussed here and summarised in Table 2.2.

Benefits

Public involvement is usually considered useful for both citizens (and, more broadly, societal actors) and policy-makers. On the one hand, it allows citizens and other non-state actors to access information, enhance their awareness about public problems, influence decisions that affect their lives, and benefit from public policies that are more in line with their will (Creighton 2005; Dietz & Stern 2008; Irvin & Stansbury 2004; Thomas 2012). On the other hand, public involvement helps policy-makers because the inclusion of citizens' inputs adds value to the process of policy-making and the resulting public decisions. The process is what actually happens and consists, to a large extent, of the relationships among actors. The result is what comes out of that process, i.e. the

Table 2.2 Benefits and costs of public involvement

	Benefits		*Costs*
Public decision	Better quality * *Substantive rationale*	↔	Poor content
Policy process	More legitimacy, trust and acceptance * *Political rationale*	↔	Lower performance
Political system	Stronger democracy * *Ethical rationale*	↔	Imperfect representation

content of a policy (or administrative) decision or initiative (Beierle & Cayford 2002; Bobbio 2004; Bollens 1993).

Several benefits brought by public involvement to policy-making have been distinguished in the literature. Three are particularly important (see Table 2.2). First, public involvement improves the "quality" of public decisions by bringing a broader spectrum of ideas and knowledge into policy-making. Second, public involvement enhances the "legitimacy" of the way public decisions are adopted; in turn, legitimacy increases "trust" in the government and public support to its activities. Third, public involvement strengthens the "democracy" of a political system (Bobbio 2004; Lee *et al.* 2013; Rowe & Frewer 2000; OECD 2001a; 2008; Thomas 2012; Ulibarri 2015). These advantages of public involvement (i.e. quality, legitimacy, trust and democracy) define three major rationales that motivate the need to engage citizens and other societal actors in policy-making: a substantive rationale, a political rationale and an ethical rationale.

The substantive (or cognitive) rationale has to do with the information, expertise and ideas that the public can bring into policy-making. Indeed, knowledge is not limited to scientists, experts and specialists: 'both the public [...] and the scientific community have substantial expertise, but expertise of different kinds and on different matters' (Dietz & Stern 2008: 148). Experts working in isolation from citizens may overlook important aspects that are, for instance, well known to the local population (Bobbio 2004). Specialists' insights and "lay" (often local) knowledge are complementary and, together, can produce better policies. In other words, public involvement leads to better policy contents by exposing policy-makers to a wider range of perspectives, priorities and values around a problem (Andersson 2008; Burby 2003; Thomas 1995).

The political (or instrumental) rationale relates to the way legitimacy and trust work. The genuine involvement of societal interests in policy-making is likely to increase the legitimacy of public decisions because they become the product of the citizens' voice. This is likely to result in citizens and other stakeholders trusting their government's voice more. Moreover, legitimacy and trust have a positive impact on policy implementation since decisions recognised as legitimate by their targeted groups face less opposition. As Creighton (2005: 18) explains: '[u]nilateral decisions are always the quickest to make but often very expensive to implement. Frequently there is so much resistance that they are never implemented at all'. While unilateral decisions often cause controversies, conflicts and delays, public involvement is likely to ease policy implementation through conflict resolution. It produces higher rates of implementation through the legitimation and acceptance of decisions, and the reduction of (existing or potential) conflicts among competing interests (Beierle & Cayford 2002; Lee 2014; Ulibarri 2015).

Finally, the ethical (or normative) rationale is strictly linked with the core of democratic life and the principle of self-determination. In a democracy, citizens, industries, interest groups, NGOs and local communities who are affected by national policies and governmental programmes have the right to express their values during policy-making and see them incorporated into public decisions (Thomas 2012). Therefore, public involvement strengthens the democratic nature of a political system through its policy and administrative decisions, and the way they are adopted (Blomgren Bingham *et al.* 2005; Irvin & Stansbury 2004; Lee *et al.* 2013).

Costs

Public involvement implies costs as well as benefits. Three major costs recur in the literature and relate to the content of decisions, managerial performance and matters of representation (Blomgren Bingham *et al.* 2005; West 2005) (Table 2.2).

Public involvement can have a negative impact on the content of public decisions. The public can be sometimes inadequately equipped with technical knowledge to deal with the complexity of some policy issues (Checkoway 1981; Thomas 1995). Moreover, public involvement could lead to trivial results since initial instances are likely to get watered down in the effort to build a consensus among actors with very different values and interests (Rowe & Frewer 2000). Hayden Lesbirel (2005: 8) argue that '[w]hile open and participatory decision processes have increasingly been seen to lead to better processes, [...] they may not lead to better outcomes'.

Public involvement can have negative impacts on the process, too. It can affect the managerial performance because it costs both time and money. Indeed, public involvement tends to slow down policy-making by introducing additional stages into an already complex process (Wilson 1999). The inclusion of multiple actors is likely to delay or, sometimes, paralyse policy-making through endless deliberations (Dietz & Stern 2008; Irvin & Stansbury 2004; Lee 2014; Thomas 2012). The organisation of a participatory process and the delay it may incur also have important financial repercussions. High costs of time and money for policy-makers can outweigh the benefits of public involvement, which explains why it can be perceived as a bureaucratic hurdle by those responsible for leading the policy process (Lee *et al.* 2013).

Finally, public involvement often poses problems of equality in the representation of citizens' and other societal interests. Those who participate often do not constitute a representative sample of the population, which makes public involvement "unrepresentative" (Thomas 1995). Important questions are raised as soon as public involvement is discussed or attempted and they all lead to the danger of imperfect representation: Who should participate and according to whom? What is the weight that is recognised to each stakeholder in the policy process? and so on. According to Thomas (2012), there is a general socio-economic bias in the participating actors, who tend to be those with more education and income. Moreover, in a general growing popular detachment from politics and institutions (see chapter 1), only stronger organised interests (namely industry) will more likely take part in a participatory process; this may result in representation unbalances and unfair decision-making (Irvin & Stansbury 2004).

The common counterargument about the costs of public involvement is that, overall, its benefits are higher than the costs. For instance, the protracted time needed for decisions may be worth if conflicts during implementation can, then, be avoided (Bobbio 2004; Irvin & Stansbury 2004; Lee 2014; Thomas 1995). However, a more realistic analysis of the benefits and costs of public involvement would recommend that public involvement in policy-making is contingent: it is desirable in some circumstances and not in others (Thomas 2012). As we have just seen, public involvement is not only good or bad. It can lead to better public decisions or pointless compromises. It can increase trust among actors but also result in inefficient decision-making. It can strengthen the democratic nature of a political system, but also perpetuate unbalances in representation. Ultimately, the pursuit of public involvement should avoid useless enthusiasm and pointless resistance. It should rather be the result of an attentive consideration about public interest. The same degree of desirable involvement – information, consultation or active participation (see above) – depends on the context (Thomas 2012).

Public involvement and policy implementation

We have defined public policies as government decisions and efforts to address public problems (Dye 1972; Howlett 2011). They are usually defined by a collection of documents that are produced by various institutions at different governmental levels (i.e. national and subnational[3] governments). Laws, rules, and various other official acts and practices cumulatively constitute a public policy (Birkland 2001; Howlett & Ramesh 2003; May 2012).

Primary laws adopted by elected officials in national parliaments only define the main legal framework that governs a given policy field. This framework is usually quite general and lacks the details needed for the execution of national policies. Once adopted by legislators, national legislation needs to be specified and executed by the administrative organisation of the state, i.e. the bureaucracy with its public agencies (Creighton 2005). This is policy implementation: a process of execution of policy decisions contained in national laws that follows the development of legislation (or policy formulation) (Howlett & Ramesh 2003). Policy implementation translates laws into action through a complex set of legal acts such as rules and regulations,[4] administrative routines and social practices with the purpose of achieving the objectives[5] defined in those laws (Hupe & Hill 2006; O'Toole 2012; Sabatier 1980). In the framework of implementation, public agencies conduct regulatory, planning, development and licensing activities (Lowry & Eichenberg 1986).

Administrative acts such as rules and regulations are also called "delegated legislation":[6] they are issued on the basis of a delegation of legislative authority attributed by the legislator (i.e. national parliaments) to public agencies (Page 2001; Rakar & Tičar 2015). Delegated legislation is intended to articulate, specify, refine, complement and shape the substance of primary legislation; in other words, rules implement laws (Kerwin & Furlong 2011). By supplementing the enactment of laws with rules, the "administrative decision-making" that issues them is a continuation of the legislative process. It constitutes, thus, the most important way in which public agencies contribute to the definition of national policies and play a key role as political actors in the policy process (Balla 2005; Lee 2014; Beierle & Cayford 2002; Thomas 2012). Besides issuing delegated legislation, national public administrations also carry out a wide range of operations during policy implementation. Civil servants adopt plans, administer programme activities, deliver services associated with a given public policy, authorise individual projects, etc. (Lee *et al.* 2013). This is the operationalisation of public policies (Napolitano 2007; West 2005).

Through the production of delegated legislation and the operationalisation of public policies, administrative officials have a large number of powers. In particular, the increasing decision-making role of national bureaucracies represents an important challenge in democratic political systems. The governmental agencies that specify laws through delegated legislation are not elected by the citizens; they are accountable to the delegating authorities but usually exercise considerable discretion beyond the letter of the law (Dietz & Stern 2008; Kerwin 1999). Therefore, in the democratic circuit citizens–parliament–government–administration, it is crucial that those affected by the decisions and actions of unelected bureaucrats can have direct influence on the administrative decision-making and operationalisation activities (Creighton 2005). This argument justifies the need for public involvement during policy implementation. Indeed, public involvement constitutes the indirect way to ensure the accountability and legitimacy of public agencies during the development of rules and other administrative activities (Balla 2005; Kerwin & Furlong 2011; Napolitano 2007; Thomas 1995).

The important role of citizens and target groups during the execution of public policies has been acknowledged for long time by the academic research on policy implementation. After a first wave of studies that looked at implementation as a mere process of administrative execution of political decisions taken in central governments, it has become clear that the sole leadership of central policy-makers cannot explain the complex dynamics of implementation (Barrett 2006; Younis & Davidson 1990). This "top-down approach" had overlooked the impact of lower-level officials and target groups on the execution of public policies (Howlett & Ramesh 2003; Matland 1995). Negotiation and consensus between policy-makers and administrative implementing agencies, and participatory mechanisms between the latter and target groups became the focus of a second wave of studies on policy implementation (Barrett 2006; Parsons 1995). This research adopted a "bottom-up perspective" and has conceptualised implementation as an open and dynamic process, where the bottom of the bureaucracy delivering the service – i.e. street-level bureaucrats – as well as the target groups of a given policy became relevant (Andresen *et al.* 1995; Maarse 1984; Matland 1995).

Particularly, Hjern and Porter (1981) stressed the importance of interactions between various (government and non-government) organisations involved in policy implementation, which they called "implementation structures". These implementation structures cross organisational borders and include clusters of public and private actors that are targeted by or interested in the same public programme, and form, thus, collaborative networks. The validity of this approach and the salience of inter-organisational relations for implementation has received abundant confirmation by the policy literature (Blomgren Bingham *et al.* 2005; Geurts & Joldersma 2001; Hanf & O'Toole 1992; Klijn & Koppenjan 2000; 2012; Howlett 2000; 2011; May 2012; O'Toole 2012). The bottom-up approach has also given particular relevance to the implementation structures operating at the local level (Winter 2012b).

Despite the important insights coming from the bottom-up strand of policy research, the implementation of national policies remains a complex process that depends on both central guidance (and control) and inter-organisational ties (e.g., citizens' reaction and centre-local relations) (Klijn 1996; Maarse 1984; Parsons 1995; O'Toole 2000; Winter 2006; 2012b). Some scholars have, thus, synthesised both approaches to study implementation. Winter's (1990; 2003; 2012a) integrative analytical framework is particularly interesting since it explains policy implementation and its results by looking at the whole policy-making process, yet through few clusters of variables: policy formulation, policy design and implementation process (in a given socio-economic context).

Policy formulation is the process of generation and assessment of possible actions that can tackle a public problem. These actions must not only be technically capable of correcting a problem and administratively feasible, but also politically acceptable to public opinion. Indeed, conflicts that are present during policy formulation continue into the implementation process that will follow (Winter 2003). Policy design is the content given to a specific public policy as (mainly) defined in primary laws (Schneider & Ingram 1990). The design of policies addressing highly technical issues – such as RWM – has usually been grounded in technical research (engineering analysis, risk assessment, geological screening, etc.). However, socio-political variables strongly affect policy implementation and they should not be neglected in the content given to public policies (Kraft 2000). The implementation process consists of the set of interactions that take place among various state and non-state actors, at the national and local level. These interactions are characterised by varying levels of commitment and coordination within public agencies, among them, and between them and target groups (Winter 2003).

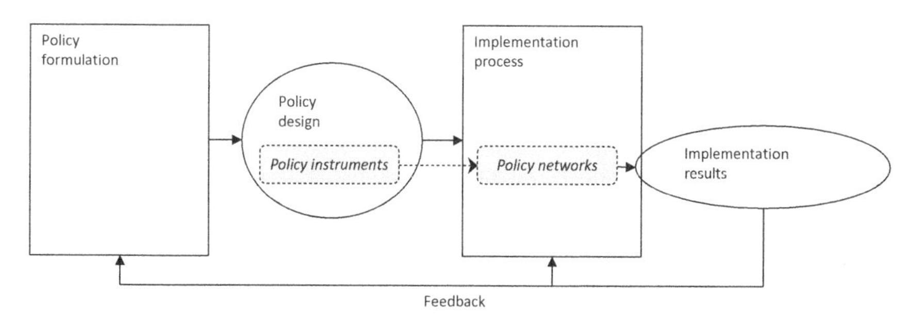

Figure 2.2 Analytical framework
Source: Adapted from Winter (2012a: 258)

Figure 2.2 simplifies the analytical framework developed by Winter (1990; 2003; 2012a) for the purpose of the book. This adaptation offers a simple but wide-ranging analytical tool to arrange several insights on public involvement. Indeed, useful considerations related to public involvement can be made for each one of the analytical components explaining policy implementation – policy formulation, policy design and the implementation process (as we will see in chapter 4). In particular, we will focus on the implementation process and its tie with policy design, for which further conceptual clarifications are provided in the following sections.

Implementation process: public involvement and policy networks

We have argued that the way governments make policies in the modern (Western) world has changed over the last decades. Public policies across a wide range of areas no longer emanate from a single authority but rather result from complex interactions among multiple public and private organisations. This new mode of producing and executing collective decisions through horizontal networks of public, private and non-profit organisations takes the name of *governance* (Blomgren Bingham *et al.* 2005; Klijn & Koppenjan 2012; Thomas 2012; van Asselt & Renn 2011).

This shift from government – where activities are decided and executed by institutions with formal authority and legal power – to governance goes hand in hand with the development of public involvement (Stoker 1998). Like public involvement, governance redefines the relations between state and society: it reflects the will of policy-makers and public administrators to seek "power with" the citizens rather than "power over" the citizens (Cooper 1984). The concept of governance emphasises the inter-organisational nature of public policies in modern times: governments engage the public in policy-making through horizontal interactions and a series of collaborative arrangements (Kasymova & Lauer Schachter 2014).

In fact, the presence of inter-organisational connections in policy-making is well known in the literature on policy implementation since the bottom-up approach, and the work of Hjern and Porter (1981) (see above). Their idea that implementation structures – understood as collaborations (or partnerships) among private, semi-public bodies, public agencies, national and local governments – are at the heart of the execution of public policies (Stoker 1998; Thomas 2012) has been revamped through the newer concept of "policy networks"[7] (Hanf & O'Toole 1992; Klijn 1996; 2008; Winter 2012b).

A policy network consists of a complex web of linkages among government agencies and societal organisations (Hanf & O'Toole 1992; Klijn 2008; Rhodes 1984; Skogstad 2005). These actors assemble around a policy issue with different interests and objectives but are mutually dependent because they share the resources needed to take a decision, put it into practice and solve that issue (Bobbio 2004; Klijn 1996). Resource dependency is the core factor that initiates and sustains networks among actors with a different perception on problems' definition and solution (Börzel 1997; Klijn 1996). Resources are both material and immaterial assets such as: knowledge (understood as information, evidence and expertise); money (i.e. funds); authority or power (including leadership, political support and public legitimacy); and organisation (e.g., structure and personnel) (Bobbio 2004; Klijn 2007; O'Toole 2012; Peterson 2003).

To sum up, the development and implementation of public policies take place across a complex set of (governmental and non-governmental) organisations (i.e. policy networks) that are mutually dependent to reach decisions and solve public problems (Börzel 1997; Klijn 1996; 2007; 2008; Klijn & Koppenjan 2012; OECD 2017b; Van Gils & Klijn 2007). In this context, implementation can improve if patterns of cooperation and collaborative arrangements emerge among public and private organisations involved in the implementation process. Intergovernmental relations and the creation of mechanisms that ensure coordination across layers of government also become very important (May 2012; O'Toole 2012). Both inter-organisational and intergovernmental relations during the implementation process can be changed and improved by governments through the use of specific policy instruments and their inclusion in policy design (Börzel 1997; May 2012; Stoker 1998; Winter 2003).

Policy design: public involvement and policy instruments

In the context of the shift from government to governance and a new mode of developing and executing public policies through policy networks, it is important to understand how citizens and all relevant stakeholders can participate in these networks (Thomas 1995). During policy implementation, agencies can open the decision-making process to the influence of interested and affected parties in ways that can be defined by policy design (Dietz & Stern 2008; Winter 2003). Policy design specifies the objectives of a public policy and the tools that governments use to reach those objectives (Howlett 2011; Howlett *et al.* 2009; Schneider & Ingram 1990). Some of these tools, i.e. the *substantive* implementation instruments (such as sanctions, taxes, subsidies, etc.) are used during implementation to intervene on the substance of a socio-economic system by affecting the production, distribution, and consumption of goods and services in society. Other types of policy instruments can, instead, be used to affect the same process of implementation. These *procedural* implementation instruments alter the constellations of actors involved in a public policy (or policy networks) and their interactions by influencing the political behaviour of their members (Howlett 2000; 2011; Shroff *et al.* 2012).

Therefore, procedural implementation instruments are crucial for public involvement during policy implementation (Schneider & Ingram 1990): they can be used by governments to promote networks' formation, create new interactions within policy networks, manipulate existing relationships, institutionalise inter-organisational interactions, regulate conflicts and alter actors' policy positions (Hanf & O'Toole 1992; Howlett 2000; 2011; Howlett *et al.* 2015;

Shroff *et al.* 2012). Procedural implementation instruments have, nonetheless, been less studied by scholarly research than their substantive counterpart (Howlett 2011); this calls for 'more systematic assessment, inventories, categories and models of procedural policy tools' (Howlett 2000: 424).

A useful distinction among procedural implementation instruments is the one proposed by Howlett (2000; 2011) that builds on the study of Hood (1983) on substantive tools. According to Hood (1983), governments dispose of few types of resources that they can employ for policy instruments: knowledge, money, authority and organisation (see also Shroff *et al.* 2012; Winter 2012b). Based on this distinction, Howlett (2000; 2011) identifies four types of procedural implementation instruments.

First, "procedural informational instruments" are used to alter the behaviour of policy network members through the use of knowledge. This category of instruments consists of information disclosure and access to documents (Howlett 2011; Howlett *et al.* 2009; Shroff *et al.* 2012).

Second, "procedural financial instruments" are techniques which involve the transfer of treasure resources to individuals, firms and organisations with the aim of altering the nature of the policy process. They can consist of the provision of money for the creation or mobilisation of interest groups, known as advocacy funding (Howlett 2011; Howlett *et al.* 2009; Shroff *et al.* 2012).

Third, "procedural authoritative instruments" involve the exercise of government authority to assure preferential treatment to certain actors in the policy process. These tools mobilise specific policy actors through their special recognition, for instance in advisory mechanisms such as public consultations and hearings, advisory bodies, etc. (Howlett 2011; Howlett *et al.* 2009; Shroff *et al.* 2012).

Fourth, "procedural organisational instruments" rely upon the use of the organisational resources of governments, such as structures and personnel, in order to affect the policy process. They mainly consist of institutional reorganisation (or reform): governments create new agencies or reconfigure existing administrative structures with the aim of affecting interactions in the community of policy actors (Howlett 2011; Howlett *et al.* 2009; Shroff *et al.* 2012).

In the words of Howlett (2000: 420), this classification (or taxonomy) 'is useful insofar as it [...] allows a virtually unlimited number of instruments to be placed in a limited number of general categories'. I will come back to policy instruments in greater detail in chapter 5 where it will be clear that a classification of existing (participatory) instruments is needed to analyse public involvement in the domain of RWM.

Concluding remarks

National legal frameworks set the design of public policies. Policy implementation specifies this design through rules, regulations, programmes, plans, projects and a large amount of activities that give execution to national legislation and can generate conflicts among the actors involved. The book looks at public involvement during the implementation of public policies for the management of RW. It does so by emphasising the process. Rowe and Frewer (2000) warn that there can be situations where public involvement is visible in the process, but it does not lead to any actual influence of citizens and other stakeholders in the final result (i.e. public decision or activity). Yet, the process is an important component; as put by Reed (2008: 2421) 'the quality of a decision is strongly dependant on the quality of the process that leads to it'.

In the implementation process, different types of interactions can be established among the actors involved. Policy-makers and public administrators can intervene on these relations through policy design. They can use procedural implementation instruments to foster collaborative behaviours, ameliorate conflicts and ease the achievement of policy objectives (Howlett 2000; O'Toole 2012). Indeed, policy implementation is shaped by choices of policy design (May 2012); the analytical framework borrowed and adapted from Winter (1990; 2003; 2012a) conceptualises these connections.

The analytical framework also unveils that policy implementation is more than a managerial, administrative and technocratic activity (May 2003). The implementation process is made of interactions among multiple actors and is under the pressure of a variety of organisations with competing interests: political elites (at national and subnational level), implementing agencies, economic interests, target groups, etc. (Parsons 1995). After the adoption of a public policy, its implementation continues, thus, the political game among these actors (Bardach 1977; Winter 2012b). This "political" game consists of 'patterns of power and influence between and within organisations' (Morgan 1990: 52); it determines who gets what, when, and how, which is at the core of politics (Lasswell 1936). Therefore, policy implementation is "policy politics" (May 2012). Even when policies are adequately designed, their implementation can fail if it does not take into account the realities of power, defined as 'the ability of groups opposed to the policy to block the efforts of its supporters' (Morgan 1990: 52).

Notes

1 An important distinction is the one between public involvement and public deliberation. Public deliberation is commonly understood as a way of revising preferences, reconciling diverging points of view and producing well-informed opinions through debate, discussion and the exchange of arguments and new information (Delli Carpini *et al.* 2004; Michels & De Graaf 2010). The book focuses on public involvement and does not deal with public deliberation.
2 For instance, the NEA (2013c) prefers to distinguish between these terms. Openness indicates an attitude and consists of the willingness to listen, change and adapt. Transparency refers, instead, to a process, namely the process of making actions visible by enabling people to access and understand information.
3 The subnational level does not only refer to the local level. Depending on the national institutional context, intermediate levels (i.e. regions, provinces, departments, etc.) can be found between the central and local levels of government. For sake of simplification, the book focuses, though, on the national and local levels only.
4 The terms "rule" and "regulation" can be used interchangeably (West 2005).

5 Policy objectives (or goals) indicate the desirable situation that a policy intends to achieve (Howlett & Ramesh 2003).
6 The term is rather general but useful for international comparisons where researchers have to deal with the "substantial and institutional heterogeneity" of delegated legislation (Rakar & Tičar 2015). The term is also useful for looking at the EU as a region of 28 different national systems.
7 The academic literature has abundantly investigated the concept of policy network (e. g., Hill & Hupe 2009; Klijn 1996; 2007; Klijn & Koppenjan 2012; Schneider 1987; Skogstad 2005) but a full review falls out of the scope of this section.

References

Andersson, K. (2008) *Transparency and Accountability in Science and Politics. The Awareness Principle*, Palgrave MacMillan, Basingstoke and New York.

André, P. (2006) "Public Participation – Best Practice Principles", in *IAIA Special Publications Series*, No. 4.

Andresen, S., Skjoerseth, J. B. and Wettestad, J. (1995) *Regime, the State and Society: Analyzing the Implementation of International Environmental Commitments*, Working Paper, International Institute for Applied Systems Analysis, Laxenburg.

Arnstein, S. R. (1969) "A Ladder of Citizen Participation", in *Journal of the American Institute of Planners*, Vol. 35, No. 4, pp. 216–224.

Balla, S. J. (2005) "Between Commenting and Negotiation: The Contours of Public Participation in Agency Rulemaking", in *I/S: A Journal of Law and Policy*, Vol. 1, pp. 59–94.

Bardach, E. (1977) *The Implementation Game*, MIT Press, Cambridge MA.

Barrett, S. M. (2006) "Implementation Studies: Time for a Revival?" in Budd, L., Charlesworth, J. and Paton, R. (Eds) *Making Policy Happen*, Routledge, New York.

Beierle, T. C., and Cayford, J. (2002) *Democracy in Practice. Public Participation in Environmental Decisions*, Resources for the Future, Washington DC.

Birkland, T. A. (2001) *An Introduction to the Policy Process – Theories, Concepts, and Models of Public Policy Making*, M. E. Sharpe, Armonk-London.

Bishop, P. and Davis, G. (2002) "Mapping Public Participation in Policy Choices", in *Australian Journal of Public Administration*, Vol. 61, No. 1, pp. 14–29.

Blomgren Bingham, L., Nabatchi. T. and O'Leary, R. (2005) "The New Governance: Practices and Processes for Stakeholder and Citizen Participation in the Work of Government", in *Public Administration Review*, Vol. 65, No. 5, pp. 547–558.

Bobbio, L. (2004) *A piu' voci – Amministrazioni pubbliche, imprese, associazioni e cittadini nei processi decisionali inclusivi*, Edizioni Scientifiche Italiane, Rome.

Bollens, S. A. (1993) "Restructuring Land Use Governance", in *Journal of Planning Literature*, Vol. 7, No. 3, pp. 211–226.

Börzel, T. A. (1997) "What's So Special About Policy Networks? – An Exploration of the Concept and Its Usefulness in Studying European Governance", in *European Integration Online Papers*, Vol. 1, No. 16.

Burby, R. J. (2003) "Making Plans that Matter: Citizen Involvement and Government Action", in *Journal of the American Planning Association*, Vol. 69, No. 1, pp. 33–49.

Checkoway, B. (1981) "The Politics of Public Hearings", in *The Journal of Applied Behavioural Science*, Vol. 17, No. 4, pp. 566–582.

Cooper, T. L. (1984) "Citizenship and Professionalism in Public Administration", in *Public Administration Review*, Vol. 44, Special Issue March, pp. 143–151.

Creighton, J. L. (2005) *The Public Participation Handbook. Making Better Decisions Through Citizen Involvement*, Jossey-Bass, San Francisco.
Delli Carpini, M. X., Cook, F. L. and Jacobs, L. R. (2004) "Public Deliberation, Discursive Participation, and Citizen Engagement: A Review of the Empirical Literature", *Annual Reviews of Political Science*, Vol. 7, pp. 315–344.
Dietz, T. and Stern, P. C. (2008) *Public Participation in Environmental Assessment and Decision Making*, The National Academy Press, Washington DC.
Dye, T. R. (1972) *Understanding Public Policy*, Prentice-Hall, Upper Saddle River, NJ.
Geurts, J. L. A. and Joldersma, C. (2001) "Methodology for Participatory Policy Analysis", in *European Journal of Operational Research*, Vol. 128, pp. 300–310.
Hanf, K. and O'Toole, L. J. (1992) "Revisiting Old Friends: Networks, Implementation Structures and the Management of Inter-organizational Relations", in *European Journal of Political Research*, Vol. 21, pp. 163–180.
Hayden Lesbirel, S. (2005) "Transaction Costs and Institutional Change", in Hayden Lesbirel, S. and Shaw, D. (Eds) *Managing Conflict in Facility Siting*, Edward Elgar, Cheltenham and Northampton.
Hjern, B. and Porter, O. (1981) "Implementation Structures: A New Unit of Administrative Analysis", in *Organization Studies*, Vol. 2, No. 3, pp. 211–227.
Hill, M. and Hupe, P. (2009). *Implementing Public Policy*. SAGE Publications Ltd, London.
Hood, C. (1983) *The Tools of Government*, The MacMillan Press Ltd, London and Basingstoke.
Howlett, M. (2000) "Managing the 'Hollow State': Procedural Policy Instruments and Modern Governance", in *Canadian Public Administration*, Vol. 43, No. 4, pp. 412–431.
Howlett, M. (2011) *Designing Public Policies. Principles and Instruments*, Routledge, Abingdon.
Howlett, M. and Ramesh, M. (2003) *Studying Public Policy – Policy Cycles and Policy Subsystems*, Oxford University Press, Oxford.
Howlett, M., Ramesh, M. and Perl, A. (2009). *Studying Public Policy – Policy Cycles and Policy Subsystems*, Oxford University Press, Oxford.
Howlett, M., Mukherjee, I. and Woo, J. J. (2015) "Thirty Years of Instrument Research: What Have We Learned and Where Are We Going", Paper Presented at the International Conference of Public Policy (ICPP), 3 July, Milan, Italy.
Hupe, P. L. and Hill, M. (2006) "The Three Action Levels of Governance: Re-framing the Policy Process Beyond the Stages Model", in Peters, B. G. and Pierre, J. (Eds) *Handbook of Public Policy*, Sage Publications, London.
Irvin, R. A. and Stansbury, J. (2004) "Citizen Participation in Decision Making: Is It Worth the Effort?", in *Public Administration Review*, Vol. 64, No. 1, pp. 55–65.
Joss, S. (1999) "Public Participation in Science and Technology Policy- and Decision-making – Ephemeral Phenomenon or Lasting Change?" in *Science and Public Policy*, Vol. 26, No. 5, pp. 290–293.
Kasymova, J. T. and Lauer Schachter, H. (2014) "Bringing Participatory Tools to a Different Level", in *Public Performance & Management Review*, Vol. 37, No. 3, pp. 441–464.
Kerwin, C. (1999) *Rulemaking: How Government Agencies Write Law and Make Policy*, Congressional Quarterly, Inc., Washington DC.
Kerwin, C. M. and Furlong, S. R. (2011) *Rulemaking: How Government Agencies Write Law and Make Policy*, Congressional Quarterly, Inc., Washington DC.
Klijn, E.-H. (1996) "Analyzing and Managing Policy Processes in Complex Networks: A Theoretical Examination of the Concept Policy Network and Its Problems", in *Administration and Society*, Vol. 28, No. 1, pp. 90–119.

Klijn, E.-H. (2006) "Managing Stakeholder Involvement in Decision-Making. A Comparative Analysis of Six Interactive Processes in The Netherlands", Paper presented at the Conference on Governance and Performance: Organizational Status, Management Capacity and Public Service, 15–16 March, Birmingham.

Klijn, E.-H. (2007) "Managing Complexity: Achieving the Impossible? Management between Complexity and Stability: A Network Perspective", in *Critical Policy Analysis*, Vol. 1, No. 3, pp. 252–277.

Klijn, E.-H. (2008) "Governance and Governance Networks in Europe: An Assessment of 10 Years of Research on the Theme", in *Public Management Review*, Vol. 10, No. 4, pp. 505–525.

Klijn, E.-H. and Koppenjan, J. F. M. (2000) "Public Management and Policy Networks. Foundation of a Network Approach to Governance", in *Public Management*, Vol. 2, No. 2, pp. 135–158.

Klijn, E.-H. and Koppenjan, J. F. M. (2012) "Governance Network Theory: Past, Present and Future", in *Policy and Politics*, Vol. 40, No. 4, pp. 587–606.

Kraft, M. E. (2000) "Policy Design and the Acceptability of Environmental Risks: Nuclear Waste Disposal in Canada and the United States", in *Policy Studies Journal*, Vol. 28, No. 1, pp. 206–218.

Lasswell, H. D. (1936) *Politics: Who Gets What, When, How*, Peter Smith Publishers, Gloucester, MA.

Lee, J. (2014) "Public Meetings for Efficient Administrative Performance in the United States", in *Public Performance & Management Review*, Vol. 37, No. 3, pp. 388–411.

Lee, M., Armeni, C., de Cendra, J., Chaytor, S., Lock, S., Maslin, M., Redgwell, C. and Rydin, Y. (2013) "Public Participation and Climate Change Infrastructure", in *Journal of Environmental Law*, Vol. 25, No. 1, pp. 33–62.

Lowry, K. and Eichenberg, T. (1986) "Assessing Intergovernmental Coordination in Coastal Zone Management", in *Policy Studies Review*, Vol. 6, No. 2, pp. 321–329.

Luyet, V., Schlaepfer, R., Parlange, M. B. and Buttler, A. (2012) "A Framework to Implement Stakeholder Participation in Environmental Projects", in *Journal of Environmental Management*, Vol. 111, pp. 213–219.

Maarse, H. (1984) *Some Problems in Implementation Analysis*, EGPA Occasional Papers, Conference on Policy Implementation with Special Reference to Agriculture, 3–5 September, Dublin.

Matland, R. E. (1995) "Synthesizing the Implementation Literature: The Ambiguity-Conflict Model of Policy Implementation", in *Journal of Public Administration Research and Theory*, Vol. 5, No. 2, pp. 145–174.

May, P. J. (2003) "Policy Design and Implementation", in Peters, B. G. and Pierre, J. (Eds) *Handbook of Public Administration*, SAGE Publications, London, Thousand Oaks, Delhi.

May, P. J. (2012) "Policy Design and Implementation", in Peters, B. G. and Pierre, J. (Eds) *The SAGE Handbook of Public Administration*, 2nd Edition, SAGE, Los Angeles and London.

Michels, A. and De Graaf, L. (2010) "Examining Citizen Participation: Local Participatory Policy Making and Democracy", in *Local Government Studies*, Vol. 36, No. 4, pp. 477–491.

Morgan, C. (1990) "Asbestos Policy and Practice in a Local Authority", in Younis, T. (Ed.) *Implementation in Public Policy*, Dartmouth, Aldershot.

Munro-Clark, M. (1992) (Ed.) *Citizen Participation in Government*, Hale and Iremonger, Sydney.

Napolitano, G. (2007) (Ed.) *Diritto amministrativo comparato*, Giuffré, Milan.

NEA (2013c) *Stakeholder Confidence in Radioactive Waste Management: An Annotated Glossary of Key Terms*, OECD, Paris.

NRC (2003) *One Step at a Time: The Staged Development of Geologic Repositories for High-Level Radioactive Waste*, The National Academic Press, Washington D.C.

O'Connor, M. and van den Hove, S. (2001) "Prospects for Public Participation on Nuclear Risks and Policy Options: Innovations in Governance Practices for Sustainable Development in the European Union", in *Journal of Hazardous Materials*, Vol. 86, pp. 77–99.

OECD (2001a) *Citizens as Partners. OECD handbook on information, consultation and public participation in policy-making*, OECD, Paris.

OECD (2001b) *Engaging Citizens in Policy-making: information, consultation and public participation*, OECD, Paris.

OECD (2005) *Public Sector Modernisation: Open Government*, OECD, Paris.

OECD (2008) *Mind the Gap: Fostering Open and Inclusive Policy Making*, OECD, Paris.

OECD (2017a) *Trust and Public Policy – How better governance can help rebuild public trust*, OECD, Paris.

OECD (2017b) *Policy Advisory Systems – Supporting Good Governance and Sound Public Decision Making*, OECD, Paris.

O'Toole, L. J.Jr. (2000) "Research on Policy Implementation: Assessment and Prospects", in *Journal of Public Administration Research and Theory*, Vol. 10, No. 2, pp. 263–288.

O'Toole, L. J. (2012), "Interorganizational Relations and Policy Implementation", in Peters, B. G. and Pierre, J. (Eds) *The SAGE Handbook of Public Administration*, SAGE, Los Angeles and London.

Page, E. (2001) *Governing by Numbers. Delegated Legislation and Everyday Policy-Making*, Hart Publishing, Oxford and Portland.

Parsons, W. (1995) *Public Policy. An Introduction to the Theory and the Practice of Policy Analysis*, Edward Elgar, Cheltenham and Northampton.

Peterson, J. (2003) *Policy Networks*, Political Science Series, Institute for Advanced Studies, Vienna.

Pollitt, C. and Hupe, P. (2011) "Talking About Government. The Role of Magic Concepts", in *Public Management Review*, Vol. 13, No. 5, pp. 641–658.

Rakar, I. and Tičar, B. (2015) "The Rulemaking Procedure – Definition, Concepts and Public Participation", in *Danube: Law and Economics Review*, Vol. 6, No. 2, pp. 109–118.

Reed, M. S. (2008) "Stakeholder Participation for Environmental Management: A Literature Review", in *Biological Conservation*, Vol. 141, pp. 2417–2431.

Rhodes, R. A. W. (1984) "Power Dependence, Policy Communities and Intergovernmental Networks", in *Public Administration Bulletin*, Vol. 49, pp. 4–31.

Rowe, G. and Frewer, L. J. (2000), "Public Participation Methods: A Framework for Evaluation", in *Science, Technology, & Human Values*, Vol. 25, No. 1, pp. 3–29.

Sabatier, P. A. (1980) "The Implementation of Public Policy: A Framework of Analysis", in *Policy Studies Journal*, Vol. 8, No. 2, pp. 538–560.

Schneider, V. (1987) "The Structure of Policy Networks", Paper presented at the "ECPR Workshop", April.

Schneider, A. and Ingram, H. (1990) "Behavioral Assumptions of Policy Tools", in *The Journal of Politics*, Vol. 52, No. 2, pp. 510–529.

Shroff, M. R., Jones, S. J., Frongillo, E. A. and Howlett, M. (2012) "Policy Instruments Used by States Seeking to Improve School Food Environments", in *American Journal of Public Health*, Vol. 102, No. 2, pp. 222–229.

Skogstad, G. (2005) "Policy Networks and Policy Communities: Conceptual Evolution and Governing Realities", Paper presented at the Workshop on Canada's Contribution to Comparative Theorizing, London (Ontario, Canada).

Stoker, G. (1998) "Governance as Theory: Five Propositions", in *International Social Science Journal*, Vol. 50, No. 155, pp. 17–28.

Thomas, J. C. (1995) *Public Participation in Public Decisions: New Skills and Strategies for Public Managers*, Jossey-Bass, San Francisco.

Thomas, J. C. (2012) *Citizen, Customer, Partner: Engaging the Public in Public Management*, Routledge, Abingdon and New York.

Thurston, W. E., MacKean, G., Vollman, A., Casebeer, A., Webre, M., Maloff, B. and Bader, J. (2005) "Public Participation in Regional Health Policy: A Theoretical Framework", in *Health Policy*, Vol. 79, pp. 237–252.

Ulibarri, N. (2015) "Tracing Process to Performance of Collaborative Governance: A Comparative Case Study of Federal Hydropower Licensing", in *Policy Studies Journal*, Vol. 43, No. 2, pp. 1–26.

van Asselt, M. B. A. and Renn, O. (2011) "Risk Governance", in *Journal of Risk Research*, Vol. 14, No. 4, pp. 431–449.

van Gils, M. and Klijn, E.-H. (2007) "Complexity in Decision Making: the Case of the Rotterdam Harbour Expansion. Connecting Decisions, Arenas and Actors in Spatial Decision Making", in *Planning Theory and Practice*, Vol. 8, No. 2, pp. 139–159.

West, W. (2005) "Administrative Rulemaking: An Old and Emerging Literature", in *Public Administration Review*, Vol. 65, No. 6, pp. 655–668.

Wilson, D. (1999) "Exploring the Limits of Public Participation in Local Government", in *Parliamentary Affairs*, Vol. 52, No. 2, pp. 246–259.

Winter, S. (1990) "Integrating Implementation Research", in Palumbo, D. J. and Calista, D. (Eds) *Implementation and the 'Policy Process – Opening Up the Black Box*, Greenwood Press, New York, Westport, CT and London.

Winter, S. (2003) "Introduction", in Peters, B. G. and Pierre, J. (Eds) *Handbook of Public Administration*, SAGE Publications, London, Thousand Oaks and Delhi.

Winter, S. C. (2006) "Implementation", in Peters, B. G. and Pierre, J. (Eds), *Handbook of Public Policy*, Sage Publications, London.

Winter, S. (2012a), "Implementation", in Peters, B. G. and Pierre, J. (Eds), *Handbook of Public Policy*, Sage Publications, London.

Winter, S. (2012b) "Implementation Perspectives: Status and Reconsideration", in Peters, B. G. and Pierre, J. (Eds) *The SAGE Handbook of Public Administration*, SAGE, Los Angeles and London.

Younis, T. and Davidson, I. (1990) "The Study of Implementation", in Younis, T. (Ed.) *Implementation in Public Policy*, Dartmouth, Aldershot.

3 The institutional challenge, key issues and stakeholders' needs

Radioactive waste management (RWM) is a highly technical issue with important social and political aspects that have often been neglected in the past (chapter 1). Indeed, three major challenges characterise RWM: the technical management of radioactive waste (RW); the response to social concerns; and the institutional integration of both these aspects in the process of collective decisions, which constitutes the focus of the book (see Introduction). In order to better understand the institutional challenge and the socio-political dimension of RWM, we start our investigation on public involvement by exploring the major concerns of stakeholders from the field across the EU.

As put by Thomas (2012), in any effort to introduce, develop or understand public involvement it is important to first know in detail the problems and expectations of the publics that are involved: Do we know what they want? More broadly, we need to understand what stakeholders expect from public involvement, which weaknesses they face and which areas for improvements they indicate.

The chapter analyses the data collected through a survey conducted across the EU on a wide range of stakeholders involved in national RWM systems: national policy-makers and governmental departments, municipalities and local authorities, national regulatory bodies and implementing agencies, industrial organisations, advisory and consultative bodies, scientific research institutes, civil society associations and NGOs, and other organisations (e.g., sectoral and professional associations, and consultancies). The survey was designed to explore the major issues and needs perceived by these different categories of actors with regard to public involvement in RWM. The survey results indicate several important themes, thus suggesting relevant directions for investigation.

Stakeholders' views: identification of emergent themes

The stakeholders of a national system for the management of RW include a broad range of actors and organisations: policy-makers at the national and subnational levels; regulatory and implementing agencies; industrial organisations (such as NPP operators); advisory and consultative bodies; scientific research institutes; civil society associations and NGOs; and other organisations (e.g., sectoral and professional associations, and consultancies) (Di Nucci *et al.* 2015; Yanev 2009).

The IAEA (2011b) defines roles for those actors who have formal responsibilities for RWM. National governments establish the legal and regulatory framework. They play a key role in the public information and participation of citizens and all actors involved in RWM. The regulatory body is responsible for all regulatory matters – including licensing applications and their approval – and for this purpose it interacts with operators and the implementing agency. Regulators have also a legal obligation to inform stakeholders about their activity. The implementing agencies – also referred to as Waste Management Organisations (WMOs) – carry out the RWM policies established by their governments. They, too, have an obligation of public information and participation.

The views of stakeholders about public involvement in RWM were collected through a survey conducted in 2015.[1] Surveys are commonly used as data-collection methods to 'describe, compare, or explain individual and societal knowledge, feelings, values, preferences, and behaviours' (Fink 2009: 11). The survey discussed in this chapter was designed to understand stakeholders' opinions, attitudes and behaviours about public involvement in RWM. The survey had an exploratory nature and wanted to solicit spontaneous answers from respondents. For this reason it has relied on an open-ended question that would elicit a large variety of responses:[2]

> 'In your opinion, what relevant questions about public participation in RWM still need to be answered? In other words, which aspects of public participation in RWM need to be better understood?'

With the purpose of capturing a broad picture of stakeholders' needs and concerns about RWM, the survey has used a broad definition of public participation (which was included in the questionnaire): 'Public participation means the involvement of stakeholders in the decision-making processes that affect their interests or in which they are interested.'[3] For the reasons explained in chapter 2, public participation and public involvement are used as synonyms in the questionnaire. However, respondents clearly distinguished in their answers between public information and more active forms of public participation. The distinction was kept in the analysis as shown below.

Respondents were invited to provide their opinion about public involvement in RWM, and a description of key issues that still remain open or needs that are not yet met in the pursuit and execution of public involvement in RWM. More than 270 organisations from the RWM domain were contacted. With a response rate of about 40 per cent,[4] responses have ensured a good coverage of categories of stakeholders in the Member States (MSs) of the EU (see Figure 3.1).

The answers were encoded so that information could be extracted, summarised and structured along arguments and category of stakeholder.[5] Texts were, indeed, analysed and systematised into "emergent themes". Themes were then linked to form a coordinated picture. Far from being comprehensive about the multifaceted problem of public involvement in RWM, the chapter discusses five core themes emerging from the survey (Figure 3.2):

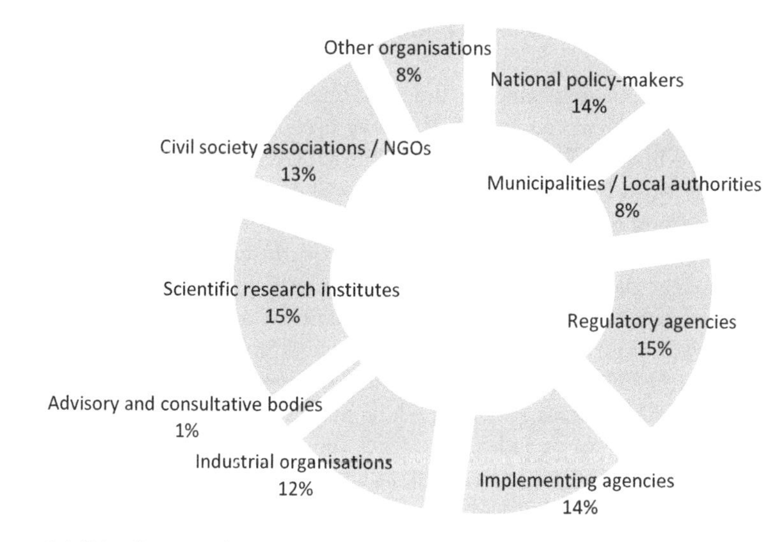

Figure 3.1 Distribution of responses per category of stakeholders

- Public information;
- Public participation;
- Resources;
- Participants;
- Dialogue and trust.

The survey responses have helped to narrow down the investigation about public involvement in RWM to a few themes. Indeed, the access to data from 28 MSs has made it possible to trace and reveal general features and similarities about major problems commonly perceived across countries. The analysis remains descriptive and limited to the survey respondents with no claim of inference to *all* stakeholders. The discussion of responses presented in this chapter summarises and displays public comments in order to provide the maximum amount of information without introducing interpretation or judgement and, thus, avoid any bias. Therefore, the narrative used to present the analysis collates and synthesises the original answers but does not introduce any evaluation on the responses provided.[6] In some cases, additional supporting information is taken from the literature or recalled from previous chapters.

Public information: safety and risk perception

Public involvement can take place with varying degrees of intensity according to the objective that policy-makers and public administrators decide to pursue. The lowest level of citizens' involvement in policy-making is information, a one-way channel of communication that allows citizens and other stakeholders to know about governmental decisions and actions (see chapter 2). Survey respondents argue that information is pivotal in the field of RWM, and it needs to be "sufficient" and "correct".

The need for an adequate amount and good quality of information is due to two main features that characterise RWM in the eyes of laypeople. As we said in chapter 1, RWM facilities are a special type of LULUs; they are aimed at managing the hazardous waste (first feature) of a contested activity such as nuclear energy production (second feature). The hazard that characterises RWM facilities distinguishes them from other non-hazardous LULUs. It follows that stakeholders demand sufficient and correct information particularly with regard to the safety of RWM. Safety of RW storage and disposal emerges as a common concern for all actors involved, from policy-makers to public administrators, from industrial organisations to NGOs. Moreover, sufficient and correct information about safety is crucial for RWM because – like the whole nuclear energy field – it is a domain where negative opinions, prejudices and fears abound.

Laymen continue to have many misconceptions about RWM and the risk it implies. Therefore, they need to be provided with thorough explanations about the safety measures put in place to manage RW, the possible consequences in case of accidents and the technical solutions available to protect the population. The information provided should answer basic but important questions that populate citizens' concerns: "What is radioactivity?", "How is RW generated?", "How long is the waste really dangerous?", "How is RW isolated, stored and ultimately disposed?". Respondents from different organisations and countries agree that providing clear answers to these questions and citizens' concerns about safety is the only way to help them understand the actual risk associated with RW.

Indeed, a strong discrepancy exists, in RWM, between actual risks and risk perception. The risk assessed by scientists and the risk perceived by non-scientists is very different; the degree of actual risk that RWM brings along is often misunderstood by laymen. For instance, the same technical distinction between LLW, ILW and HLW is not understood by the general public that sees these different types of waste as radioactive and, therefore, equally dangerous (chapter 1).

The discrepancy between the risk perception of experts and laymen is a well-known problem in the literature (Boholm 2008) and certain types of facilities are commonly associated with high risk in public perception. This applies not only to RWM facilities; chemical plants constitute another relevant example. As explained by Armour (1991: 29): 'There are substantial differences between the risk estimates of experts and laypersons and these differences result, in large part, from differences between the risk perceptions of experts and those of the public'. The consequence is that although experts may agree that a given well-designed and well-managed hazardous facility poses limited risks, host communities and the general public tend to base its opinions, attitudes and behaviours on different risk estimates.

This difference is crucial. Renn (1998: 60) explains that '[i]ndividuals respond according to their perception of risk and not according to an objective risk level or the scientific assessment of risk'. Therefore, hostility often amplifies under the perception of risk rather than the real risk itself (Kuhn & Ballard 1998). Social resistance has obvious political repercussions and stands as a major policy challenge in all democratic nations. Public opposition to hazardous facilities has often caused policy impasses in many countries, with disagreements, conflicts and delays surrounding their siting and development.

The problem seems more acute in RWM. As noted by Weingart (2007: 29), 'the scientific community's beliefs about radioactive safety in general are dramatically different from those of most of the general public. The gaps appear deeper and wider than the differences accompanying other public issues'. As we argued in chapter 1, the field of nuclear energy is highly technical and its technology unknown to the many. Ignorance creates fear, irrespective of how much evidence is produced and shown by scientists, experts and specialists. The impact of the past amplifies the feeling of danger. The result is that in RWM, "safe" and "acceptable" are not interchangeable attributes (Weingart 2007). The former belongs to the domain of science and facts, where scientific analysis investigates permissible levels of risk. The latter has to do with public confidence and relates to the world of society where risk is assessed on the basis of existing beliefs, values and preferences (Renn 1998).

Correcting wrong perceptions is not an easy task and such challenge is well known to national WMOs; one of them asks 'How [can we] face effectively wide spread half-true information on radioactivity and radiation?'. It is, indeed, recognised that, because of the strong role of emotions involved in RWM, the mere use of scientific and technical knowledge to inform the public will not dissolve people's fears about RWM. 'The words "radiation", "radioactive", and "nuclear" have too much power' (Weingart 2007: 361). Fear for radioactivity and nuclear energy dates back decades (see chapter 1). One research organisation clearly explains,

> There is certainly no direct link between increased scientific understanding and a public position for or against different strategies of nuclear waste disposal. This is not due to the public being poorly informed, but rather due to cultural cognition of expertise and historical and cultural perception of hazards to regions selected to host a geologic repository.

People's perception of risk is influenced by multiple factors that are intertwined with each other along a complex web of causal relations that social scientists have not yet completely untangled. However, ensuring public information as part of the work of legislators and government administrators involved in RWM seems to constitute an important factor in this web of causalities. Two major challenges are faced in the provision of information about RWM to the general public.

First of all, civil society organisations claim that scientific knowledge about safety should be complete and simplified. Although the point is acknowledged also by public authorities, many survey respondents agree that it is difficult to deliver simplified information on RWM because of its technical and scientific complexity. The result is that complete but vulgarised information about RWM is often missing, as pointed out by a research institute. A possible solution could be to use tailored communication – but what types of communication channels are most suitable for different target groups remains a point of debate. It is the opinion of the author that insights from the discipline of risk communication and behavioural sciences might help to find possible solutions.

A second challenge in the delivery of information lies in the problematic pursuit of a right balance between transparency towards the public and protection of sensitive information for security reasons. What and how much information should be delivered or made accessible constitutes a major concern, particularly for regulators. At present, following the terrorist threat experienced in the EU, considerations of nuclear security can make information disclosure particularly problematic for political elites responsible for the nuclear field and RWM.

To sum up, respondents agree that ensuring public information is a key element in RWM since it will help to clarify and correct misunderstandings about RWM and nuclear energy that are common among laymen. Therefore, it is acknowledged that better communication is needed towards the general public. Yet, unsolved issues still exist about public information, namely the pursuit of a good balance between completeness and simplification, and transparency and security (Figure 3.2).

Public participation and stakeholders' involvement beyond information

Most respondents acknowledge the importance of public participation, or involvement, in RWM. As noted by a policy-maker: '[i]f asked, every stakeholder sees the importance of public participation around radioactive waste management'.

However, respondents from the nuclear industry stressed that the concept and rationale of public involvement, and the way they apply to the field of RWM, needs to be better understood. According to some of them, public participation implies that not only technical aspects but also socio-economic considerations are taken into account to decide technical solutions in RWM. On this point, a few industrial organisations expressed some scepticism about the actual benefit brought by public involvement into the highly technical content of RWM solutions. Some regulatory bodies shared the same opinion. For instance, it was argued, matters of safety assessment should be the responsibility of national regulators and technical experts since they need to be based on factual data and scientific findings rather than citizens' opinions, beliefs and emotions. The assumption that the public does not have adequate technical knowledge to ensure good policy results is one of the arguments often raised against public involvement (as discussed in chapter 2).

With an opposite view on the issue of public participation, civil society organisations believe that governmental decisions are still too often taken "in the dark" with low levels of public involvement. According to these respondents,

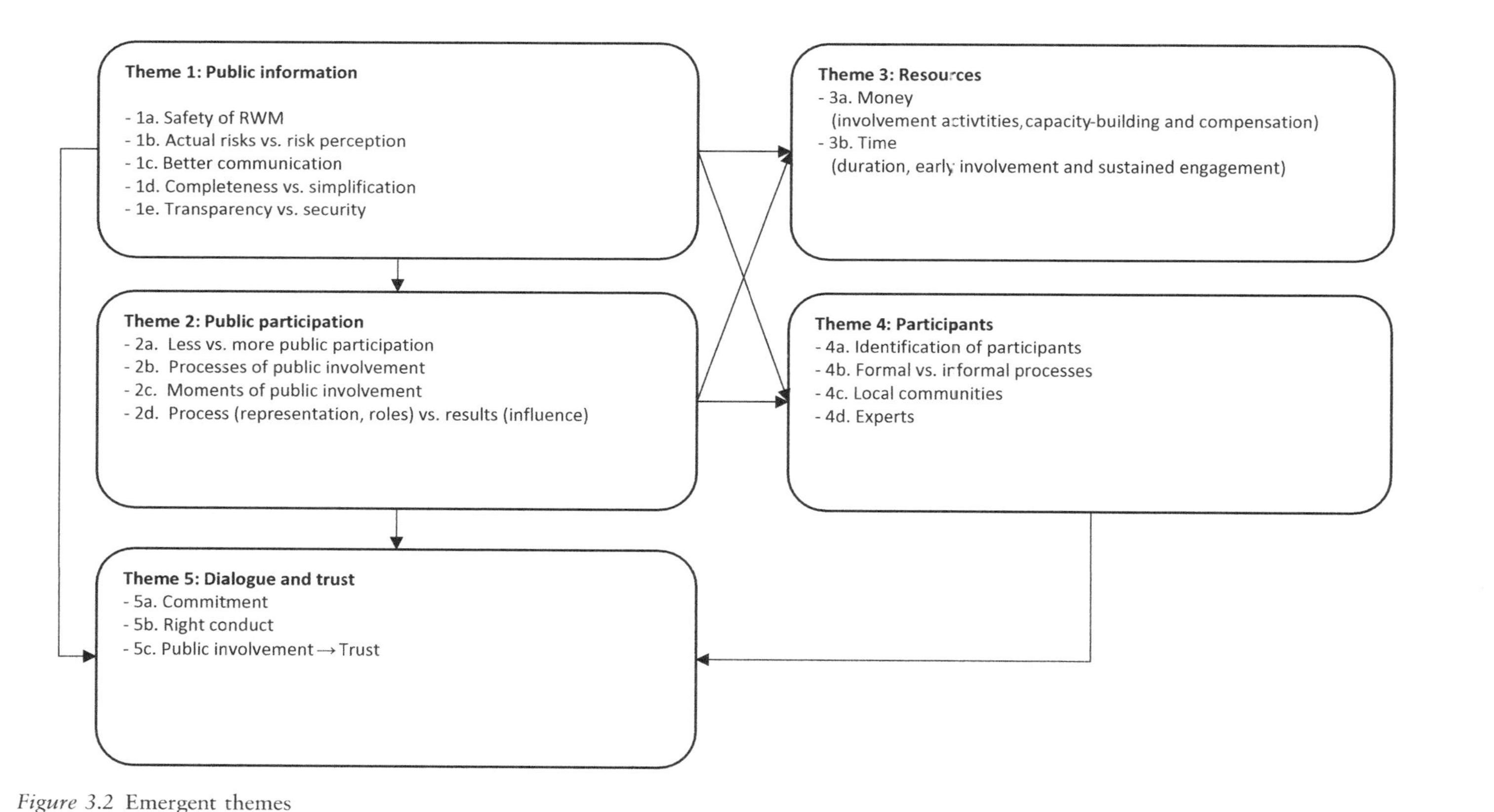

Figure 3.2 Emergent themes

decision-makers tend to take public opinion into account only if it is in line with decisions already taken (informally) by government and implementing agencies. Several civil society associations and NGOs also believe that citizens' concerns and protection are often neglected to the benefit of industrial interests.

These organisations call, thus, for more public involvement as well as a better understanding about how the principles of information, consultation and active participation are followed in the different MSs of the EU. Along the same line, other respondents among policy-makers, regulatory bodies and implementing agencies note that they would like to have more insights on formal and informal processes of public involvement that can be used to empower citizens in national policy-making and, consequently, establish or restore trust in national institutions and government agencies.

Survey respondents have also expressed their views about the moments when public involvement should take place. Some respondents argue that public participation is needed to debate RWM in the broader framework of the role of nuclear energy in a country's energy mix. This clearly refers to the very first phase of the policy cycle, i.e. policy formulation (see chapter 2). According to other respondents, public involvement is needed to generate an open discussion and inform the public about decisions that concern the management of RW facilities along all phases of their life cycle (siting, construction, operation, closure and post-closure). This is policy implementation (chapter 2).

A final point stressed by some respondents, namely implementing agencies and NGOs, is how to determine the success of public involvement. In other words, it is important to understand what qualifies public involvement as "successful". Public involvement, particularly in the form of consultation and active participation, can impact on the (decision-making) process – i.e. how decisions are handled – and the result – i.e. the content of the decision (see chapter 2).

Some respondents suggest that the effects of public involvement on process are more important than the ones on result. From this point of view, what matters is the inclusion in decision-making of a broad range of stakeholders, particularly those usually underrepresented. As said by a policy-maker, '[a]re the possibilities for participation used by the broad public or rather from well-known interest groups (environmental organisations, citizen initiatives, lobbyist groups etc.)?'. What also matters for the success of the process is the clear definition of roles and responsibilities of the different actors involved, as argued by a regulator.

Some other respondents see, instead, the success of public involvement in the result; hence, it must be ensured that the civil society (e.g., associations, NGOs and local communities) can influence what is produced by the decision-making. The focus is, here, on the "real effects" of public involvement in decision-making, i.e. the policy, strategy and legal/regulatory acts ruling RWM. For these respondents, it is important that the public feels that it has become the "co-author of the decision". Public participation must be evident not only in the process but also in the result so that there is a tangible effect of public involvement in RWM policies, legal provisions, decision-making and strategic actions. However, as we saw above, how much say the public should have in technical decisions (e.g., facility siting and licence renewal) is still open to debate rather than common ground of consensus.

To sum up, the rationale and benefits of public involvement for RWM may still need to be fully understood by some organisations involved in RWM solutions. National differences in political cultures certainly play a role in this respect. However, the responding stakeholders understand the importance to distinguish success in the process of public involvement from success in the final results; the effects of public involvement can, indeed, be located at these two different levels. While balanced representation and clear separations of role seem pivotal for a successful process, influence and authorship in the adopted decisions is, instead, fundamental if we look at success by focusing on results (Figure 3.2). As explained in chapter 2, the book looks at the (implementation) process in particular (chapter 2), but does not neglect considerations on results when possible. With a focus on the process, aspects that according to respondents need further investigation relate to when and how public involvement in RWM needs to take place. In other words, we need to better understand the moments in the policy cycle when public involvement in RWM can occur and the ways it can be put into practice.

Resources: funds and time

Public involvement implies costs as discussed in general in chapter 2. In the specific domain of RWM, some survey respondents have stressed the danger of poor content of public decisions and imperfect representation as reported in the previous section. Another cost of public involvement is the lower performance in the policy process due to the additional resources required by participatory processes (see Table 2.2)

In policy-making, resources include a broad range of physical and immaterial assets: information, funds, leadership, appropriations, equipment, personnel, talent, energy, time, etc. (Vedung 2006). We have reduced these assets to four main types – knowledge, money, authority and organisation – and argued that they are crucial for public involvement. In particular, financial resources emerge as a key element in the literature on public involvement (see chapter 2). Survey respondents have confirmed resources as an important aspect of public involvement in RWM and highlighted the implications of public involvement in terms of money (Figure 3.2).

Financial resources are imperative for public involvement for several reasons. First, they are important to support activities of public information. Second, the availability of funds helps NGOs and local communities to take part in public debates and decision-making. Third, financial resources can be used for capacity-building in favour of civil society through the organisation of training and discussions with independent experts.

According to some respondents, financial resources are important also as compensation for the local communities hosting a RWM facility. These respondents argue that appropriate investments and benefits need to be identified for the hosting communities so that an added value is created for the RWM facility they host. However, in this case, funds are not directly linked to public involvement; they rather function as incentives, as we will see in chapter 4.

No matter what use is made of this money (i.e. funds for public involvement or incentives for hosting communities), any funding related to RWM should be dealt with in a transparent way by indicating both the sources and the uses of the funds.

Some organisations involved in the survey have highlighted the salience of time in public involvement. In the disciplinary field of public administration, time is often considered as an administrative input, a resource (e.g., Lee 2014). It is also acknowledged as an important cost of public involvement (Wilson 1999). In line with the general consideration we made about the costs of public involvement (chapter 2), time has also been reported by respondents as a key resource for participatory process in RWM. Two main reasons motivate the salience of time: it is needed for the prolonged decision-making process and the lengthy acquisition of knowledge on relevant issues (Figure 3.2).

First, sufficient time is necessary for decision-making on RWM, particularly under more participatory approaches that must include multiple views. Public involvement is likely to prolong decision-making by adding further stages and deliberations. Particularly, some respondents among policy-makers and the industry are wary of these effects of public involvement on the duration of the decision-making process. Strong concerns exist about possible delays that RW projects might incur because of participatory processes. This will imply additional costs in terms of money, too.

Second, an adequate amount of time is needed so that all participants, particularly from civil society and local communities, can be sufficiently informed and learn about all the aspects at stake. Some actors may lack the knowledge to grasp technical aspects and will have to develop their own expertise.

Time has been discussed in the survey responses not only as a key resource for public involvement. It has also been the object of broader considerations regarding the temporal dimension of RWM, and the need for prompt and sustained engagement.

With regard to prompt engagement, early involvement of the public is pivotal if we want that the voice of citizens plays a role in public decisions. The point was stressed by NGOs and research organisations. They argue that national representatives, local authorities, local stakeholders and NGOs should all be involved in the (very) early stages of decision-making process, before any decision on RWM is taken. However, involving the public *too* early seems unfeasible. If a decision on RWM (e.g., for the construction of a disposal facility), is foreseen and planned for a distant future, then it is difficult to attract the attention of citizens and involve them in an issue that is not perceived as urgent.

The problem is well known to those studying public involvement. In his work on public meetings, Adams (2004: 50) argues that '[m]otivating a group of citizens to attend a meeting to discuss an issue that will be decided far in the future is difficult'. Policy-makers, regulatory bodies and implementing agencies in the RWM domain explain that citizens tend to mobilise mainly when they are faced with the contingency of a concrete project. Mobilising the public seems more difficult when the urgency of the problem is not yet perceived.

With regard to sustained engagement, the main consideration emerging from the survey is that it is challenging to maintain public attention and involvement in RWM projects over a prolonged period of time. RWM projects imply decades of work from the very start to their realisation and operation (see chapter 1). Therefore, we need to design a steady stakeholders' involvement process that lasts for more than one generation and is capable of maintaining societal attention and surviving governmental changes. On the one hand, people may lose interest over time under consultation overload and participation fatigue. On the other hand, political majorities are volatile in many countries.

Participants: fair representation and competent participation

Several organisations which took part in the survey have raised the correct identification of participants as an important aspect in public participation. Any effort of public involvement needs to clarify, first of all, who the legitimate stakeholders that will have to be involved are. It is, indeed, not always clear for some respondents who constitutes (or represents) the "public". Is it the members of national parliaments, NGOs or municipalities?

The danger of imperfect representation is acknowledged by the academic literature on the topic (e.g., Thomas 2012) and represents one of the costs of public involvement (chapter 2). In some cases, formal rules have been established so that who needs to be involved (as well as when and how) is defined on a legal basis (by laws or regulations). This is what happens, for instance, for public consultations conducted in the framework of a national Environmental Impact Assessment (EIA) (see chapter 5). However, more often, no rules have been established in the policy design and public involvement has developed informally and out of any legal provision (see chapter 4). These informal processes leave considerable freedom to public administrators in the definition of participants. Consequently, such processes call for careful considerations about who needs to be involved in order to avoid any discretion in the identification of participants. Any mistake at this level would delegitimise the entire effort of public involvement.

In the case of an informal process, respondents warn that the selection of participants must be transparent and has to ensure a good balance through the presence of all stakeholders. First, selection criteria need to be established to clarify who is entitled to participate. It must be clear to all stakeholders how such criteria have been adopted and by whom they were decided. Second, the selection of participants should ensure a wide representation. Balanced representation constitutes one of the major concerns emerging from the survey. Both public authorities (namely implementing agencies) and society (through NGOs) have insisted that participation must be designed to involve a broad spectrum of publics and not a small number of organised – often strong – interests.

In particular, the presence of stakeholders from the local level has received much attention from survey respondents. They are nonetheless aware that ensuring a "genuine" local participation represents several challenges. For example, it implies that the geographical area that needs to be involved with regard to a specific RWM facility is correctly identified. In this geographical area, then, various categories of stakeholders from the local community need to be engaged without neglecting any actor (see chapter 6).

Notwithstanding the importance generally acknowledged for societal interests and local actors, some regulators argue that the highly technical nature of RWM calls, first of all, for the presence in any practice of public involvement of experts "who understand these issues".

In conclusion, any participatory effort needs a careful reflection upon who needs to participate in order to ensure a broad and balanced engagement of citizens. Criteria for selecting the legitimate participants may already be established by national laws (and rules) or still await transparent clarification for those processes that have developed from more informal settings. The presence of the local community or communities (directly or indirectly affected by a RWM facility) and the inclusion of experts emerge as equally important in the definition of legitimate participants in RWM decision-making (Figure 3.2). The ultimate goal should be, indeed, to ensure both fair representation and competent participation.

Dialogue and trust

A final emergent theme has to do with dialogue. Creating dialogue among stakeholders is crucial for RWM because it reveals the reasons and values behind diverging positions. Boholm (2008: 2) explains that '[b]y means of dialogue, pluralities of viewpoints, evaluations and prioritizations can be considered which promotes sensible decision-making on collective and often controversial matters imbued by risk and uncertainty'. Dialogue often leads to constructive relationships among stakeholders.

However, there cannot be any dialogue without a shared commitment to a constructive exchange among all actors (see NEA 2013c). According to survey responses, the major obstacle faced by industry when it tries to engage different stakeholders in dialogue is the presence of strong views from opponents to nuclear energy. These conflictual situations can hardly be solved; as argued by a national regulator:

> Much good work has already been done on developing approaches to public participation in the field of RWM but an area that remains difficult is building an appropriate level of engagement with some of the parties opposing a particular RWM project or regulatory decision relating to an

> existing facility. Such parties sometimes want to remain outside the consultation process. In some cases, they can present their own interpretations of the information and data supporting a regulatory decision, which can suggest an increased level of uncertainty and potential harm.

In the absence of shared commitment, any attempt to develop dialogue will fail. According to some responses, experiences of public debate often result into a sterile exchange of well-known arguments among participants. These failing experiences lack any sincere intention of creating an atmosphere of real mutual learning. Some respondents think that public debate is not always aimed at finding agreed solutions; it rather creates inconclusive – and sometimes aggressive – discussions that only generate more misunderstanding. In particular, a regulator explains that,

> No matter how often and how strongly pure facts are explained, there will always be people requesting more and more discussions. [...] As a consequence the general public feels as there are continuous problems and dangers related to anything radioactive. This fear from radioactivity is unreasonably higher than fear from any other similar potentially dangerous technology.

This situation would, thus, require a right conduct from all stakeholders. Considerations of right conduct and correct behaviour are usually addressed to governments and media. These actors are expected to deliver information based on strong scientific evidence and concrete data, and are often blamed if they fail to report correctly about RWM issues. But – some regulatory bodies argue – "good" behaviour should also be practised by all other actors involved in RWM.

Respondents suggest that the core of good behaviour for a constructive dialogue is the acknowledgment by all participants in a decision-making process that any opinion is important and should be taken into due account. Some methods to improve dialogue were also suggested in the survey. One method could be employing external facilitators and mediators during discussions. A second possibility would be relying on independent experts or expert panels that could provide targeted communities with an objective interpretation of technical information and data.

These methods can certainly be useful to help dialogue among stakeholders. However, commitment and right conduct need trust as a prerequisite. Trust among stakeholders is crucial for dialogue: there can be no dialogue in the absence of trust (see Petts 2001). If actors are not willing to trust each other and consider other positions as legitimate, we can only have a dialogue of the deaf.

A lack of trust characterises the nuclear field in general, and RWM in particular (see chapter 1). This is confirmed by the survey. Respondents have stressed that societal actors and decision-makers are often diffident about each other. The need for building or rebuilding trust and confidence in the relationships with citizens is among the most urgent and complex challenges identified across the responses. Certainly, the question 'How can the existing public confidence/trust be maintained and preserved?' scores high on the agendas of both regulators and implementers.

Most respondents seem to agree that developing a culture of transparency (between citizens, experts and public authorities) and independence (of regulators, experts and local authorities from project owners) is a key step if we want to restore trust and confidence in RWM. As a regulator clearly explained:

> The safe management and final disposal of spent fuel and radioactive waste very much depends on public confidence or at least acceptance in the decision making process. A national systematic approach with long term strategies and planning as well as procedures for formal consultations and public insight is vital for the overall confidence and trustworthiness of both industry and regulatory authorities in the eyes of the public and local communities. The independence and integrity of the regulatory body is important. A fully accountable regulatory authority that is trustworthy in upholding high safety standards also gains the trust needed for an active public participation.

To sum up, RWM needs more constructive dialogue among stakeholders. Dialogue can develop and be constructive only if it starts from mutual recognition of the parties and relies on the presence of trust among them. In its turn, trust needs public involvement, independent experts and transparent institutions (Figure 3.2).

Concluding remarks

In the past, national institutions have often taken a technocratic approach to RWM and focused mainly on technical aspects for ensuring safety. Meanwhile, citizens have developed a number of concerns about RWM that only partially take into account the scientific understanding of actual risks. The results of a survey conducted on RWM stakeholders across the EU highlight some of these social concerns and important issues related to public involvement in RWM. More precisely, the data collected through the survey suggest five major themes: public information; public participation; resources; participants; dialogue and trust (Figure 3.2). These emergent themes help our investigation on public involvement in RWM by narrowing down our focus on a few researchable aspects of a much broader topic.

Several other aspects were briefly mentioned by the respondents (i.e., retrievability and reversibility,[7] knowledge transfer, intergenerational equity, etc.), but they recur less frequently among the responses and have been elaborated less clearly by respondents.

The chapter concludes with some final considerations about the limitations experienced during data collection and the way they have been circumvented. Although the survey has reached out to a large amount of diverse organisations, data collection was partially affected by language barriers, different levels of familiarity with public involvement, and respondents' bias.

First, language represented a problem, particularly during communication with local stakeholders. Although such a barrier was mitigated to a significant extent through translations, it affects the number and extensiveness of survey responses from the local level (see Figure 3.1). Municipalities faced language difficulties more than other stakeholders (e.g., ministries and industrial organisations). Therefore, a focus group was organised at a later stage of the research to overcome this limitation and dig into the local dimension of public involvement in RWM. (The insights gained through the focus group are discussed in chapter 6.)

Second, the stage of RWM and public involvement at which MSs are varies significantly between countries. There is a marked trend towards a higher rate of response than average in those MSs where public involvement practices have already been established. Some stakeholders appeared wary of the usefulness of sharing information on their public involvement practices in RWM despite much of the information already being in the public domain. This confirms the weak culture of trust and confidence that still affects the nuclear field in some MSs. However, it is not the purpose of the book to provide an analysis on a national basis (see Introduction); other works with a comparative approach (e.g., Brunnengräber *et al.* 2015) deal with national differences.

Finally, the information given by respondents to the survey questionnaire has been accepted at face value and it was not the intention of the author to verify or refuse collected responses. These answers invariably suffer from the subjectivity bias of respondents. The degree of subjectivity also varies in importance between respondents, introducing an unquantifiable bias into studies of this type. (For similar considerations in the literature, see Hosch *et al.* 2011.) Undoubtedly, the results provide insights about perceptions of respondents. However, the goal of our analysis was not to evaluate organisations or rank countries on the basis of these responses, but to have a sense of the challenges for public involvement that are still open (or perceived as such) in national RWM systems.

In conclusion, because of the response rate and the diversity of respondents, the survey has provided a good representation of the EU's RWM system as a whole and valid evidence for analysis on key issues and stakeholders' needs.

Notes

1 The survey was part of the research activity that I conducted as a civil servant of the European Commission (EC) (see Preface). At first, desk research was used to map the organisations involved in RWM in the EU. An important input at this stage came from documents produced by international organisations involved in the nuclear field (i.e. IAEA, NEA and EC): country profiles and reports were the basis for this stakeholder mapping exercise. A list of relevant organisations was compiled for the 28 MSs of the EU. The list was refined and updated through informal interviews (via phone calls) to each one of the entries to verify the private and public organisations active in the field and important for the study. Representatives from the listed organisations who had

responsibilities for RWM and relations with the public were selected to participate in the survey. They also suggested other important players missing in the list that was expanded accordingly through a snowball procedure (on a similar methodology see Pforr 2002). This led to a list of 274 stakeholders; they all received a copy of the survey questionnaire and their responses were collated in a dataset. I am very thankful to Samuel Young and Robert Langmuir for their help in this effort of data collection. For sake of confidentiality, the identity of individuals and organisations that responded to the survey is not disclosed in the book. The content of the responses will be cited and quoted without mentioning the source. Any reference to national contexts or specific facts was voluntarily omitted. The purpose of the survey was to identify common problems and trends in RWM with regard to public involvement rather than assessing national performances.

2 Open-ended questions allow participants to express their own opinion and provide an answer in their own words without limiting respondents to choose among a set of pre-established possible alternative options provided in the questionnaire. It follows that open-ended questions avoid the bias that may result from suggesting possible answers to individuals (Fink 2009; Reja *et al.* 2003; Roberts *et al.* 2014).

3 This definition is a simplification of the more elaborate one explained in chapter 2 where public involvement is defined as an organised process adopted by elected officials, government agencies or other public-sector organisations to engage citizens and other stakeholders in the formulation, adoption and implementation of public policies (Joss 1999; Wilson 1999).

4 The exact response rate was 42.3%, which is equivalent to 116 responding organisations out of the 274 that were contacted.

5 I would like to thank Annabarbara Friedrich for her support and accuracy during data analysis. We have worked as "independent analysts" for credibility checks (on this methodological point, see Timulak 2009: 597–598). We started the whole analysis at the same time but worked independently and met at the end of each step of the analysis to reach a consensus. First, we read each response and discovered major topics. Second, we created categories for each of these topics. Third, we reasoned upon these categories to check whether they could be either combined or split into sub-categories in order to identify more clearly emergent themes. Fourth, we used these themes for coding the content of the responses. It was often the case that one single open-ended response was a mixture of themes; in this case, all of the themes have been retained in the analysis. Our coding has been done primarily manually, although we have relied on a word frequency tool to validate our choices. The coded responses were reviewed at different times and independently by the two of us in order to ensure objectivity in the analysis.

6 About the difference between analysing public comment and evaluating it, see Creighton (2005). In the discussion of data, the use of percentages has also been avoided as it is recommended for surveys relying on open-ended questions: data are not uniform and, thus, difficult to be analysed statistically. Open-ended responses call for qualitative (rather than quantitative) analysis (Reja *et al.* 2003; Roberts *et al.* 2014).

7 Retrievability means that RW is disposed in a way that it can be monitored and, if needed, recovered. Reversibility of RW repository means that previous decisions and actions taken for the planning or development of deep geological disposal can be changed at any stage of the programme, for instance if new technological options become available (Di Nucci *et al.* 2015).

References

Adams, B. (2004) "Public Meetings and the Democratic Process", in *Public Administration Review*, Vol. 64, No. 1, pp. 43–54.

Armour, A. M. (1991) *The Siting of Locally Unwanted Land Uses: Towards a Cooperative Approach*, Pergamon Press, Oxford.

Boholm, Å. (2008) "New Perspectives on Risk Communication: Uncertainty in a Complex Society", in *Journal of Risk Research*, Vol. 11, No. 1–2, pp. 1–3.

Brunnengräber, A., Di Nucci, M. R., Isidoro Losada, A. M., Mez, L. and Schreurs, M. (2015) (Eds) *Nuclear Waste Governance – An International Comparison*, Springer, Berlin

Creighton, J. L. (2005) *The Public Participation Handbook. Making Better Decisions Through Citizen Involvement*, Jossey-Bass, San Francisco.

Di Nucci, M. R., Brunnengräber, A., Mez, L. and Schreurs, M. (2015) "Comparative Perspective on Nuclear Waste Governance", in Brunnengräber, A., Di Nucci, M. R., Isidoro Losada, A. M., Mez, L. and Schreurs, M. (Eds) *Nuclear Waste Governance – An International Comparison*, Springer, Berlin, pp. 25–43.

Fink, A. (2009) *How to Conduct Surveys. A Step-by-Step Guide*, SAGE, Los Angeles.

Hosch, G., Ferraro, G., and Failler, P. (2011) "The 1995 FAO Code of Conduct for Responsible Fisheries: Adopting, Implementing or Scoring Results?", in *Marine Policy*, Vol. 35, No. 2, pp. 189–200.

IAEA (2011b) *Disposal of Radioactive Waste*, Safety Standards Series No. SSR-5, International Atomic Energy Agency, Vienna.

Joss, S. (1999) "Public Participation in Science and Technology Policy- and Decision-making – Ephemeral Phenomenon or Lasting Change?" in *Science and Public Policy*, Vol. 26, No. 5, pp. 290–293.

Kuhn, R. G. and Ballard, K. (1998) "Canadian Innovations in Siting Hazardous Waste Management Facilities", in *Environmental Management*, Vol. 22, No. 4, pp. 533–545.

Lee, J. (2014) "Public Meetings for Efficient Administrative Performance in the United States", in *Public Performance & Management Review*, Vol. 37, No. 3, pp. 388–411.

NEA (2013c) *Stakeholder Confidence in Radioactive Waste Management: An Annotated Glossary of Key Terms*, OECD, Paris.

Petts, J. (2001) "Evaluating the Effectiveness of Deliberative Processes: Waste Management Case-studies", in *Journal of Environmental Planning and Management*, Vol. 44, No. 2, pp. 207–226.

Pforr, C. (2002) *The 'Makers and Shapers' of Tourism Policy in the Northern Territory of Australia. A Policy Network Analysis of Actors and Their Territorial Constellations*, Proceedings of the 2002 CUATHE Conference.

Reja, U., Lozar Manfreda, K., Hlebec, V. and Vehovar, V. (2003) "Open-ended vs. Closed-ended Questions in Web Questionnaires", in *Developments in Applied Statistics*, Proceedings of Peer-Reviewed Scientific Conference Contributions, University of Ljubljana.

Renn, O. (1998) "Three Decades of Risk Research: Accomplishments and New Challenges", in *Journal of Risk Research*, Vol. 1, No. 1, pp. 49–71.

Roberts, M. E., Stewart, B. M., Tingley, D., Lucas, C., Leder-Luis, J., Gadarian, S., Albertson, B. and Rand, D. (2014) "Structural Topic Models for Open-Ended Survey Responses", in *American Journal of Political Science*, Vol. 58, No. 4, pp. 1064–1082.

Thomas, J. C. (2012) *Citizen, Customer, Partner: Engaging the Public in Public Management*, Routledge, Abingdon and New York.

Timulak, L. (2009) "Meta-analysis of Qualitative Studies: A Tool for Reviewing Qualitative Research Findings in Psychotherapy", in *Psychotherapy Research*, Vol. 19, No. 4–5, pp. 591–600.

Vedung, E. (2006) "Evaluation Research", in Peters, B. G. and Pierre, J. (eds.) *Handbook of Public Policy*, Sage Publications, London.

Weingart, J. (2007) *Waste Is A Terrible Thing To Mind*, Rivergate Books, New Brunswick, NJ.

Wilson, D. (1999) "Exploring the Limits of Public Participation in Local Government", in *Parliamentary Affairs*, Vol. 52, No. 2, pp. 246–259.

Yanev, Y. (2009) "Nuclear Knowledge Management", in *International Journal of Nuclear Knowledge Management*, Vol. 3, No. 2, pp. 115–124.

4 General principles for public involvement

The peaceful use of nuclear energy in the European Union (EU) is governed by the Euratom Treaty which established the European Atomic Energy Community (Euratom) in 1957 (chapter 1). The Euratom Community is a separate legal entity from the EU, but is governed by the same institutions. In the framework of Euratom, the European Commission (EC) deals with nuclear activities with a focus on three major aspects: nuclear safety, nuclear security and nuclear safeguards. Nuclear safety is about the safe operation of nuclear installations and is complemented by radiation protection and radioactive waste management (RWM). Nuclear security relates to the physical protection of nuclear material and installations against intentional malicious acts (e.g., sabotage and theft). Nuclear safeguards are measures to ensure that nuclear materials are used only for the peaceful purposes declared by the users.[1]

In addition, the EC finances nuclear research through multi-annual Euratom Framework Programmes (FPs) that run in parallel with the larger FPs of the EU.[2] Since 2000, the Euratom FPs have dedicated political attention and economic support to public involvement in RWM and the complex set of questions that this implies. Several national experiences have become the object of case studies researched by social scientists in collaboration with practitioners and experts from several Member States (MSs). It is clear from these studies that a one-fits-all solution for good or better public involvement in RWM does not exist. However, the diversity of social and political contexts that characterises the EU[3] offers a useful pool of knowledge and experience from which we can extract general principles and indications for political action and policy change for all EU countries.

The chapter extracts the knowledge about public involvement in RWM developed by the Euratom research programmes over the last twenty years and synthesises the major lessons learnt. Several research projects have investigated the social dimension of RWM and produced useful insights on matters of participation. The findings of these projects are analysed and systematised in the chapter and used to define a list of general principles for public involvement. Such principles are meant to work as indications for promoting and enhancing public involvement in the formulation, design and implementation of RWM policies.

Lessons from the Euratom Framework Programmes. A synthesis of principles

The stakeholders responding to our survey on public involvement in RWM across the EU (chapter 3) have pointed out issues and needs that they perceive as still open, unmet and relevant in the field. From these responses, five emergent themes were identified: public information; public participation; resources; participants; dialogue and trust (Figure 3.2). This chapter is based on the assumption that there are certain conditions, referred to as "general principles", that can give indications for each one of these themes with the aim of improving public involvement in RWM. These principles would play, thus, an important role for the success of public involvement in RWM despite the contextual differences of national practices that characterise the EU.

Principles and practices belong to different levels of abstraction. Practices are tangible and visible behaviours (Bardach 2012). They are sensitive to their context – since they heavily depend on social, political and temporal factors – and, for this reason, they can hardly travel across countries. Although practices are context-bound, they share common principles of general and abstract nature (Bobbio 2004). With their higher level of abstraction, principles can travel across countries. In other words, while practices of public involvement cannot be easily replicated from one context to another, principles can provide indications for improvement and guidance for actions that can be shared by policy makers and practitioners (OECD 2015; Webler *et al.* 2001). This chapter deals with principles; practices constitute, instead, the topic of the next two chapters.

The goal of this chapter is, indeed, to abstract general principles for public involvement that can allow a more transparent, more participatory and, overall, an improved management of RW by providing policy directions on the five emergent themes of our investigation. Such principles are extracted from the research projects funded by the Euratom FPs that have specifically addressed public involvement in RWM (Table 4.1): COWAM (2000–2003) and RISCOM II (2000–2003) under the Fifth Framework Programme; ARGONA (2006–2008), CIP (2007–2009) and COWAM2 (2004–2006) under the Sixth Framework Programme; InSOTEC (2011–2014) and IPPA (2011–2013) under the Seventh Framework Programme. The chapter builds on the findings developed by these projects as they were presented in their final reports.[4] In addition to these EU-funded projects, insights developed by the CARL project – which falls outside the Euratom funding scheme – have been taken into account because of the relevance of the project.[5]

The insights developed by these Euratom research projects add to the large number of qualitative studies about public involvement in RWM that have increased throughout the years both in the scientific and grey literature. Case studies have been conducted across many EU countries and have provided a large body of evidence for which we still lack a comprehensive and systematic review aimed at identifying common findings. As in many disciplinary areas, such growth of studies calls for a "cumulative assessment" of research findings at a certain moment (Timulak 2009). Cumulative assessments respond to a practical need; as

Table 4.1 Euratom projects on public involvement in RWM

Funding scheme	*Project name*	*Countries involved*	*Duration*
Fifth Framework Programme			
	COWAM Community Waste Management	Belgium, Czech Republic, Finland, France, Germany, Slovenia, Spain, Sweden, Switzerland, United Kingdom.	2000–2003
	RISCOM II Transparency and Public Participation in Radioactive Waste Management	Czech Republic, France, Finland, Sweden, United Kingdom.	2000–2003
Sixth Framework Programme			
	ARGONA Arena for Risk Governance	Belgium, Czech Republic, France, Finland, Norway, Slovakia, Sweden, United Kingdom.	2006–2008
	CIP COWAM in Practice	Belgium, France, Romania, Slovenia, Spain, United Kingdom.	2007–2009
	COWAM2 Community Waste Management 2	France, United Kingdom, Switzerland, Spain.	2004–2006
Seventh Framework Programme			
	InSOTEC International Socio-Technical Challenges for implementing geological disposal	Belgium, Czech Republic, Finland, France, Germany, Hungary, Norway, Slovenia, Spain, Sweden, United Kingdom.	2011–2014
	IPPA Implementing Public Participation Approaches in Radioactive Waste Disposal	Bulgaria, Czech Republic, France, Finland, Germany, Hungary, Poland, Romania, Slovakia, Slovenia, Sweden, United Kingdom.	2011–2013

Source: Personal elaboration based on DG RTD (2005; 2007; 2012)

put by Thomas and Harden (2008: 5), policy-makers and practitioners 'are interested in the answers that only qualitative research can provide but are not able to handle the deluge of data that would result if they tried to locate and read all the relevant research themselves'. In other words, faced with the overload of data and information that characterises the contemporary world, synthesis and simplification of the available knowledge is key to policy-making.

Synthesising qualitative studies has emerged as an important methodology to bring research closer to policy-makers. For the development of more informed public policies, these syntheses – or qualitative "meta-analyses"[6] – are extremely important. They are secondary (qualitative) analyses of existing primary qualitative studies in a given research topic aimed at providing a concise and comprehensive interpretation of a complex set of findings. Qualitative meta-analyses pull together contents from previous primary studies, aggregate their essential findings and translate them into a new conceptualisation, i.e. a new line of argument that goes beyond the original content (Thomas & Harden 2008; Timulak 2009).[7] These integrations constitute, thus, conceptual innovations in the sense that they are more than the sum of the parts (Thorne *et al.* 2004). Meta-analyses provide novel interpretations of primary findings. An example of meta-analyses is the ones focusing 'on the more abstract principles present in primary studies' (Timulak 2009: 593).

In line with this methodological approach, the chapter examines the research on public involvement in RWM funded by the Euratom scheme over almost two decades[8] and provides a systematisation of general principles for public involvement in RWM (see Table 4.2). For this systematisation we rely on the analytical framework proposed by Winter (1990; 2003; 2012a) and explained in chapter 2 (Figure 2.2). Empirical analysis in policy research is, indeed, guided by theoretical models or, more frequently, frameworks for analysis (Winter 2012b). Winter's analytical framework has been chosen because it focuses on policy implementation without neglecting how a public policy is formulated (policy formulation) and shaped (policy design). Policy formulation and policy design need to be taken into account together with the implementation process in order to fully understand policy implementation (chapter 2). On this basis, we can argue that general principles for public involvement must guide the formulation, design and implementation of public policies, although we will look in detail at public involvement during policy implementation.

The next sections present these principles for each component of the analytical framework. We will then put the principles in relation with the five themes presented in chapter 3.

Principles for public involvement during policy formulation

Policy formulation is the process of generation and assessment of all possible ways to solve a public problem. It is during policy formulation that alternative possible actions are identified and analysed in order to inform the subsequent policy decisions in the most accurate way. Governments decide which action is feasible in the light of the technical, administrative and political constraints identified at this stage.

Table 4.2 General principles for public involvement in RWM

Policy formulation	*Policy design*	*Implementation process*
Principle 1	**Principle 4**	**Principle 7**
Acknowledging the social dimension	Clarifying roles among organisations	Promoting partnering and voluntarism
Principle 2	**Principle 5**	**Principle 8**
Ensuring early involvement	Foreseeing instruments for public involvement	Adopting a flexible process
Principle 3	**Principle 6**	**Principle 9**
Creating a national-local debate	Providing adequate resources	Building trust

Constraints can come from the tractability (or "intellectual complexity") of the problem addressed – some public problems are, indeed, more difficult to understand and solve (chapter 1). Other constraints consist of the financial and institutional capacity of the state since government action depends on the amount of available state resources (i.e., knowledge, money, authority and organisation). Finally, governments are limited in the pursuit of problem solutions by the configuration of actors around given policy options. Such configuration depends on the contingent system of values and beliefs, the political parties in power, the expected socio-economic impacts of government action (Howlett *et al.* 2009; Winter 2003) and the amount of conflict that public decisions around a given problem can generate among stakeholders ("political malignancy") (Sabatier 1980; Underdal 2000; 2002; Victor *et al.* 1998).

In other words, the action to be taken must not only be technically capable of correcting a problem and administratively feasible but also politically acceptable in the eyes of the public opinion. In particular, political acceptability has to do with the opposition that a specific decision and course of action may generate. It is proven by policy research that conflicts among actors that emerge during policy formulation are likely to continue during the implementation process that follows (Winter 2003).

Therefore, it is crucial that legislators and bureaucratic agencies formulating a public policy have contact with a broad base of affected groups. Inputs from affected citizens should be taken into due account possibly through as broad as possible public consultation (Howlett *et al.* 2009). Although the focus of the book is not on policy formulation, it cannot be neglected that contacts with target groups should be established already at this stage. The Euratom research stresses three core principles that can be put in relation with the formulation of national policies for RWM (Table 4.2):

- Principle 1: Acknowledging the social dimension;
- Principle 2: Ensuring early involvement;
- Principle 3: Creating a national-local debate.

Social dimension

RWM has traditionally been considered as a technical topic and dealt with by national authorities on the basis of the engineering advice coming from nuclear experts who put safety and risk assessment at the centre of their considerations. However, the dominance of this "nucleocracy" (Lehtonen 2015) has failed to take into account that RWM is a multifaceted problem characterised not only by technical complexity, but also by a strong emotive component about risk and nuclear energy (chapter 3). The lack of adequate information, appropriate communication and public involvement in policy-making around the management of RW from the side of national policy-makers and implementing agencies has generated social distrust and caused strong opposition from citizens and local communities to several policy initiatives in the past decades (chapter 1).

The Euratom social research analysed in this chapter warns that issue-framing and problem-solving related to RWM cannot be addressed from a mere techno-scientific perspective. RWM has a social component consisting of social values, national traditions and public concerns that should be taken into account during the development of a national policy together with technical aspects (i.e. type of waste, properties of containers for storage/disposal, etc.) and safety issues. Policy-makers, regulatory bodies, implementing agencies and the scientific community should involve affected actors from the society (i.e. the general public, NGOs and local communities) in the debate that frames complex public problems like RWM and in the search for technical solutions. It has become clear that safety issues cannot be debated only on the basis of facts and scientific evidence. The technical effort sustained for the purpose of ensuring safety in RWM also has to take into account values and the perception of risk existing among laymen. This perception often differs from the view of experts (see chapter 3).

* **Principle 1: Acknowledging the social dimension** – Policy-makers, regulatory bodies, implementing agencies and the scientific community should take into account the social dimension of RWM in the formulation of a national policy.

Early involvement

Public involvement can take place both in the formulation of a national policy and in its implementation through specific programmes and projects (chapter 2). The scientific literature (e.g., Michels & De Graaf 2010: 481) stresses that any effort of participatory policy-making 'operates under the premise that citizens and other stakeholders take an active role in the policy process at an early stage'. This applies to RWM, too, as expressed by stakeholders from the field (chapter 3). The social research developed under the Euratom FPs points out that citizens and other stakeholders should participate at the earliest phase of policy-making (on the same point, see also NEA 2015).

Early involvement is understood as engagement of the public in the development of a national policy for RWM. Therefore, inputs from citizens and all interested actors must already be taken into account during policy formulation. The public needs to engage much earlier than in the execution of national policies, or policy implementation. In line with policy research (e.g., Winter 2003), the Euratom projects confirm that early involvement of the civil society in policy-making already during policy formulation is beneficial for the entire policy process since it creates broader support for policy decisions.

* **Principle 2: Ensuring early involvement** – Citizens and other stakeholders should take an active role in the policy process at an early stage, i.e. in the formulation of public policies for RWM.

National–local debate

We have stated that the social dimension needs to be taken into account in the formulation of policies for RWM and public involvement needs to take place already at the early stage of policy-making. These considerations are particularly important with regard to the engagement of local stakeholders. The inclusion of local actors is pivotal for public involvement in RWM, as has been highlighted by the same organisations involved in the field (see chapter 3). The academic literature acknowledges that public involvement at the local level means engaging local authorities and their communities not only in the delivery of services but much earlier in the formulation of national policies (Wilson 1999).

The Euratom project consortia investigating the topic confirm that local involvement is fundamental to ensure that better policies are developed even before the local population is engaged for the implementation of these policies through programmes, plans and projects. It follows that policy formulation for RWM should rely on an inclusive debate that runs in parallel at both the national and local level. Such debate needs to start at policy formulation and continue, later, during the preparation of national programmes, and the design and execution of projects.

* **Principle 3: Creating a national–local debate** – Policy formulation for RWM should rely on an inclusive debate that runs in parallel at both the national and local level.

Principles for public involvement in policy design

Policy design is the content of a public policy as defined in the legislation of a country (chapter 2). Policy design emerges from policy formulation and requires to be successfully implemented. The capability of governments to implement policy designs depends on many technical, administrative and political factors (Howlett 2011).

Policy design in the domain of RWM has traditionally been informed by technical research (i.e. engineering analysis, risk assessment, geological screening, etc.) (chapter 1). However, socio-political variables should also be taken into account in the content given to public policies. These variables have to do with the set of actors, ideas and interests that converge into policy-making, shape the content of a policy with specific expectations and strongly affect its implementation (Kraft 2000).

Policy design contains several elements. It defines the objectives of a public policy, or policy goals, and identifies a mix of tools, or policy instruments, that will be employed to reach those policy goals. The instruments selected may affect the same implementation process, since certain instruments – i.e. the procedural implementation instruments – determine the formation of a particular organisational (or implementation) structure (chapter 2). A policy design also designates the (governmental or non-governmental) organisations responsible for achieving the objectives. Finally, it allocates the resources required for the related tasks (May 2012). Among the findings that result from the Euratom research on public involvement in RWM, three have to do with policy design (Table 4.2):

- Principle 4: Clarifying roles among organisations;
- Principle 5: Foreseeing instruments for public involvement;
- Principle 6: Providing adequate resources.

Clarity of roles

Policy design designates the governmental and non-governmental organisations responsible for executing and achieving specific policy objectives. The academic literature on policy implementation specifies that the organisational structure in charge of a given public policy should be clearly identified and its responsibilities precisely defined in order to ease implementation (Dunsire 1990; May 2003; Mitchell 1990; Winter 2006).

Clarity in relation to the identification of responsible organisations is also relevant for public involvement in RWM as it emerges from stakeholders' survey responses (chapter 3). The same Euratom social research highlights the importance of clarifying, in the policy design, the entire organisational structure of the national RWM system, which includes both types of actors and their roles. Therefore, national policies for RWM should specify which organisations and bodies are responsible for issuing laws and regulations, implementing the legislative and regulatory framework, monitoring and controlling relevant activities, funding these tasks, etc. National RWM policies should also ensure clarity about the requirements and procedures for public involvement.

* **Principle 4: Clarifying roles among organisations** – National policies for RWM should clarify the organisational structure of a national RWM system including the requirements and procedures for public involvement.

Instruments for public involvement

Policy design identifies two types of policy instruments, i.e. substantive implementation instruments and procedural implementation instruments (chapter 2). The former affect the production, distribution and consumption of goods and services. The latter alter actors' behaviours and interactions within policy networks and, thus, influence the process of implementation (Howlett 2000; 2011; Shroff *et al.* 2012).

The Euratom projects suggest that any national RWM policy should include a set of instruments for public involvement in its design. Procedural implementation instruments are crucial for public involvement during the execution of public policies because they can modify interactions among the actors involved in policy implementation. They are tools that governments use to create new interactions among actors, improve existing relationships and eventually solve conflicts (Hanf & O'Toole 1992; Howlett *et al.* 2015; Schneider & Ingram 1990).

Public involvement can be either foreseen by the national legislation[9] or take place *extra legem*. In the latter case, instruments for public involvement are not included in the law (or delegated legislation), but are introduced in the practice by public administrators to respond to an actual need for public involvement. This happens, for instance, when public administrators decide to broaden the list of actors involved in a given decision beyond what is requested by the law of a country. Therefore, involvement is not only limited to formal processes (Bobbio 2004).

In the domain of RWM, the Euratom research shows that instruments for public involvement are often included, defined and required by national legislation ("formal process") (see chapter 5). However, in many cases, instruments for public involvement have been adopted and used beyond legal requirements and without any change in the legislative framework ("informal process"). In other words, national legislative frameworks in the EU's MSs can foresee (through legal provisions) or ignore (by omissions) spaces for the involvement of the general public, (concerned) local communities and other stakeholders in the decision-making around RWM.

Both formal and informal processes present advantages and disadvantages. A formal process has a legal, thus stronger, basis but can become too rigid to allow creative inputs, particularly from those types of stakeholders that are less familiar with institutional settings. By contrast, an informal process can more easily adapt to new inputs and changes; yet, it depends completely on the good will of the actors involved. Finally, informal processes of public involvement may be less rigid and, thus, facilitate citizens' engagement and dialogue among actors.

However, there are a number of possible reasons why stakeholders may decide not to take part in an informal process of public involvement. First, the results of an informal process are often non-binding for decision-makers so that the whole process can appear meaningless to some stakeholders. Second, societal actors (like NGOs) and local communities may be willing to maintain their autonomy and, for this reason, refuse to take part in a process where the developer of a contested project is also present. Third, even when autonomy is guaranteed, a stakeholder can refuse to participate in a process in which their "opponents" take part, for the purpose of delegitimising the same process. Fourth, stakeholders may lack trust in the neutrality of the process or its organiser.

In the light of these considerations, we can, then, argue that foreseeing formal processes in the law may ensure not only the right of public involvement but also a duty of commitment from all the parties, the lack of which can compromise any effort of dialogue (as indicated by the survey results of chapter 3). Despite the advantages of informal processes, it seems important that procedural implementation instruments are included already in the policy design. It is important to bear in mind, though, that the results of any process of public involvement – either formal or informal – are not legally binding. The input from stakeholders needs to be included in a public decision to have practical effects (Bobbio 2004).

Finally, irrespective of how procedural implementation instruments have been adopted in the EU (formally or informally), a rich amount of such tools exist in the policy practice. The procedural implementation instruments used in RWM in the EU are analysed in detail in chapter 5 and 6.

* **Principle 5: Foreseeing instruments for public involvement** – A national RWM policy should include in its design instruments which allow and ensure public involvement.

Adequate resourcing

Research on public involvement in RWM conducted under the Euratom funding scheme points out that an adequate amount of resources needs to be made available and accessible for stakeholders. We have explained that, in policy science, resources are understood as physical and immaterial assets used and mobilised to formulate and implement policies (Knoepfel *et al.* 2007; Vedung 2006). They include knowledge (i.e. information, evidence and expertise), money (i.e. funds), authority or power (including leadership, political support and public legitimacy) and organisation (e.g., structure and personnel) (Bobbio 2004; Klijn 2007; O'Toole 2012; Peterson 2003). Knowledge, money and authority have explicitly been addressed by the findings of the Euratom research. While we look at authority later in this chapter (under principle 7), let us discuss the first two types of resources here.

Knowledge constitutes a key asset for public involvement. Adequate information is important for societal interests and local communities because these actors need to build their capacity if they are expected to be involved in policy-making through more participatory processes. Particularly at the local level, individuals and groups from the civil society often lack technical expertise, communication skills and organisational capabilities. Local actors are, thus, in need of more knowledge to grasp the complexity of RWM and enter in a fair dialogue with national agencies and decision-makers. Furthermore, once public and local involvement is allowed (either formally or informally), societal interests and local communities also need to be made aware of which entry points they have into the national policy-making and learn how to use them.

Public involvement requires money, too (see chapter 2). Therefore, national authorities should provide adequate financial means to groups from the civil society and local communities. Local authorities need financial resources so that they can deploy sufficient means for the information and participation of their citizens. Local communities also need money in order to be able to consult experts on their own initiative and arrange training (if needed) to better understand the complexity of RWM. Likewise, NGOs need funds to make their engagement possible in practice and not only on paper.

Financial resources are often used as compensation. Hazardous facilities usually create inequities because of the unbalance between benefits (often distributed nationally) and costs (usually born by the hosting local community) (see Introduction). Such unbalance can be reduced by means of financial compensation, or "community benefits" offered to the hosting communities. However, such cash transfer is not aimed at public involvement (as pointed out in chapter 3). Some NGOs have even denounced the use of community benefits as a form of bribery. Financial compensations rather need to be integrated in a broader plan of local development that includes infrastructures, employment, etc. (Kasperson 2005; Kuhn & Ballard 1998). Only in this way can the RWM facility become an integral component of the life of a local community and a pivot for local economic growth.

* **Principle 6: Providing adequate resources** – National authorities should make sure that an adequate amount of resources are available for public involvement and that they are accessible by local communities in particular.

Principles for public involvement during the implementation process

During the last decades, public policies have become the result of interactions among multiple actors, from state and society, interested in a common public problem (i.e. policy networks). In particular during the execution of national laws (i.e. policy implementation), governmental and non-governmental actors depend on shared resources for the realisation of given policy objectives. The implementation process consists of the set of relations that take place among various state and non-state organisations at all levels of governance – from the national to the local level – for the execution of national policies (chapter 2).

These inter-organisational relations are characterised by varying levels of commitment and coordination between the actors involved from government agencies, street-level bureaucrats and target groups (Winter 2003). Governmental actions can manipulate these relationships and promote collaborative patterns through the use of dedicated policy instruments (see Principle 4). The findings of the Euratom social research on RWM suggest ways to complement the application of these instruments and improve the inter-organisational relations that constitute the implementation process (Table 4.2):

- Principle 7: Promoting partnering and voluntarism;
- Principle 8: Adopting a flexible process;
- Principle 9: Building trust.

Partnering and voluntarism

According to the Euratom research results, public involvement during policy implementation is more influential when it embodies principles of "partnering" and "voluntarism", and takes, thus, the form of active participation (chapter 1).

Partnering means that the public agencies in charge of policy implementation accept that they should collaborate and share some degree of authority and power with their non-state counterparts. By the partial concession of this resource – i.e. authority – to non-state actors, organised groups and citizens become "partners" of the public agency (Bobbio 2004; NEA 2010a; 2013c; Thomas 2012). Through partnering arrangements or "partnerships", problem definition and solution in RWM are, thus, jointly owned by agencies, experts and citizens (NEA 2010d).

Public–private partnerships can be formally foreseen by legislative/regulatory acts or established informally. The so-formed partnership bodies can take different structures (see chapter 5), but are usually concluded among national public agencies, organised groups and citizens. Particularly, the inclusion of the national regulatory authority and implementing agency is of major importance since these public bodies possess the knowledge, information and expertise to answer questions and concerns raised by citizens and other stakeholders.

Partnering requires also that central authorities and the implementing agency are willing to actively involve and cooperate with local governments and administrations in any relevant process of decision-making. Indeed, partnerships are primarily played out at the local level; hence, local communities are an important part of a partnership arrangement. In these "inter-governmental partnerships" (Lowry & Eichenberg 1986), also known as centre–local partnerships or – more simply – local partnerships, it is vital that the presence of the local community reflects the actual composition of the local fabric to ensure legitimacy for the partnership. A balanced representation of the local fabric should include local elected representatives, local economic actors, trade unions, and community representatives from the public at large. Yet, it often remains difficult to define in practice who is representative and accountable to specific components of the local community (see chapter 3).

Local partnerships can carry out important tasks. They allow local communities to access scientific evidence and gather knowledge from multiple viewpoints. They interact with experts, conduct studies and analyses, formulate local requirements for a specific project, and design community benefit packages. They inform local elected representatives so that local politicians are better prepared to carry out dialogue with national authorities. They interact with the regional and national institutions, provide recommendations to the competent authorities, and monitor project developments. They can strive to involve the silent majority, lead and structure dialogue at the local level, and train their members (on these points, see also NEA 2010a).

A local partnership links both the public and private actors at the local level, and the centre and local level of governance. The creation of a local partnership, though, does not say much about the outcome, intended as actual engagement of the local population and local authorities in the development and implementation of public policies. Therefore, local partnerships can be an effective way to include local stakeholders in policy-making or simply a way of assembling local actors (Lowndes & Sullivan 2004). The same organisations involved in RWM are aware that public involvement can take place in the process without any influence on the result (chapter 3).

Furthermore, the Euratom social research warns that local communities should be empowered through voluntarism. The principle of voluntarism is embodied in arrangements where the national government (or the national implementing agency) invites local communities to participate in a siting process. Voluntary siting consists of a process during which locations are considered for facility siting 'only upon the request of local residents or officials' (Weingart 2007: 9). This expression of interest is usually preceded by a preliminary screening based on technical criteria and aimed at identifying adequate areas.

Voluntarism is also embodied in the veto power that can be granted to local communities in some countries. At a precise moment in the decision-making process, a local community is then allowed to express its decision to withdraw from a siting process (NEA 2010d). According to the Euratom research, local communities seem more willing to participate in site selection when they are granted a veto power, which acknowledges them as genuine partners in dialogue and decisions. It is important, though, that local involvement continues after the siting stage, in the decision-making about construction, operation, closure and post-closure.

Finally, partnering and voluntarism are beneficial for RWM also because they contribute to create that sense of familiarity with hazard and societal control over risk that has been highlighted as key for RWM (on this point, see also NEA 2004a).

* **Principle 7: Promoting partnering and voluntarism** – Policy-makers, regulatory bodies and implementing agencies should promote active participation through partnering and voluntarism.

Process flexibility

An important principle that applies to the implementation process is flexibility in decision-making. The Euratom projects have recommended that RWM decision-making should be structured along stages and proceed per steps, for instance the ones explained in chapter 1 for a deep geological disposal (DGD). These stages, or steps, are meant to be reversible, adjustable and open to stakeholders' inputs. Decision-making "per stages" suggested by the Euratom experience is in line with the major insights developed by the Nuclear Energy Agency (NEA) under the notion of "stepwise approach" (see chapter 7).

For the success of this flexible decision-making, it is important to clearly identify stages and milestones, as well as the roles of the different actors involved at each stage. It is also important that clear rules specify when the decision-making process can move to the next step – this can occur on the basis of agreed criteria. At the end of each stage, several possible options should be foreseen in order to avoid dead ends. The result is that important decisions are not taken in one single moment but emerge from numerous smaller decisions in which the concerned actors are constantly involved. Making choices by stages facilitates adaptation to inevitable changes that can modify technical, legal, economic, social and political conditions (see also NEA 2004a).

With this approach, the evolution of a decision or a project is thoroughly discussed at both national and local level. The national–local debate recommended for policy formulation (see above) should, indeed, continue throughout the entire policy process. This helps citizens, local communities and other stakeholders gain familiarity with RWM institutions and technologies, and become better informed and more competent. According to the Euratom research, flexibility in decision-making empowers stakeholders with opportunities to review and eventually modify earlier decisions if experience shows that they have adverse or unwanted effects (see also NEA 2013c). For instance, local communities can cautiously ponder their participation in a RWM project at each single step of its development and be entitled to block or reverse a decision at the end of any stage.[10]

Although this type of decision-making has its advantages, it also implies costs, namely in terms of time. Sufficient time is needed so that stakeholders and local communities can grasp the issues at stake, develop dialogue and build their input (chapter 2). With every increase in the number of steps, the duration and costs of the process are likely to increase, too. Therefore, it is important that rules are established in order to balance between the need to revisit decisions and the need to bank progress and move forward. The long extension of a process may, indeed, induce a "stakeholder fatigue" and the withdrawal of individuals who have other responsibilities (see chapter 3).

* **Principle 8: Adopting a flexible process** – RWM decision-making should be structured along stages and proceed per steps that are reversible, adjustable and open to stakeholders' inputs.

Trust

We stated that policy design shapes policy implementation and that procedural implementation instruments can be used to promote collaborative behaviour among the actors involved in the implementation process (chapter 2). Notwithstanding the importance of design choices for the functioning of policy networks, O'Toole (2012: 299) points out that 'when levels of trust are low, it may be difficult to get a true interorganizational effort off the ground'. Without trust, multi-actor processes can become dialogues of the deaf where actors discuss from very different frames and are not willing to consider other views and perspectives.

All interactions involved in the implementation process – at the central level, local level and between the two – are heavily impacted by trust. Therefore, in the absence of trust, dialogue among actors is weak, public involvement is difficult and the same functioning of policy networks is jeopardised (chapter 2).

The topic has been debated by several project consortia, addressed in many Euratom projects and recurs in their results and conclusions. The emerging picture is that there is a general degree of scepticism of local communities and the general public towards national authorities, implementing agencies and the nuclear industry. Reasons for this lack of trust in the nuclear field have already been discussed in chapter 1. The core message to take from the Euratom research is the need for building trust and rebuilding it where it has already been lost.

Beside this relation between trust and public involvement where the latter is eased by the former, i.e. "from trust to public involvement", RWM stakeholders have stressed the salience of the inverse causality "from public involvement to trust" (see chapter 3). In other words, trust emerges as both the result of public involvement and one of its enablers. A whole chapter (chapter 7) is dedicated to the relevance of trust in RWM and its relations with public involvement and social acceptance. There, we will see whether and how trust can be built or rebuilt.

* **Principle 9: Building trust** – Trust should be built or rebuilt where it has already been lost.

Concluding remarks

RW has traditionally been managed from a technical and technological perspective (chapter 1). However, the conflictual nature of RWM has brought its social dimension to the centre of the political debate. Policy-makers, public administrators and managers from the industry acknowledge nowadays that the technical and social dimensions of RWM are intertwined. This socio-technical nature of RWM brings along many challenges and makes public involvement unavoidable.

Many factors relevant for public involvement (e.g., legal and institutional frameworks, policy style and the political culture) are contextual and specific to each individual country of the EU; hence, a one-fits-all solution cannot be provided for all MSs. However, the Euratom FPs and the projects financed under these funding schemes have developed useful insights about public involvement in RWM. The chapter has synthesised this large amount of research and organised its major findings in common principles for the formulation, design and implementation of public policies.

The list of principles (Table 4.2) is also useful to provide initial direction for the critical areas (or emergent themes) identified by stakeholders: public information and participation, resources, participants and trust (chapter 3). Table 4.3 puts these themes in relation with the principles explained in this chapter for each component of our analytical framework. The resulting grid will be helpful for the analysis of national practices and local experiences that follow in chapters 5 and 6. Few aspects can be stressed about each emergent theme.

First, the strong emotions that RWM elicits in people and the risk perception of citizens (often distorted by personal beliefs about nuclear energy) makes public information and participation crucial for RWM. Therefore, a social dimension (made of values, national traditions and public concerns) needs to be acknowledged and taken into due account during policy formulation through the engagement of affected actors from society (i.e. the general public, organised interest, NGOs and local communities) (*Principle 1*).

Second, public and local involvement need to start early in the process (*Principle 2*) and continue in small steps throughout the entire policy- and decision-making (*Principle 8*), from the formulation of a national policy to the execution of localised projects. In order to make public involvement possible, national RWM policies should have a clear design in terms of instruments for public involvement (*Principle 5*).

Third, changes in policy designs may be needed to allow adequate support in terms of resources available for public involvement (*Principle 6*). Only with sufficient resources, can inclusive decision-making processes be put in practice. A fair interplay between national state actors and public/local interests implies that, for instance, adequate financial support is provided for activities of public

Table 4.3 Combined table

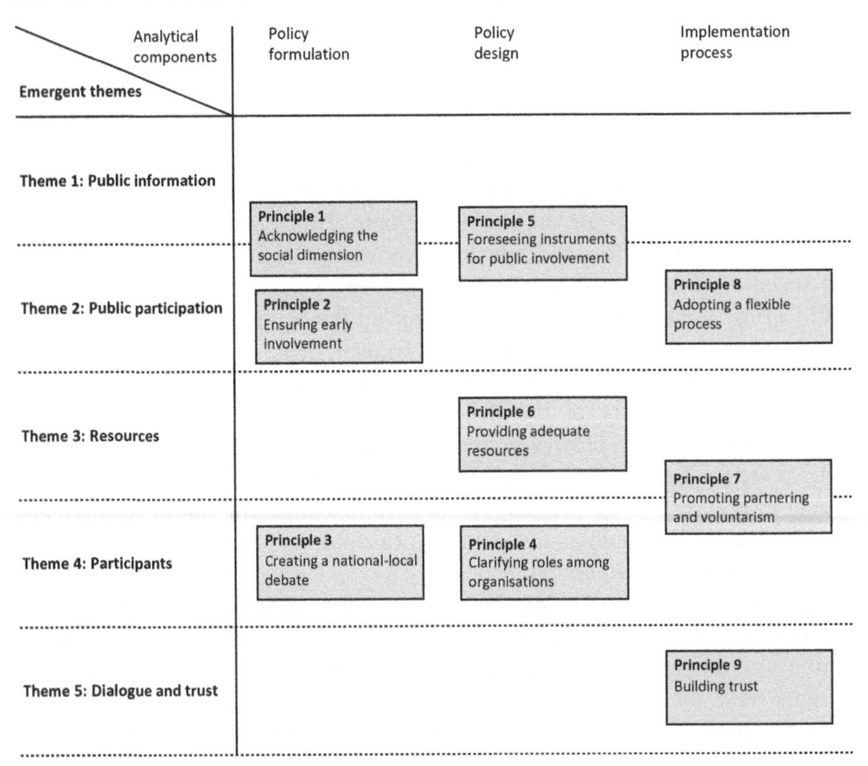

Emergent themes \ Analytical components	Policy formulation	Policy design	Implementation process
Theme 1: Public information	**Principle 1** Acknowledging the social dimension	**Principle 5** Foreseeing instruments for public involvement	
Theme 2: Public participation	**Principle 2** Ensuring early involvement		**Principle 8** Adopting a flexible process
Theme 3: Resources		**Principle 6** Providing adequate resources	**Principle 7** Promoting partnering and voluntarism
Theme 4: Participants	**Principle 3** Creating a national-local debate	**Principle 4** Clarifying roles among organisations	
Theme 5: Dialogue and trust			**Principle 9** Building trust

information, more active participation and capacity building. Resources also include authority (chapter 2); more power needs to be shared with non-state actors in decision-making in order to ensure actual citizens and stakeholders' influence during the implementation process. Policy instruments should facilitate and promote active participation (through partnering and voluntarism) during policy implementation (*Principle 7*).

Fourth, stakeholders have stressed the need of ensuring (either formally or informally) a balanced and transparent representation of a broad range of interests so as to give adequate recognition to all parties, from competent experts to local concerns (chapter 3). The Euratom projects stress the importance of identifying clear roles in decision-making (*Principle 4*) and, in particular, empowering local actors to express their views throughout the entire policy cycle from policy formulation with the creation of an national–local debate (*Principle 3*) to policy implementation through collaborative arrangements (*Principle 7*).

Fifth, trust represents an important requirement for constructive dialogue among stakeholders about issues and solutions. In the RWM and nuclear domain there is large space for improvement of trust. Efforts in the direction of building or re-building trust are recommended by the Euratom projects as an important principle to enhance public involvement in the field (*Principle 9*).

In the following chapters, we discuss to what extent and how some of these principles (namely those relating to policy design and implementation process) are reflected in national practices and local experiences of public involvement across the EU. This is important for any policy-maker or public administrator embarking on the journey of public involvement. Indeed, Dietz and Stern (2008: 15) explain that:

> The main challenge facing practitioners is to find a way to implement the principles of good public participation practice. [...] Practical experience makes clear, however, that implementing the principles can be much more difficult in some contexts than others, and that different contexts present different challenges for public participation.

Notes

1 See https://ec.europa.eu/energy/en/topics/nuclear-energy (last access: 14.02.2018).
2 See http://ec.europa.eu/research/energy/euratom/index_en.cfm?pg=fission§ion=history (last access: 01.02.2016).
3 Also two non-EU states have been included in some of the projects funded under the Euratom FPs and used for this chapter, namely Norway and Switzerland (see Table 4.1).
4 For two of these projects (i.e. ARGONA and CIP), specific guidelines produced by the project consortia have also been used. The OBRA project (2006–2008) was not included in this review because it assessed the feasibility of creating an observatory

on the governance of RWM in the EU rather than elaborating policy directions for public involvement.

5 The CARL network supported a comparative social science research project focusing on stakeholder involvement in RWM and the effects this generates on the decision-making process. The countries involved were Belgium, Sweden, Slovenia and the United Kingdom. The research project ran from October 2004 till December 2007.

6 Many more terms exist to refer to these synthesising efforts: meta-synthesis, meta-ethnography, meta-narrative, meta-study, meta-interpretation, etc. (Ring *et al.* 2010). The objective of the chapter, though, is not to discuss these different approaches.

7 The step of going beyond the content of primary studies differentiates meta-analysis from traditional literature review (Thomas & Harden 2008).

8 In the light of this explanation, there can be no selection bias about the primary studies selected for the meta-analysis. However, arbitrary choices could have been made about the aspects prioritised and principles extracted. In other words, some features of the primary studies (i.e. the project reports) could have been emphasised to the detriment of others. In order to ensure the meta-analysis with "credibility checks" (Timulak 2009) and, thus, avoid neglecting or overlooking some primary findings, the core content of the chapter was reviewed by researchers from the Euratom project consortia (Table 4.1) and practitioners from the relevant services of the EC. The latter includes the project officers of the Directorate-General for Research and Innovation (DG RTD) who had been directly involved in the development, monitoring and assessment of the different projects. An initial version of this chapter was, indeed, published as a policy report of the EC and a journal article (Ferraro & Martell 2015a; 2015b). This chapter builds on that report and add some newer considerations. Any misinterpretation is the sole responsibility of the author.

9 In this case, however, it may happen that the legal requirements for citizens' involvement are so vaguely defined in the primary legislation of a country that it is up to the implementer to give them practical application. A large space for discretion is, thus, left to the administrators (Thomas 1995).

10 Future generations, too, should be allowed to reconsider the decisions taken by their predecessors.

References

Andersson, K. (2014) *Implementation of Transparency and Participation in Radioactive Waste Management Programmes*, Final Summary Report, IPPA Project.

Andersson, K., Westerlind, M., Atherton, E., Besnus, F., Chataîgnier, S., Engström, S., Espejo, R., Hicks, T., Hedberg, B., Hunt, J., Laciok, A., Leskinen, A., Lilja, C., O'Donoghue, M., Pierlot, S., Wene, C.-O., Vira, J. and Yearsley, R. (2003) *Transparency and Public Participation in Radioactive Waste Management*, RISCOM II Final report, RISCOM II Project.

Bardach, E. (2012) *A Practical Guide for Policy Analysis. The Eightfold Path to More Effective Problem Solving*, SAGE, London.

BergmansA., Elam, M., Kos, D., Polič, M., Simmons, P., Sundqvist, G. and Walls, J. (2008) *Wanting the Unwanted: Effects of Public and Stakeholder Involvement in the Long-Term Management of Radioactive Waste and the Siting of Repository Facilities*, Final Report Carl Project.

Bobbio, L. (2004) *A piu' voci – Amministrazioni pubbliche, imprese, associazioni e cittadini nei processi decisionali inclusivi*, Edizioni Scientifiche Italiane, Rome.

Cooperative Research on the Governance of Radioactive Waste Management (2007), Final synthesis report, COWAM 2 Project.

DG RTD (2005) *Euratom FP6 Research Projects and Training Activities – Nuclear fission and radiation protection*, Volume I, Directorate-General for Research, Office for Official Publications of the European Communities, Luxembourg.

DG RTD (2007) *Euratom FP6 Research Projects and Training Activities – Nuclear fission and radiation protection*, Volume III, Directorate-General for Research, Office for Official Publications of the European Communities, Luxembourg.

DG RTD (2012) *Euratom FP7 Research & Training Projects – Nuclear fission and radiation protection*, Volume III, Directorate-General for Research, Office for Official Publications of the European Communities, Luxembourg.

Dietz, T. and Stern, P. C. (2008) *Public Participation in Environmental Assessment and Decision Making*, The National Academy Press, Washington DC.

Dunsire, A. (1990) "Implementation Theory and Bureaucracy", in Younis, T. (Ed.) *Implementation in Public Policy*, Dartmouth, Aldershot.

Ferraro, G. and Martell, M. (2015a) *EURATOM Projects, radioactive waste management and public participation: What have we learnt so far? A synthesis of principles*, Publications Office of the European Union, Luxembourg.

Ferraro, G. and Martell, M. (2015b) "Radioactive Waste Management and Public Participation in the EU. Lessons learnt from the EURATOM Research Framework Programmes", in *International Journal of Nuclear Power*, Vol. 60, No. 12, pp. 708–713.

Gadbois, S. (2010), *Final Report*, CIP Project.

Hanf, K. and O'Toole, L. J. (1992) "Revisiting Old Friends: Networks, Implementation Structures and the Management of Inter-organizational Relations", in *European Journal of Political Research*, Vol. 21, pp. 163–180.

Howlett, M. (2000) "Managing the 'Hollow State': Procedural Policy Instruments and Modern Governance", in *Canadian Public Administration*, Vol. 43, No. 4, pp. 412–431.

Howlett, M. (2011) *Designing Public Policies. Principles and Instruments*, Routledge, Abingdon.

Howlett, M., Mukherjee, I. and Woo, J. J. (2015) "Thirty Years of Instrument Research: What Have We Learned and Where Are We Going", Paper Presented at the International Conference of Public Policy (ICPP), 3 July, Milan, Italy.

Howlett, M., Ramesh, M. and Perl, A. (2009). *Studying Public Policy – Policy Cycles and Policy Subsystems*, Oxford University Press, Oxford.

International Socio-Technical Challenges for implementing geological disposal (2014), Project Final Report, InSOTEC Project.

Jonsson, J. P. and Andersson, K. (2010) (Eds), *Towards implementation of transparency and participation in radioactive waste management programmes*, ARGONA Final Report.

Kasperson, R. E. (2005) "Siting Hazardous Facilities: Searching for Effective Institutions and Processes", in Hayden Lesbirel, S. and Shaw, D. (Eds) *Managing Conflict in Facility Siting*, Edward Elgar, Cheltenham and Northampton.

Klijn, E.-H. (2007) "Managing Complexity: Achieving the Impossible? Management between Complexity and Stability: A Network Perspective", in *Critical Policy Analysis*, Vol. 1, No. 3, pp. 252–277.

Knoepfel, P., Larrue, C., Varone, F. and Hill, M. (2007) *Public Policy Analysis*, The Policy Press, University of Bristol, Bristol.

Kraft, M. E. (2000) "Policy Design and the Acceptability of Environmental Risks: Nuclear Waste Disposal in Canada and the United States", in *Policy Studies Journal*, Vol. 28, No. 1, pp. 206–218.

Kuhn, R. G. and Ballard, K. (1998) "Canadian Innovations in Siting Hazardous Waste Management Facilities", in *Environmental Management*, Vol. 22, No. 4, pp. 533–545.

Lehtonen, M. (2015), "Megaproject Underway. Governance of Nuclear Waste Management in France", in Brunnengräber, A., Di Nucci, M. R., Isidoro Losada, A. M., Mez, L. and Schreurs, M. (Eds) *Nuclear Waste Governance – An International Comparison*, Springer, pp. 117–138.

Lowndes, V. and Sullivan, H. (2004) "Like a Horse and Carriage or a Fish on a Bicycle: How Well do Local Partnerships and Public Participation go Together?" in *Local Government Studies*, Vol. 30, No. 1, pp. 51–73.

Lowry, K. and Eichenberg, T. (1986) "Assessing Intergovernmental Coordination in Coastal Zone Management", in *Policy Studies Review*, Vol. 6, No. 2, pp. 321–329.

May, P. J. (2003) "Policy Design and Implementation", in Peters, B. G. and Pierre, J. (Eds) *Handbook of Public Administration*, SAGE Publications, London, Thousand Oaks and Delhi.

May, P. J. (2012) "Policy Design and Implementation", in Peters, B. G. and Pierre, J. (Eds) *The SAGE Handbook of Public Administration*, 2nd Edition, SAGE, Los Angeles and London.

Michels, A. and De Graaf, L. (2010) "Examining Citizen Participation: Local Participatory Policy Making and Democracy", in *Local Government Studies*, Vol. 36, No. 4, pp. 477–491.

Mitchell, R. C. B. (1990) "The Implementation of Education Policy: School Councils", in Younis, T. (Ed.) *Implementation in Public Policy*, Dartmouth, Aldershot.

NEA (2004a) *Learning and Adapting to Societal Requirements for Radioactive Waste Management. Key findings and Experience of the Forum on Stakeholder Confidence*, OECD, Paris.

NEA (2010a) *The Partnership Approach to Siting and Developing Radioactive Waste Management Facilities*, OECD, Paris.

NEA (2010d) *Partnering for Long-term Management of Radioactive Waste. Evolution and Current Practice in Thirteen Countries*, OECD, Paris.

NEA (2013c) *Stakeholder Confidence in Radioactive Waste Management: An Annotated Glossary of Key Terms*, OECD, Paris.

NEA (2015) *Implementing Stakeholder Involvement Techniques*, OECD, Paris.

Nuclear Waste Management from a Local Perspective – Reflections for a Better Governance (2003), Final Report, COWAM Project.

OECD (2015) *Stakeholder Engagement for Inclusive Water Governance*, OECD, Paris.

O'Toole, L. J. (2012), "Interorganizational Relations and Policy Implementation", in Peters, B. G. and Pierre, J. (Eds) *The SAGE Handbook of Public Administration*, SAGE, Los Angeles and London.

Peterson, J. (2003) *Policy Networks*, Political Science Series, Institute for Advanced Studies, Vienna.

Ring, N., Ritchie, K., Mandava, L. and Jepson, R. (2010) *A guide to synthesising qualitative research for researchers undertaking health technology assessments and systematic reviews*, NHS Quality Improvement Scotland.

Sabatier, P. A. (1980) "The Implementation of Public Policy: A Framework of Analysis", in *Policy Studies Journal*, Vol. 8, No. 2, pp. 538–560.

Schneider, A. and Ingram, H. (1990) "Behavioral Assumptions of Policy Tools", in *The Journal of Politics*, Vol. 52, No. 2, pp. 510–529.
Shroff, M. R., Jones, S. J., Frongillo, E. A. and Howlett, M. (2012) "Policy Instruments Used by States Seeking to Improve School Food Environments", in *American Journal of Public Health*, Vol. 102, No. 2, pp. 222–229.
Thomas, J. C. (1995) *Public Participation in Public Decisions: New Skills and Strategies for Public Managers*, Jossey-Bass, San Francisco.
Thomas, J. C. (2012) *Citizen, Customer, Partner: Engaging the Public in Public Management*, Routledge, Abingdon and New York.
Thomas, J. and Harden, A. (2008) "Methods for the Thematic Synthesis of Qualitative Research in Systematic Reviews", in *BMC Medical Research Methodology*, Vol. 8, No. 45.
Thorne, S., Jensen, L., Kearney, M. H., Noblit, G. and Sandelowski, M. (2004) "Qualitative Metasynthesis: Reflections on Methodological Orientation and Ideological Agenda", in *Qualitative Health Research*, Vol. 14, No. 10, pp. 1342–1365.
Timulak, L. (2009) "Meta-analysis of Qualitative Studies: A Tool for Reviewing Qualitative Research Findings in Psychotherapy", in *Psychotherapy Research*, Vol. 19, No. 4–5, pp. 591–600.
Underdal, A. (2000) "Science and Politics: the Anatomy of an Uneasy Partnership", in Andresen, S., Skodvin, T., Underdal, A. and Wettestad, J. (Eds) *Science and Politics in International Environmental Regimes – Between Integrity and Involvement*, Manchester University Press, Manchester and New York.
Underdal, A. (2002) "One Question, Two Answers", in Miles, E. L., Underdal, A., Andresen, S., Wettestad, J., Skjaerseth, J. B. and Carlin, E. M. (Eds) *Environmental Regime Effectiveness – Confronting Theory with Evidence*, The MIT Press, Cambridge and London.
Vedung, E. (2006) "Evaluation Research", in Peters, B. G. and Pierre, J. (eds.) *Handbook of Public Policy*, Sage Publications, London.
Victor, D. G., Raustiala, K. and Skolnikoff, E. B. (1998) "Introduction and Overview", in Victor, D. G., Raustiala, K., and Skolnikoff, E. B. (Eds) *International Environmental Commitments – Theory and Practice*, The MIT Press, Cambridge and London.
Webler, T., Tuler, S. and Krueger, R. (2001) "What Is a Good Public Participation Process? Five Perspectives from the Public", in *Environmental Management*, Vol. 27, No. 3, pp. 435–450.
Weingart, J. (2007) *Waste Is A Terrible Thing To Mind*, Rivergate Books, New Brunswick, NJ.
Wilson, D. (1999) "Exploring the Limits of Public Participation in Local Government", in *Parliamentary Affairs*, Vol. 52, No. 2, pp. 246–259.
Winter, S. (1990) "Integrating Implementation Research", in Palumbo, D. J. and Calista, D. (Eds) *Implementation and the Policy Process – Opening Up the Black Box*, Greenwood Press, New York, Westport, CT and London.
Winter, S. (2003) "Introduction", in Peters, B. G. and Pierre, J. (Eds) *Handbook of Public Administration*, SAGE Publications, London, Thousand Oaks and Delhi.
Winter, S. C. (2006) "Implementation", in Peters, B. G. and Pierre, J. (Eds), *Handbook of Public Policy*, Sage Publications, London.
Winter, S. (2012a), "Implementation", in Peters, B. G. and Pierre, J. (Eds), *Handbook of Public Policy*, Sage Publications, London.
Winter, S. (2012b) "Implementation Perspectives: Status and Reconsideration", in Peters, B. G. and Pierre, J. (Eds) *The SAGE Handbook of Public Administration*, SAGE, Los Angeles and London.

5 National practices of public involvement

We have explained the concept of public involvement and contextualised it within the domain of radioactive waste management (RWM) (chapters 1 and 2). The objective was to free the topic from ambiguity and confusion. However, even when citizens' engagement seems to be clear at a conceptual level, it can still remain not well understood in an operational sense. As put by Creighton (2005: xvi), '[e]fforts to study public participation empirically have been sporadic and sometimes unconvincing to those actually conducting everyday programs'. The point is also raised by many stakeholders from RWM who stressed the need to better understand how the public can be involved *in practice* (chapter 3).

A thorough analysis of national practices of public involvement is made possible by the National Programmes (NPs) that each Member State (MS) has adopted in compliance with the Council Directive 2011/70/Euratom (the "Waste Directive"). This Directive provides a comprehensive and legally binding framework for the harmonisation of national policies dealing with the management of spent fuel (SF) and radioactive waste (RW) from all civilian activities, from generation to disposal, in a safe and responsible way. Article 10 disciplines matters of "transparency" in compliance with the Aarhus Convention (see Introduction) and calls for MSs to ensure public information (art. 10.a) and participation (art. 10.b) in RWM (see chapter 1). National arrangements and instruments to guarantee and promote public information and participation in policy-making should be specified in the NPs.

The Waste Directive stipulates, indeed, that every MS shall establish and maintain a national policy that describes the approach taken for the management of SF and RW as well as an associated National Programme (NP) for the implementation of the national policy through a concrete plan of action. MSs were required to transpose the Waste Directive by summer 2013 and put in place a NP by summer 2015.[1] All 28 MSs have submitted to the European Commission (EC) these programmatic documents about their management of SF and RW (either in final or draft form at the time of writing).

The chapter analyses national practices of public involvement in RWM across the EU. It focuses on policy implementation (chapter 2), investigates the use of procedural implementation instruments and develops an inventory of how MSs pursue and realise information, consultation and active participation in the management of RW. The chapter also assesses whether and to what extent national experiences align with general principles for public involvement (chapter 4) in relation to emergent themes (chapter 3). Before looking into national practices, the chapter provides an overview on the enactment of the principle of transparency in national legal frameworks.

The right of public information and participation in national legislations

The Aarhus Convention (1998, 2001) calls for its contracting parties to promote public information and participation during the formulation of a policy and its implementation (through delegated legislation, programmes and activities). The EC is party to the Convention, which applies to nuclear activities including RWM (see Introduction). In line with the Aarhus Convention, the right of public information and participation in RWM are foreseen by most national legal frameworks of the MSs[2] of the EU. Reference to public involvement – or transparency or openness (see chapter 2) – is present in national laws with a broad scope or in legislative acts specific to policy domains such as environment, energy or nuclear energy, RWM and radiation protection (see Table 5.1).

In the first case, public involvement in RWM is ensured by the same national laws that govern public information in general. These laws take different denominations in different MSs. They usually go under the names of Access to Public Information Act, Act on Free Access to Information, Act on Openness of Government Activities, Law on Provision of Information to the Public, Freedom of Information Act, etc. As a common feature, these national laws acknowledge the right of the public to request and receive information held by the public administration. In other words, they discipline both the right to access information and the right to be provided with information from the competent public bodies (i.e. the national regulatory authorities for the domain of RWM).

Table 5.1 The right of public information and participation in national legislations

Right of public information and participation in national legislation	*Number of MSs*
General primary laws	13
Environmental laws	14
Energy laws	1
Nuclear laws	12
RWM laws	6
Radiation protection laws	10

Note: The table shows how many MSs refer to the right of public information and participation in each different type of national legislation. Any single MS may refer to this right in several types of legislation.

In the second case, public access to information is foreseen by national laws that govern specific domains. This happens for instance for the environmental field where national governments have adopted Environmental Protection Acts, Environmental Codes, Environmental Information Acts, etc. These acts refer to public involvement and call for its application across all environmental matters, including RWM. Usually MSs have included the right of public information in laws that govern energy (e.g., Energy Acts) and nuclear energy, in general (i.e. Atomic Acts, Atomic Energy Acts, Nuclear Energy Acts, Nuclear Safety Acts, etc.), or RWM, in particular. Legal obligations of information on radiological emergency are also contained in national acts that are specific to radiation protection (e.g., Radiation Protection Acts).

To sum up, national legislations enacted in the 28 MSs contain provisions for the right of public information and participation, in compliance with the Waste Directive and the Aarhus Convention. However, looking solely at the national legislation that ensures transparency in RWM provides us with a limited view on how public involvement is actually conducted in practice in the management of RW across the MSs of the EU. Furthermore, informal practices of public involvement have often been established even *extra legem*, i.e. out of any legal framework (see chapter 4). Therefore, it is important to move from an overview on legal prescriptions to the analysis of concrete practices. For this purpose the information contained in the NPs is particularly useful. Indeed, the NPs provide a rich amount of data with regard to both formal and informal processes of public involvement, from public information to consultation and active participation.

National practices across the EU: an inventory of instruments

In chapter 4, we defined practices as tangible and visible behaviours (Bardach 2012). More precisely, practices of public involvement are the ways chosen to engage people (Thurston *et al.* 2005). They are described by scholars and practitioners in many interchangeable ways: approaches, instruments, means, mechanisms, methods, practices, procedures, processes, techniques, tools, etc. In line with the policy literature, the book uses the term instruments or – more correctly – procedural implementation instruments (see chapter 2).

Public involvement during policy implementation includes many of these instruments; they aim at informing, consulting and actively engaging the public (Balla 2005). Rowe and Frewer (2000) stress that several aspects of the instruments used to provide information have been the object of research, for instance in the field of risk communication. In this area, scholars have studied the best way to present information, the best medium to transmit information, and the best people to provide information. The two authors point out that '[l]ess research, however, has been conducted on mechanisms for involving the public at higher levels of input into decision making' (Rowe & Frewer 2000: 6). Particularly for the field of RWM, little systematic analysis is available on the actual use of procedural implementation instruments. Therefore, the chapter analyses the use of various instruments by which the public and all stakeholders can be involved, not only informed, in RWM during policy implementation. The pool of knowledge offered by the 28 national contexts that form the EU provides a good basis for such effort.

The chapter develops an inventory of procedural implementation instruments used by MSs in RWM along the degrees of public involvement they aim to achieve: information, consultation and active participation (see chapter 2). For this purpose, the empirical information contained in the NPs has been organised through the analytical insights on public involvement produced by scientific literature (e.g., Creighton 2005; Bobbio 2004; Depoe *et al.* 2004; Thomas 2012), policy reports (e.g., OECD 2015), international projects (i.e. Implementing Public Participation Approaches in Radioactive Waste Disposal[3]) and professional associations (such as the International Association for Public Participation[4]).

The chapter is descriptive and explanatory rather than prescriptive or normative. It aims at analysing instruments for public involvement used in RWM as they emerge from national experiences across 28 political systems. The chapter does not intend to act as a guide to action: it does not suggest how interactions should take place, nor does it suggest how engagement should be practised. (Policy recommendations are elaborated in chapter 8.)

A comprehensive discussion of *all* possible instruments for public involvement is, also, not the purpose of the chapter; several reasons motivate this choice. First, the large variety of instruments for informing, consulting and engaging the public faces problems of space limitations, which precludes a detailed analysis. Second, distinctions between instruments for public involvement are not always clear-cut: empirically, borders between instruments are, often, blurred; instruments are applied somewhat differently in different contexts; and many variants of more recurrent instruments exist. Third, these instruments are in constant evolution; hence, full coverage is ambitious. Fourth, limiting the analysis to a few types can simplify discussion. Fifth, we only look at RWM and the instruments reported by MSs.

The last point leads to a final important consideration: absence of evidence is not evidence of absence. The chapter analyses the information provided by MSs in their NPs. Therefore, we cannot assume that the absence of information on the use of some of these instruments in the official documents implies that they are certainly not used. The following sections and the information represented in Figure 5.1 are based on the data contained in the NPs and supporting documents (i.e. the available national reports).

Policy implementation and instruments for information

A first category of instruments is the one used to inform the public. The goal of these instruments is to provide balanced and objective information in order to help citizens understand problems and alternatives, opportunities and solutions (see chapter 2). As reported in the NPs, the provision of information on matters of nuclear safety and radiation protection constitutes a general obligation for any legal person who is carrying out RWM activities in all MSs.

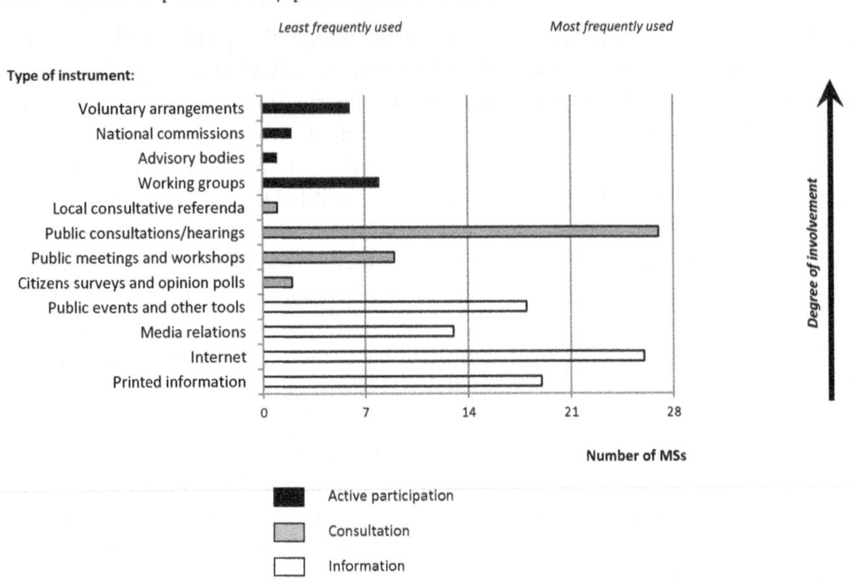

Figure 5.1 Instruments for public involvement in RWM across the EU
Note: The figure shows how many MSs have reported to use a given instrument.

In particular, the provision of information constitutes one of the key responsibilities of national regulators. National regulators are responsible for the provision of information to the public concerning the safety and security of nuclear energy decisions and activities, including those related to the management of SF and RW. The public can also request acts issued by the national regulator on the basis of the right of public access to official records unless such acts are covered by secrecy. In some MSs, documents about the licensing procedure of nuclear and RWM facilities are made public by the regulatory authorities as requested by national laws.[5]

National laws in the EU also assign a legal obligation of information to the licence holders, i.e. the operators of nuclear facilities or the national Waste Management Organisation (WMO) for RWM facilities. Some MSs specify that licence holders have a duty to inform both the general public and the affected local community. Finally, other bodies, usually at ministerial level, are also responsible for the provision of information.

Information is provided by MSs through several information dissemination instruments that can be grouped into four main categories (Figure 5.1):

- printed information;
- internet;
- media relations;
- public events and other tools.

Printed information

Printed information constitutes one of the easiest and most familiar methods used to communicate and increase awareness about a public problem. It can provide a short overview of a topic or present more detailed insights of an issue at stake. The major advantage of printed information is that it can be easily distributed – by handing it out into letterboxes and via mail (Creighton 2005; Smutko & Addor 2012 – see also IAP2 and IPPA).

Printed information is frequently used by EU MSs for conveying messages about RWM to the public. It takes several forms: short publications (e.g., newsletters), leaflets and brochures. Printed information can also take the form of more elaborate types of written documents, namely studies and reports (e.g., annual, progress and technical reports). The same NPs are often issued as instruments that inform the public about national policies and plans for the management of SF and RW. Some MSs have disseminated their NPs also online, through media and in information sessions.

Internet: websites and social media

The instruments available for information provision and access have expanded since the 1990s with the development of the internet. New information technologies have largely contributed to the dissemination of public information and knowledge (Napolitano 2007; Thomas 1995). In the field of RWM, MSs have reported about their increasing use of the internet with the purpose of building awareness and providing information about RWM policy developments, projects and related issues. The main use of the internet consists of corporate websites. Their advantage is that an enormous amount of information can be provided to a very large number of users in a free and easily accessible way (Lee 2014 – see also IAP2 and IPPA).

Websites serve different uses. They can work as information repositories that provide access to documents and reports. They are a channel to broadcast information about meetings or events. They constitute a virtual space where interested citizens can post opinions and feedbacks, discuss an issue, and comment about alternatives under consideration (Creighton 2005; Smutko & Addor 2012; West 2005).

In recent years, the internet has broadened its applications. Opportunities for sharing information have increased with the development of social media (OECD 2003b; Thomas 2012). Social media are virtual platforms and applications that enable users to create and exchange content. This virtual social networking allows citizens to express their demands on governments more easily (Michels & De Graaf 2010). The most popular social media are Facebook, YouTube and Twitter, to name but a few. In several MSs, some organisations involved in RWM are already using social media and blogs as their channel of communication with citizens.

A barrier to the utilisation of websites and social media for information provision and access is represented by age, with the older population less familiar and more reluctant to use the internet in their daily life. Such limitation needs to be taken into account in all policy areas, including RWM.

Media relations

MSs have reported in their NPs that media relations are often used by WMOs to inform the public. Media relations include several instruments: press releases, press conferences, newspaper articles or inserts, national official journals, TV programmes, etc.

Press releases disseminate information quickly to a large number of people; they can raise publicity and awareness. Press conferences have the benefit that all media is reached at one setting; it is a good medium for informing about the latest developments of a project or to give statements related to recent events. Newspaper articles can help to increase the awareness of a certain issue among a broad audience; they can be used to inform the public about project updates and important events or to give background information. Newspaper inserts aim, instead, to reach and inform the majority of people in a targeted geographic area about a given issue; for instance, they can be used to increase awareness about a policy or project proposal. National official journals are often used to inform citizens about new regulations (as well as new legislation). Finally, TV programmes can be used as an important tool to reach out to the national audience (through a national broadcaster) or local communities (through local TV channels) (Creighton 2005; Smutko & Addor 2012 – see also IPPA).

Public events and other tools

MSs can decide to provide information about RWM through public events such as exhibitions, public conferences, information sessions, seminars, public presentations, etc. These different formats share the common objective of providing information and raising awareness. Public events are gathering opportunities intended only to provide information to the public without the stakeholders' interaction that characterises consultation techniques (e.g., public meetings and workshops – see below).

Public events used by MSs for RWM also include open days. Open days (e.g., open house events and site visits) allow those promoting development initiatives to present them to a wider public and secure reactions in an informal manner. The venue (which can be the same site selected for a facility) is usually arranged with a number of displays that explain the project (final proposal or options) by using a variety of interactive display techniques. Open days can be organised at any stage of the design and development process. They can last from a few hours to several weeks. The organisers will be present to deal with queries and engage in informal debate. Open days are meant to promote a relaxed atmosphere and enable staff to tailor responses according to the needs/questions of the public. This allows the discussion of sensitive topics and the creation of useful connections for the future (Creighton 2005; Smutko & Addor 2012 – see also IAP2 and IPPA).

Finally, another tool mentioned by MSs in their NPs is information centres. An information centre is an office established to distribute information (for instance about a specific RWM project), respond to inquiries and act as a focal point for discussion. They are located either at the selected site of a RWM facility or in the centre of the nearest town (see IAP2 and IPPA).

Policy implementation and instruments for consultation

The second category of instruments for public involvement is aimed at consultation. Instruments for consultation are employed when policy-makers and public administrators want to know and understand the needs and concerns of interested actors. These instruments are, indeed, used to receive and compile feedback and opinions from the public about government decisions and actions (see chapter 2). While the previous category of instruments is used by public agencies to provide information to non-state actors, instruments for consultation bring the knowledge of laymen and relevant stakeholders (which constitutes an important resource) into the policy-making.

In RWM, consultation of the public and other stakeholders takes different forms that vary across MSs. These forms span from informal settings to more institutionalised practices, from ad hoc initiatives to regular mechanisms of consultation. We have discussed the major differences between informal and formal public involvement in chapter 4 in general. In particular, informal consultation refers to discretionary, ad hoc, and unstandardised contacts with the interested parties. This type of consultation is less cumbersome and more flexible than more institutionalised forms of consultation. However, it may suffer from limited transparency and accountability. Formal consultation has, instead, a legal basis (in national laws or regulations), is more systematic and structured, and occurs regularly; the feedback obtained is formally recorded.

From the NPs we understand that MSs tend to rely on the following instruments of consultation (Figure 5.1):

- citizen surveys and opinion polls;
- public meetings and workshops;
- public consultations and public hearings;
- local consultative referenda.

Citizen surveys and opinion polls

Citizen surveys and opinion polls are used by few MSs to test public opinion about specific RWM projects. These instruments can generate useful information and evidence from citizens that may influence public programmes and projects. As explained by Creighton (2005: 128), surveys and opinion polls ‘permit a quantitative assessment of viewpoints in the community'. They enable the measurement of attitudes and characteristics of a group through the use of a structured questionnaire applied to a representative sample of the population. More precisely, in the case of surveys, questionnaires may include open-ended questions allowing respondents to offer their own views more extensively than in opinion polls.

Both surveys and opinion polls can be conducted through several means – i.e. by phone, mail and internet – in order to reach out to a large number of people. They can be arranged ad hoc or take place periodically. In the latter case, provided that the same questions are retained, surveys and opinion polls can be used for longitudinal studies to monitor change over time.

Despite the useful insights on citizens' orientations that they provide, these two instruments have some pitfalls. First, the selected sample may not be representative or comprehensive of a whole population. Second, questions need to be formulated in a simple and straightforward way to facilitate understanding; hence, the information gathered can be simplistic and superficial. Third, the rate of response may be too low to allow any conclusion. Fourth, the results are often not comparable (Creighton 2005; Smutko & Addor 2012 – see also IAP2 and IPPA). Fifth, they do not allow dialogue and debate between state actors and the public. Sixth, they do not facilitate wide and active participation of citizens; they are, indeed, relatively passive and aimed at gaining a general view without any space for debate (Adams 2004; Kasymova & Lauer Schachter 2014; Rowe & Frewer 2000; Thomas 1995; Wilson 1999).

Public meetings and workshops

Some MSs have mentioned public meetings and workshops among the instruments that they use for public involvement in RWM. They consist of the gathering of citizens who want to have more information from a designated speaker or expert, ask questions, express their opinions and concerns on a decision or a project, and give comments (e.g., Bobbio 2004; Creighton 2005; Smutko & Addor 2012; Thomas 2012 – see also IAP2 and IPPA). They are usually organised by the national regulatory body or the implementing agency in order to meet citizens in general, or specific local communities concerned by RWM plans and facilities in particular.

Access is open to all citizens who participate as individuals rather than representatives of groups. The main purpose is the exchange of information: agencies inform citizens about their activities and citizens provide personal opinions on the agency policy. Public meetings and workshops are often informal and heavily interactive since they aim at the active exchange of information among participants. They are a way 'to convey information about public opinion to officials' (Adams 2004: 46) but allow for communication and discussion among stakeholders, too (Lee 2014).

Public meetings and workshops constitute an important instrument of consultation; they serve the purpose of obtaining and understanding informed citizens' views on controversial issues. Therefore, they allow policy-makers and public administrators to go beyond the one-directional provision of information typical of the previous set of instruments (i.e. printed information, internet, media relations and public events). They generally have a facilitator, who encourages two-way communication, and a recorder who records suggestions and issues that are revealed at the meeting.

Indeed, the outcomes can be used to develop materials on the subject for public use as well as to inform media debates on the issue. This type of tools is normally used with a view to publicise the outcome widely (Bobbio 2004; Creighton 2005; Smutko & Addor 2012). However, they are not meant to produce any shared decision (Thomas 2012). The decision-making power remains fully in the public agency (Beierle & Cayford 2002).

Public meetings can take different formats and names (e.g., public discussions, public debates, etc.) but they are commonly open to the public for which they create a venue for interaction and exchange (Lee 2014; Thomas 1995). Because public meetings are open to anyone who wishes to join in the discussion, they may face a major organisational problem: the size of the audience can be so large that interaction and discussion become difficult (Adams 2004; Thomas 1995). This instrument may also suffer from unrepresentativeness (Thomas 2012; see chapter 2).

Workshops tend to be more interactive and productive than public meetings: 'Workshops usually interest participants because they can do something other than sit and listen' (Thomas 1995: 117).

Public consultation and public hearings

Public consultation and public hearings are more formal types of consultation mechanisms than public meetings and workshops. Their strength consists of their potential to inform and listen to citizens in a formal way for improved decision-making and conflict minimisation. However, public consultations and hearings may be dominated by special interest groups; indeed, they tend to exclude disadvantaged groups. Therefore, the feedback obtained from these instruments needs to be treated carefully because it may not be representative of an entire community (Creighton 2005; Howlett 2011; Howlett *et al.* 2009).

From the NPs it is clear that public consultation is the most common instrument used by MSs to elicit societal input for RWM. During public consultation, a draft proposal (e.g., of a new rule, licence, etc.) is submitted for public (written) comments (via official journals, the internet, etc.) before it is finalised, approved and adopted (Thomas 2012). This consultative effort can be analysed by looking at the procedures, representation, available resources and results.

First, public consultation in the EU can take place in the framework of the Strategic Environmental Assessment (SEA) of policy documents governing RWM (i.e. national plans and programmes) and the Environmental Impact Assessment (EIA) of specific RWM projects. Both the SEA and EIA constitute formal procedures of citizens' engagement and are regulated by two EU Directives (see Introduction). However, their use is specified by the national legal and regulatory framework of each MS. For instance, some MSs have submitted their

NP for public consultation in the framework of a SEA; others deemed it not necessary; some others have submitted the document for public consultation out of any legal requirement. Public consultation in the framework of the EIA is often a precondition for the issuing (or amending) of licences for RWM facilities and other nuclear installations.

Public consultation in RWM is promoted by the responsible policy-making institution (e.g., at the ministerial level), the regulatory authority or the implementing agency. Experts from public relations and communication can be involved to facilitate discussions. Moreover, surveys can accompany the consultation process so that the inputs received can be used to improve future consultations.

Second, representation in the consultation process depends on the national legal and regulatory framework. As a general trend, though, we understand from the NPs that consultation in RWM has a broader base when more general issues are addressed and during the pre-selection phase. After site selection has been completed, consultation for RWM usually narrows down to the localities that are directly targeted by a project. Furthermore, if a proposed RWM project has a potential transboundary impact, third countries (that are potentially affected by the RWM project) may participate in the EIA in compliance with the Espoo Convention (see Introduction).

Third, an important supporting instrument for public consultation is the funding of NGOs aimed at their mobilisation in the framework of the EIA. However the availability of this type of funding is only reported by one MS.

Fourth, in several cases, the NPs stress that the result of the public consultation must be taken into due account and the use made (or not made) of citizen's inputs must be justified. Comments received during the consultation process are in some cases made publicly available in order to explain to what extent they have been used by policy-makers and public administrators. This reporting activity, though, has only been mentioned explicitly by a few MSs.

While public consultation is an articulated process, a public hearing constitutes a single event that is usually part of a broader process of public consultation. 'Public hearings, which are usually required by law, allow citizens to comment on a specific issue or proposal before a governmental entity makes a decision' (Adams 2004: 44). A public hearing consists of a formal meeting with scheduled presentations where interested parties can comment in person.

Public hearings aim at gathering information and feedbacks from the public on a specific topic as happens in public meetings. However, there are substantial differences between public meetings and public hearings. First, public hearings are not venues for discussion among participants. Second, members of the public are present in public hearings as representatives of an organisation or group of interest. Third, these representatives state opinions and positions that are formally recorded (Checkoway 1981; Creighton 2005; Rowe & Frewer 2000 – see also IAP2 and IPPA).

The impact of public hearings on policy developments is debatable. Two problems seem to characterise this type of instrument: representation and timeliness. In terms of representation, the often low participation rate at public hearings can produce an audience that is unrepresentative of the community. For instance, it may be over-populated with strong economic interests or extremist positions. A second problem is that public hearings often take place late in the policy development, after significant basic decisions about a proposal have, in fact, already been taken (Adams 2004; Blomgren Bingham *et al.* 2005; Checkoway 1981; Kasymova & Lauer Schachter 2014; Rowe & Frewer 2000).

Local consultative referenda

As explained in the Introduction, forms of representative and direct democracy are not discussed in the book. Referenda are commonly instruments of direct democracy. However, one special type of referendum cannot be neglected in this inventory of instruments for public involvement. MSs can indeed have consultative (or advisory) referenda at the local level, for instance for site selection. Consultative referendum during policy implementation (mentioned only by one MS) qualifies as an additional instrument of consultation (Wilson 1999). Its use, though, is compatible only with some national constitutional and legal frameworks (Creighton 2005; Rowe & Frewer 2000).

Policy implementation and instruments for active participation

A final group of instruments is used for the purpose of supporting active participation and a close collaboration between public authorities and citizens. Through these instruments, state and non-state actors work together to jointly define possible solutions. Citizens are, thus, given the authority to influence public decisions (see chapter 2). Public involvement through instruments of active participation is particularly important for those local communities that host or are likely to host the storage and disposal of RW.

In the EU, institutions exist at the local level (e.g., municipalities) and regional level (e.g., counties) that embody the principle of representative democracy and, thus, ensure the institutional representation of subnational interests in the national policy-making of MSs. In addition to these forms of representative democracy, complementary arrangements of participative democracy have been put in place in the RWM domain.

Instruments of active participation in RWM decision-making embody the principles of "partnering" and "voluntarism" (see chapter 4). The application of the principle of partnering has also led to contractual agreements between the national governments (or their implementing agencies) and local communities. Partnership agreements usually provide the local community with resources (namely, funds) to facilitate their engagement in the decision-making related to RWM. In some cases, the establishment of a local partnership has also involved the creation of new legal entities.

The principles of partnering and voluntarism take a variety of forms across the EU. Yet, all instruments included in this category have a higher degree of formality than those listed in the previous categories. Indeed, they often have a mandate within the regulatory process. The level of societal and local control exerted through these instruments varies across countries, programmes and projects. However, local empowerment is overall stronger than in the previous two categories of instruments (for information and consultation). On the basis of the information provided by MSs in their NPs, active participation of social interests and local stakeholders include the following instruments (Figure 5.1):

- working groups;
- advisory bodies;
- national commissions;
- and voluntary arrangements.

Working groups

In some MSs, active participation is made possible through the creation and operation of working groups that enable a partnership approach to decision-making. Working groups have different names, structures and objectives across MSs. However, as a common feature, they involve – in a formal way – representatives from a broad range of interests including state authorities, regulatory bodies, implementing agencies, associations of the civil society and NGOs. Working groups can be involved in the preparation of strategic documents – such as the NPs – or a specific project – like deep geological disposal (DGD).

A variation of the working groups comes in the form of local (liaison) groups or bodies, which are often called "local committees". They are established in several MSs in specific sites that host or are likely to host nuclear power plants (NPPs) or RWM facilities. Their composition varies across MSs; however they usually bring together elected officials and other representatives of the local population. These bodies facilitate information and consultation on nuclear and RWM matters. They also work as a communication channel between the licence holder, the regulator and the local population of the concerned municipalities, thus allowing some form of communities' participation in decisions concerning facilities' siting, development and operation (NEA 2009).

Finally, a third type of working group is represented by the (regional) associations of local governments. These associations are set up in the area of existing or planned RWM facilities and regroup several towns. Their purpose is to allow communication and social monitoring of RWM facilities. They transfer information on RWM facilities and activities to the local population (via printed materials, website and media relations) and give feedback from citizens to the implementing agency which is, usually, not part of these associations. The status of these associations may be formalised by the national acts ruling the use of nuclear energy.

Advisory bodies

A function similar to working groups, yet with a higher degree of institutionalisation, is the one assigned to advisory bodies (also known as advisory committees, advisory councils, etc.). Although reliance on this instrument of active participation is not very frequent for RWM across the EU, it deserves particular attention because it represents an important instrument of active participation that could be further developed and used by MSs.

Advisory bodies are formal organisations; they can be permanent or established ad hoc. Representatives from relevant societal groups sit in these bodies with the task of giving advice to governments and public agencies on specific policy issues, the operation of sectoral public programmes or broad topics (Thomas 2012 – see also IAP2 and IPPA). Therefore, advisory bodies work as important mechanisms to bring the inputs of society and interest groups into governmental decisions. They provide a venue for organised and non-organised interests to analyse specific issues and present their views. Three aspects of this procedural implementation instrument are discussed here: procedure, representation and results.

First, advisory bodies are usually small groups composed of both state and non-state actors mainly at the national level; they include government officials and parties from outside government who have a stake in the issue. Participants are usually clearly defined and consistent in time; they gather in regular meetings over years. The strength of advisory bodies lies in the fact that they generate a two-way communication between citizens and policy-makers. More precisely, they enquire about particular issues, intervene on agency proposals, propose advice and recommendations for administrative decisions and actions, and can – in some cases – issue agreed decisions as an expression of joint decision-making (Balla 2005; Beierle & Cayford 2002; Lynn & Busenberg 1995).

Second, government authorities appoint the advisory bodies and select the representatives who will sit on these bodies (Beierle & Cayford 2002). These representatives are, thus, recognised special authority and rights in the policy process (Smutko & Addor 2012). In order for advisory bodies to be effective and recognised as legitimate, their membership (i.e. the range of relevant groups represented) should be broad and balanced so that all views are fairly represented (Balla 2005; Thomas 2012). The incapacity to ensure a full representation of all interests can impact negatively on the legitimacy of the advisory body and the advice it produces (Lee 2014; Lynn & Busenberg 1995).

Third, the results of the participation that takes place through advisory bodies are normally formulated as recommendations for an agency (Beierle & Cayford 2002; Smutko & Addor 2012). In terms of actual impact on the results of decision-making, the literature reports about a "varied picture" of advisory bodies' impact on policy outcomes from more influential cases to purely fictitious ones (Lynn & Busenberg 1995). As we explained in chapter 4, if there is no will from the side of state authority to share some degree of decision-making power with the public and make it a partner in decisions, any arrangement of active participation is simply an assembly of multiple actors (Lowndes & Sullivan 2004).

National commissions

Very few MSs have reported about the establishment of national commissions for the promotion of public involvement in RWM. In general, national commissions are costly but highly visible. However, their visibility outweighs the costs due to their creation: these new governmental structures are usually set up to develop new (and better) relations with the civil society (Howlett 2011). As explained by Weingart (2007: 40),

> In general, when legislatures choose to assign tasks to new commissions instead of directing them to ongoing governmental departments, it is because they feel an added level of public respect or credibility will be afforded. The issue may receive more public prominence than would occur if it was to be just one among the many priorities that a major department has to juggle.

Voluntary arrangements

A final group of instruments for active participation includes several voluntary arrangements (also called "consent-based mechanisms") that are based on the principle of voluntarism. Only a minority of MSs has reported about the presence and use of these instruments in their RWM system. Voluntary arrangements are particularly important for intergovernmental relations, understood here as the relations between national governments and local communities (see chapter 6). These arrangements allow local communities to express their support or dissent vis-à-vis given RWM projects and, thus, actively participate in the decision-making process.

In this voluntary approach to decision-making, support or dissent can be expressed in various ways. First, local communities can be invited to voluntarily express their interest to explore the possibility of locating a RWM facility in their jurisdiction. Obviously, willing communities must first of all meet the siting criteria (see chapter 1). Second, in some cases, public support must be evident and is formally tested before moving to the next stage of development of a RWM facility. Third, a local community that participates in preliminary discussions has the right to withdraw from the siting process after full consideration. It is, indeed, important that a local community is given the chance to explore the possibility of hosting a RWM facility without incurring in any obligation (Weingart 2007). Fourth, in some MSs, a formal veto power is recognised to the municipalities with regard to the establishment of an unwanted facility. To sum up, from the information provided by MSs in their NPs, it results that voluntary approaches in the EU include several forms such as expression of interest, proof of public support, right of withdrawal and local veto. These instruments represent a radical shift away from the traditional decide–announce–defend (DAD) approach (see Introduction) that has characterised RWM and facility siting for many decades (chapter 1).

Concluding remarks

The way a policy is discussed (policy formulation) and the content it takes (policy design) largely impact on its execution (implementation process) and the results achieved (chapter 2). Chapter 4 elaborated several principles for public involvement that can improve information, consultation and active participation in policy formulation, through policy design and during the implementation process. Putting these principles into practice is not always an easy task for practitioners; levels of difficulty also vary from country to country (Dietz & Stern 2008). The chapter has looked into the practical experience of 28 MSs as reported in their NPs.

Given their executive nature and implementation function, the NPs do not provide insights on practices of public involvement during policy formulation, which anyway falls outside our focus. Some countries are developing totally new policies (see Landström & Bergmans 2015). From the few information reported in the NPs, we understand that, in some MSs, *informal* public debates (e.g., through public meetings and workshops) have taken place on several occasions and have impacted on the revision of national legislations during the amendment process. Less frequently, MSs have reported about *formal* public consultations that occurred during the process of amendment of national laws related to RWM. Once a new policy is adopted, information on new legislation is provided in national official journals.

NPs detail the implementation of national policies through concrete plans for action. The implementation process develops through a network of interactions among various state and non-state actors, located at both the national and local level, with different degrees of commitment and coordination. A wide range of practices, or procedural implementation instruments, can be used to alter and improve the set of interactions that take place during implementation. Indications concerning what types of instruments could be used for public involvement are not present in the Waste Directive. This is due to the very nature of EU Directives that set out goals that all EU countries must achieve but leave to the individual MSs to devise their own ways to reach those goals (see chapter 1).

Therefore, the chapter has discussed the procedural implementation instruments used by MSs for RWM with the purpose of providing practitioners (and scholars) with an overview on the instruments of public involvement currently used for RWM within the EU. The chapter makes no claims to exhaustiveness and acknowledges that more extensive lists of policy tools for public involvement are possible. Moreover, the objective of the chapter was descriptive – rather than normative and prescriptive.

Some key points can be highlighted at the conclusion of this chapter in relation to the emergent themes (chapter 3) and principles for public involvement (chapter 4) that should guide policy design and the implementation process (see Table 5.2).

First, MSs have legal frameworks in place to ensure public involvement and rely on several instruments that allow the information, consultation and engagement of the public and other stakeholders in RWM (*Principle* 5). Some instruments may

Table 5.2 Summary table

Emergent theme	Policy design		Implementation process	
	Principle	*National practice*	*Principle*	*National practice*
Theme 1: Public information	**Principle 5** Foreseeing instruments for public involvement	MSs have legal frameworks in place to ensure public involvement and rely on several instruments for information, consultation and active participation in RWM.		
Theme 2: Public participation			**Principle 8** Adopting a flexible process	Collaborative arrangements take different organisational structures, including consent-based processes that empower local communities at any critical step of the decision-making process.
Theme 3: Resources	**Principle 6** Providing adequate resources	Several opportunities are created for the exchange of knowledge. The availability of financial resources is not sufficient in all MSs. The concession of decision-making authority is weak.	**Principle 7** Promoting partnering and voluntarism	While the majority of MSs reported on the use of instruments for information and consultation, only almost half of MSs referred to instruments for active participation.
Theme 4: Participants	**Principle 4** Clarifying roles among organisations	Almost all MSs have clearly indicated the roles and responsibilities of the most relevant actors in the management of SF and RW and public involvement.		
Theme 5: Dialogue and trust			**Principle 9** Building trust	(Missing information)

Source: Personal elaboration. The table puts the content of NPs in relation with Table 4.3.

pose challenges of fair representation for their very nature. Anyway, all instruments have strengths and pitfalls, so that an optimal option does not exist. One single instrument is often not enough on its own and they all need to be contextualised before being applied.

Second, collaborative arrangements for more active forms of involvement can take different organisational structures. They include: working groups and committees aimed at developing proposals and negotiate benefits for the local community; advisory bodies and commissions with a more institutionalised basis; and consent-based processes that enable local communities to volunteer in and withdraw from a siting process at any critical step of the decision-making process, if they wish (*Principle 8*). However, voluntarism is still applied very rarely across the EU (see Figure 5.1).

Third, considerations can be drawn about resources (*Principle 6*), namely knowledge, money and authority. Knowledge seems to be channelled both from state authorities to the public (through information activities) and from the public to state actors (through consultation instruments). Several opportunities are created for the exchange of relevant information, both formally and informally. The availability of financial resources is, instead, not enough in all MSs and the funding of active participation is still quite poor. Financing the mobilisation of societal interests, even when processes of involvement are requested by law (e.g., for SEA and EIA), is rare. The concession of decision-making authority to citizens by the competent governmental agencies is also still quite exceptional. Authority can be shared, for instance, as a preferential status recognised to specific interests, like in the case of the partnership approach. These partnership arrangements also channel important funding to local communities for their active engagement in decision-making.

Fourth, almost all MSs have clearly indicated the roles and responsibilities of the most relevant actors in the management of SF and RW and public involvement (*Principle 4*). Particularly, the national regulatory authority and any legal person carrying out RWM activities (i.e. implementing agency, licence holder, etc.) have an obligation to provide information to the public (and the affected communities) with regard to nuclear safety and radiation protection. Activities of consultation (e.g., public meetings and workshops) are usually steered by the regulatory or implementing agencies to reach out to all citizens or specific communities. Furthermore, partnership arrangements have led to the creation of new legal entities that are formally recognised in national acts and the regulatory process. In particular, local partnerships recognise a formal role to local communities.

Fifth, NPs contain a good amount of evidence about how MSs allow and provide information and ensure opportunities for public consultation, particularly in the framework of SEA and EIA procedures (Figure 5.1). While the majority of MSs reported on the use of instruments for information and consultation, only almost half of MSs referred to instruments for active participation (*Principle 7*). It often remains unclear how MSs engage their publics in decision-making for the management of SF and RW. Explanations and examples of active participation are somehow vague, though not for all MSs. As a general remark, collaborative arrangements seem to have room for improvement in many countries of the EU.

Notes

1 By summer 2015, MSs were also expected to submit to the EC national reports on the overall implementation of the Waste Directive (see chapter 1). The available national reports have been used as background information in the writing of the chapter. Both National Programmes and implementation reports can be found here: http://www.nuclear-transparency-watch.eu/a-la-une/access-to-national-programmes-on-radioactive-waste-management.html (last access: 25.01.2017).
2 Public information can also be foreseen in national constitutions. Few MSs have reported that public access to official records is a constitutional principle that applies also to the domain of nuclear energy (including RWM).
3 The project "Implementing Public Participation Approaches in Radioactive Waste Disposal" (IPPA) was funded by the Seventh Euratom Framework Programmes (FP7) (see chapter 4) and has produced a list of tools for public involvement in RWM (see http://toolbox.ippaproject.eu/index; last access: 14.07.2015).
4 The International Association for Public Participation (IAP2) is the principal professional association in the field of public participation (Thomas 2012). Its toolbox arranges instruments of public involvement into three categories: sharing information; compiling and providing feedback; and bringing people together (see http://www.iap2.org; last access: 14.07.2015).
5 In the nuclear field, the national legislation establishes a licensing system: specific activities can be conducted only in compliance with the terms and conditions specified in the licence issued by a public authority. Compliance is verified through reporting obligations imposed on the licensee and inspections by the licensing authority. Cases of non-compliance with the terms and conditions of the licence result in the suspension or revocation of the licence, and other penalties (NEA 2012d).

References

Adams, B. (2004) "Public Meetings and the Democratic Process", in *Public Administration Review*, Vol. 64, No. 1, pp. 43–54.

Balla, S. J. (2005) "Between Commenting and Negotiation: The Contours of Public Participation in Agency Rulemaking", in *I/S: A Journal of Law and Policy*, Vol. 1, pp. 59–94.

Bardach, E. (2012) *A Practical Guide for Policy Analysis. The Eightfold Path to More Effective Problem Solving*, SAGE, London.

Beierle, T. C., and Cayford, J. (2002) *Democracy in Practice. Public Participation in Environmental Decisions*, Resources for the Future, Washington DC.

Blomgren Bingham, L., Nabatchi. T. and O'Leary, R. (2005) "The New Governance: Practices and Processes for Stakeholder and Citizen Participation in the Work of Government", in *Public Administration Review*, Vol. 65, No. 5, pp. 547–558.

Bobbio, L. (2004) *A piu' voci – Amministrazioni pubbliche, imprese, associazioni e cittadini nei processi decisionali inclusivi*, Edizioni Scientifiche Italiane, Rome.

Checkoway, B. (1981) "The Politics of Public Hearings", in *The Journal of Applied Behavioural Science*, Vol. 17, No. 4, pp. 566–582.

Council Directive 2011/70/EURATOM of 19 July 2011 establishing a community framework for the responsible and safe management of spent fuel and radioactive waste.

Creighton, J. L. (2005) *The Public Participation Handbook. Making Better Decisions Through Citizen Involvement*, Jossey-Bass, San Francisco.

Depoe, S. P., Delicath, J. W. and Aepli Elsenbeer, M.-F. (2004) (Eds) *Communication and Public Participation in Environmental Decision Making*, State University of New York Press, New York.

Dietz, T. and Stern, P. C. (2008) *Public Participation in Environmental Assessment and Decision Making*, The National Academy Press, Washington DC.
Howlett, M. (2011) *Designing Public Policies. Principles and Instruments*, Routledge, Abingdon.
Howlett, M., Ramesh, M. and Perl, A. (2009). *Studying Public Policy – Policy Cycles and Policy Subsystems*, Oxford University Press, Oxford.
Kasymova, J. T. and Lauer Schachter, H. (2014) "Bringing Participatory Tools to a Different Level", in *Public Performance & Management Review*, Vol. 37, No. 3, pp. 441–464.
Landström, C. and Bergmans, A. (2015) "Long-term Repository Governance: A Socio-technical Challenge", in *Journal of Risk Analysis*, Vol. 18, No. 3, pp. 378–391.
Lee, J. (2014) "Public Meetings for Efficient Administrative Performance in the United States", in *Public Performance & Management Review*, Vol. 37, No. 3, pp. 388–411.
Lowndes, V. and Sullivan, H. (2004) "Like a Horse and Carriage or a Fish on a Bicycle: How Well do Local Partnerships and Public Participation go Together?" in *Local Government Studies*, Vol. 30, No. 1, pp. 51–73.
Lynn, F. M. and Busenberg, G. J. (1995) "Citizen Advisory Committees and Environmental Policy: What We Know, What's Left to Discover", in *Risk Analysis*, Vol. 15, No. 2, pp. 147–162.
Michels, A. and De Graaf, L. (2010) "Examining Citizen Participation: Local Participatory Policy Making and Democracy", in *Local Government Studies*, Vol. 36, No. 4, pp. 477–491.
Napolitano, G. (2007) (Ed.) *Diritto amministrativo comparato*, Giuffré, Milan.
NEA (2009) *About the Forum on Stakeholder Confidence*, OECD, Paris.
NEA (2012d) *Nuclear Energy Today*, OECD, Paris.
OECD (2003b) *Engaging Citizens Online for Better Policy-making*, OECD, Paris.
OECD (2015) *Stakeholder Engagement for Inclusive Water Governance*, OECD, Paris.
Rowe, G. and Frewer, L. J. (2000), "Public Participation Methods: A Framework for Evaluation", in *Science, Technology, & Human Values*, Vol. 25, No. 1, pp. 3–29.
Smutko, L. S. and Addor, M. L. (2012) *Public Participation Guidelines for Park Planning*, Department of Parks and Recreation, City Of Raleigh, NC.
Thomas, J. C. (1995) *Public Participation in Public Decisions: New Skills and Strategies for Public Managers*, Jossey-Bass, San Francisco.
Thomas, J. C. (2012) *Citizen, Customer, Partner: Engaging the Public in Public Management*, Routledge, Abingdon and New York.
Thurston, W. E., MacKean, G., Vollman, A., Casebeer, A., Webre, M., Maloff, B. and Bader, J. (2005) "Public Participation in Regional Health Policy: A Theoretical Framework", in *Health Policy*, Vol. 79, pp. 237–252.
UNECE (1998) *Convention on Access to Information, Public Participation in Decision-Making and Access to Justice in Environmental Matters*, Aarhus
Weingart, J. (2007) *Waste Is A Terrible Thing To Mind*, Rivergate Books, New Brunswick (NJ).
West, W. (2005) "Administrative Rulemaking: An Old and Emerging Literature", in *Public Administration Review*, Vol. 65, No. 6, pp. 655–668.
Wilson, D. (1999) "Exploring the Limits of Public Participation in Local Government", in *Parliamentary Affairs*, Vol. 52, No. 2, pp. 246–259.

6 The involvement of local stakeholders

The analysis of National Programmes (NPs) across the European Union (EU) has shown that Member States (MSs) have legal frameworks that ensure the right of public information and participation in radioactive waste management (RWM). Furthermore, MSs rely on several instruments of public involvement to inform, consult and engage the general public, local communities and all relevant stakeholders. Chapter 5 has provided an overview of these instruments based on the information reported by MSs in their NPs. It has also assessed to what extent national practices align with general principles for public involvement in the policy design and during the implementation process, with a focus on emergent themes highlighted by stakeholders (chapter 3).

Public decisions related to RWM have a clear multilayer-governance nature. The local dimension is particularly important for the role it has during policy implementation. While the previous chapter presented the formal position of MSs on the basis of official national documents (i.e. the NPs), this chapter tries to go beyond what has been reported by MSs and focuses on the experience and perception that local communities have about the state of public involvement at the local level.

The chapter explores to what extent local communities have found their way into national decision-making on RWM, whether the instruments reported by MSs in their NPs have created actual opportunities of involvement and how interactions among actors at different levels of governance take place. Procedural implementation instruments are, indeed, aimed at opening policy networks to invite more and new participants into policy-making. The chapter discusses the relevance of the local dimension in the implementation process and add insights on public involvement in RWM from the perspective of local communities.

The salience of the local dimension in the implementation process

We have defined the implementation process as the complex set of interactions that take place between actors located within and outside the state functions at national and subnational level (chapter 2).

In the specific domain of RWM, several actors interact during the implementation process: policy-makers (i.e. national legislators, government and ministries); the national administration with its regulatory bodies[1] and implementing agencies; elected representatives from the local level, the local government and local administrative authorities; regional bodies; the nuclear industry, composed of industrial organisations – like the operators of nuclear power plants (NPP) – and sectoral/professional associations; civil society associations and NGOs active at the national or local level; the general public and citizens of the local community; advisory and consultative bodies, scientific research institutes and technical experts; media and other organisations (e.g., consultancies) (Di Nucci et al. 2015; Yanev 2009).

State actors are those organisations and bodies that have formal policy-making responsibilities in RWM recognised by the law. These include not only policy-makers and national government agencies (e.g., regulatory body and implementing agency) but also local elected representatives and local government entities. Non-state actors are usually understood as societal actors; NGOs and the citizens of the local communities belong to this category (chapter 2). Figure 6.1 shows a simplification of this large number of stakeholders interacting during policy implementation and arranges them as state and non-state actors at the national and local level.[2]

In the framework of a general shift towards governance and the development and execution of public policies by networks of interdependent actors (Blomgren Bingham *et al.* 2005; Klijn & Koppenjan 2012; Winter 2012b), local communities should be put at the heart of these policy networks in the execution of public policies (Bobbio 2004; Stoker 1998; Thomas 2012). In RWM, it results from the views of stakeholders (chapter 3) and the insights of social research conducted in the EU (chapter 4) that the local dimension plays an important role in the implementation of national RWM policies. Two main reasons explain this role.

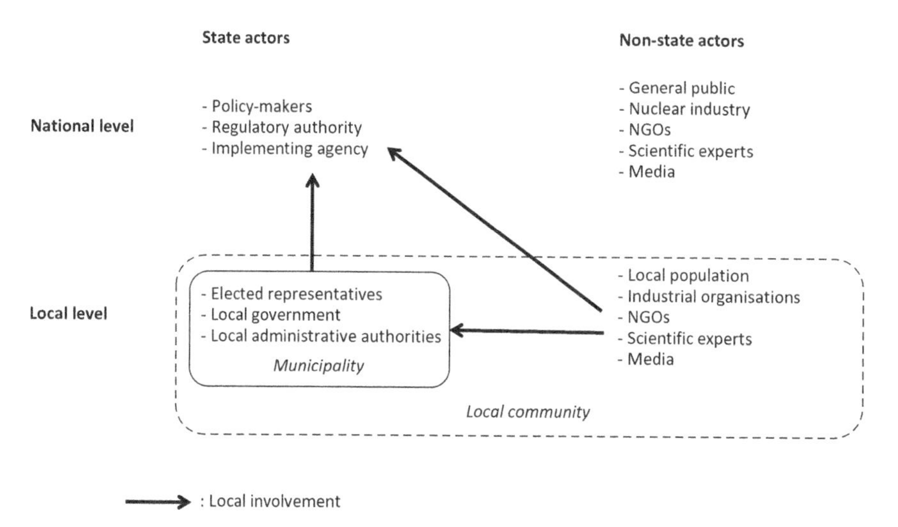

Figure 6.1 Actors involved in the implementation process

First, RWM facilities are LULUs with a hazardous nature. Like all LULUs, these facilities generate potential benefits for the entire country (i.e. the storage or disposal of hazardous waste) but concentrate their costs (i.e. environmental impact and risk) on the hosting local communities (Aldrich 2005; Hayden Lesbirel 2005; Weingart 2007). Such unbalance between benefits and costs is the major cause of local opposition to these contested projects; their development has been delayed or even halted by local conflicts on many occasions (Aldrich 2005; Armour 1991; Bollens 1993; Popper 1981).

Second, as long as political debates and policy discussions take place at the national level about possible courses of action, policy-making is less controversial. It is during policy implementation that RWM becomes more visible for the local communities that are identified as potential hosts (Weingart 2007). As clearly explained by Landström and Bergmans for deep geological disposal (DGD),

> While siting is mainly a problem addressed by national governments and implementers who must devise strategies to identify repository sites that are both geologically and politically feasible, hosting involves other actors. In hosting a [DGD], a local community becomes the site for a full-scale socio-technical experiment, never previously attempted and intended to be the only one of its kind in a country.
>
> (Landström & Bergmans 2015: 379)

Latent opposition manifests itself and rapidly increases when specific geographical areas are identified, that is during the execution of national policies through national programmes and project proposals (Weingart 2007). The involvement of local communities during policy implementation is expected to solve or deflate conflicts, ease implementation and facilitate social acceptance (Breukers & Wolsink 2007; Hilson 2002; Jobert *et al.* 2007; Walker *et al.* 2011; Wolsink 2000). Local participation can happen through constructive intergovernmental relations and the creation of opportunities that ensure coordination across layers of government (May 2012; O'Toole 2012). The presence (or absence) of opportunities for the participation of local communities seems to explain their attitude towards infrastructures and facilities that usually raise controversy better than the assumption of a selfish response ("Not in my backyard!") too often used by some academic literature.

Not In My Back Yard? Moving beyond the NIMBY syndrome

Local opposition to unwanted uses of the land has been traditionally explained by relying on the not-in-my-back-yard (NIMBY) syndrome. Introduced by O'Hare (1977), the NIMBY syndrome consists of the combined preference for a public good and the refusal to contribute to it. In other words, people are in favour of a given infrastructure but opposed to hosting it in their own area on the basis of calculated personal costs and benefits. Ultimately, the NIMBY syndrome resolves into a selfish behaviour against a common good that generates and explains local conflicts (Wolsink 2000). In case of hazardous facilities like the ones for managing radioactive waste (RW), an element of fear due to risk perception adds up to the self-interest (Armour 1991).

Several studies (e.g., Gervers 1987; Jobert *et al.* 2007; Kuhn & Ballard 1998; Walker *et al.* 2011; Wolsink 2000) have questioned, though, the explanatory value of the NIMBY syndrome that reduces local opposition to an egoistic behaviour. A more complex set of motivations lies, instead, behind local opposition to given infrastructures; multiple factors play a role: former use of the site, status and characteristics of the local economy, fairness of site selection, validity of the technical programme, economic incentives and benefits put in place, etc. In particular, these studies stress that LULUs affect inter-organisational networks of actors with a complex system of beliefs, values, ideals, norms, passions and emotions (Boholm & Löfstedt 2004). Therefore, it becomes important how decision-making processes are arranged, how decisions are taken among stakeholders and how all perspectives are taken into account.

As many other wicked problems, the management of highly contested infrastructures – including the ones for RWM – is populated by strong disagreement (in knowledge) and disputes (on values) (NEA 2012a). Through analytical simplification, we could say that two major fronts are often present around these projects. On the one hand, the organisation proposing a project (normally a private firm or government agency) has confidence in technological solutions and advancements, and is supportive of the project. On the other hand, the public, local citizens' groups and environmental organisations tend to oppose the project because of concerns of environmental justice, social inequity, fear and distrust of the credibility of proponents and governmental agencies (Aldrich 2005; Hayden Lesbirel 2005; Kuhn & Ballard 1998).

Reality is even more complex. Intricate diverging perspectives are brought into the debate, decision-making and development of locally unwanted infrastructures by the broad spectrum of actors involved. The same alliances among actors tend to change over time as a project develops (Boholm & Löfstedt 2004; Kuhn & Ballard 1998; Walker *et al.* 2011).

Therefore, interactions within these policy networks are particularly important. Lack of information provision to local residents, bad communication with the public, weak consultation and scarce active participation in the decisions and planning of a project stand out as important factors explaining why certain infrastructures are contested at the local level. Rather than reducing all explanations to the NIMBY syndrome, more attention is needed to these factors in order to resolve local opposition.

Armour (1991) suggests some options. First, the public's concerns must be taken into account. Second, the public should be included early in the process. Third, information should be provided in a clear and sufficient way. Fourth, voluntary siting should be used so that communities are identified if they are willing and able to accept a proposed facility. Fifth, incentives should be provided to the local community in order to redress the inequity in costs distribution, but these incentives should not constitute a form of bribing communities that are usually economically or socially disadvantaged.

Similar considerations apply to RWM as pointed out by stakeholders from the field (chapter 3) and researchers (chapter 4). On some of these points, we were able to collect the point of view of local communities directly from their mayors.

The perspective of local communities

The local community includes both non-state actors (such as individual citizens, industry, NGOs, etc.) and state actors of the municipality (i.e. elected representatives, local government and local authorities) (Figure 6.1). It follows that public involvement of local stakeholders has two important dimensions: it can mean citizens' participation in both local governance and intergovernmental relations. First, the local population needs to find a way to express its concerns and preferences towards the local elected representatives, government and administrative authorities. Second, local communities must be empowered to take part in national debates and decisions through these state actors. In other words, public involvement of citizens in local government is important as well as public involvement of the local government in national policy-making.

In the EU, municipalities (and regional bodies) ensure the representation of subnational interests vis-à-vis national institutions. Citizens and other stakeholders from the local community find their ways into national policy-making through their elected representatives and legitimate government agencies that are institutionally empowered to make public choices (McDaniels *et al.* 1999). However, this role and the legitimacy of local elected representatives and local authorities cannot always be taken as self-evident (Lowndes & Sullivan 2004).

Therefore, public involvement at the local level also needs to rely on the direct engagement of the local population in national decision-making through information, consultation and active collaborative arrangements. Expressions of representative democracy and forms of participative democracy can complement each other and, together, strengthen the democratic nature of a political system. Local participation should also happen beyond elected local governments, through non-electoral participatory initiatives. This chapter focuses on this aspect and presents insights from the local level about public involvement in RWM.

Such insights were collected through a workshop with local communities that host RWM facilities.[3] The workshop ran like a focus group for the purpose of data collection on experiences, achievements, challenges and drawbacks of public involvement in RWM at the local level. Eight local communities attended the workshop; they were represented by their mayors. In two cases, municipality representatives substituted the mayors and were invited in their capacity as institutional representatives of their local community. The event followed the Chatham House Rule;[4] hence, the information provided was recorded in written form and exchanged with the participants after the event but is used in this chapter without attribution to participants by means of their identity or affiliation.

Focus groups are a research technique that collects data through group interaction: several participants are interviewed simultaneously on a topic (i.e. the "focus") decided by the researcher (Morgan 1997). Group interviewing capitalises on the interactions and dynamics that take place within a group, thus proving rich experiential data and insights (Frey & Fontana 1991). The dynamics of the group discussion and interactions (along a list of questions) stimulate the contribution of each individual participant and, thus, allow us to examine a specific topic (or research question) from the point of view of the participants (Asbury 1995; Krueger 1994). The focus group develops as organised discussion that unveils ideas, opinions and perceptions of a homogenous group of participants (often the affected population) about a sensitive topic or policy problem (Kahan 2001; Frey & Fontana 1991).

This technique is useful to interpret and clarify findings from other sources, and amplify and validate previously gathered data (Frey & Fontana 1991). Focus groups are also useful to understand a phenomenon or an issue from the perspective of a specific population, particularly when this perceptive has not been sufficiently included by previous data sources (Asbury 1995). For this reason, focus groups are often used as a supplementary source of data to complement, for instance, the results of a survey (Morgan 1997). This is the use made in this book. The focus group with mayors from local communities with RWM facilities was important to collect further insights from those local stakeholders that were less responsive in a previous survey (see chapter 3, Figure 3.1).

The focus group was arranged around topics that allowed putting the answers in relation to the major themes emerging from the survey presented in chapter 3: public information, public participation, resources, participants, dialogue and trust. The theme of resources was actually addressed by the focus group while discussing public information and participation. Where possible, these results were also put in perspective with the official information provided by MSs in their NPs (chapter 5). The small number of people required by focus group dynamics was not meant to be representative of all local communities affected by RWM facilities. Yet, the workshop provided relevant experiential evidence on which our study can draw. The final objective was, indeed, to examine more closely what exactly is taking place during the implementation process in the centre–local interactions.

Public information and independent expertise

The history of nuclear energy is characterised by a loss of trust across time (chapter 1). Governmental and industrial organisations from the nuclear sector have responsibilities in this erosion of trust, particularly because of poor communication with the public in the past decades. Although the provision of information to the public represents the lowest level of citizens' involvement in policy-making (chapter 2), it has proven to be crucial for public perception. Stakeholders from the field of RWM agree that public information is pivotal given the need of correcting common misperceptions and misunderstandings about nuclear energy, its waste and the risk it brings along (chapter 3).

If adequate information on RWM is important for the general public, it is even more important for the local communities that host or will potentially host a RWM facility. The mayors participating in the focus group have added interesting insights on the issue of public information and discussed it in relation to the availability of independent expertise at the local level.

Policy-makers often rely on experts (as individuals or panels) to interpret complex scientific knowledge on a particular technical problem. According to Page (2010: 258), '[e]xpertise is a high level of familiarity with a body of knowledge and/or experience that is neither widely shared nor simply acquired'. In this broad working definition, expertise is knowledge and, therefore, it constitutes a key state resource for public policy-making together with information, ideas, etc. (see chapter 2).

In general, a certain amount of expertise in RWM is present at the local level. Inside the social fabric, members of the local community may have the educational or professional background needed to understand nuclear matters and eventually explain them to other members of the community. In the local administration, civil servants have gained enough preparation on these topics either from their education and training, or from their work even when nuclear matters do not necessarily correspond to their education and training.

Nevertheless, some local communities may lack the adequate competences and technical knowledge needed to fully understand the multiple aspects involved in RWM. We know from the results of the Euratom research (chapter 4) that the capacity of local communities (understood as knowledge and competences about nuclear matters) needs to be strengthened if these actors are expected to be involved in policy-making through more participatory processes and make a factual contribution to the decision-making on RWM.

This is particularly true when, by expertise, we mean *scientific* expertise understood as 'knowledge of a set of abstract concepts, theories governing relationships between these concepts and a range of techniques to apply insights of this body of knowledge to policy problems' (Page 2010: 259). Scientific and technical experts are essential in the provision of correct, sound and objective information on the multiple aspects of nuclear energy, including RWM, to local communities.

If adequate financial resources are made available, then local governments may decide to appoint independent (scientific) experts to enhance the community's capacity for its involvement in national decisions on nuclear matters. These independent experts can provide insights to local authorities and strengthen their position in relation to the central government and governmental (regulatory and implementing) agencies. By strengthening the local capacity to grasp and master technical matters such as RWM, independent experts can also contribute to build greater confidence in local actors in the decision-making process. We saw in chapter 3 that the provision of information to the targeted community by independent experts may also be a way to improve dialogue. Therefore, in some countries, panels or committees of experts are set up at the local level to provide scientific advice on nuclear and RWM matters.

However, it is not always easy to identify *independent* experts that could sit in these committees and advise local communities. Adams and Hairston (1995) warn that expertise often comes with a bias strictly linked to its source: the reliability of experts depend on their employer, financial support, type of professional training, etc. The majority of mayors involved in the focus group have acknowledged that the concept of independence is ambiguous and can be misleading; everyone is, indeed, dependent on the sources from where we gain our knowledge. This applies to any domain, not only the nuclear field. As put by Wilsdon and Willis (2004: 40) '[s]upposedly "objective" reports by "experts" are actually carefully and subjectively framed according to the outlook of the experts themselves, and the questions they choose to answer'.

In the light of this consideration, some participants have pointed out that independence is, indeed, relative; what really matters is using a plurality of sources of information and comparing them. Triangulation of data – rather than absolute independence of experts – seems to be, thus, a more feasible way to obtain more objective information on nuclear matters, including RWM.

Municipalities tend to collect data and opinions from different parties, mainly scholars from academic institutions and experts from research centres of their own country. However, this implies that municipalities from small MSs have at their disposal a small pool of experts from which they can search for independent advice. Indeed, many of the available experts have often already worked for national governmental agencies or the same national nuclear industry. In response to this constraint of small MSs, participants argued that the establishment of funds made available by the central government for local communities would allow the latter ones to hire international experts from abroad and build their own competence.

Two additional ways could be pursued by local communities in order to strengthen their own capacity in RWM. First, they can learn from one another *across* MSs through linkages and exchanges of experience("inter-state connections").[5] Second, they could network *within* a single country to share similar problems and discuss possible solutions ("intra-state connections"). This last type of linkage would eventually form a sufficient critical mass of engagement at the local level that could, ultimately, enhance local influence on national policy-making.

Public participation and collaborative arrangements

MSs have legal frameworks in place that ensure public involvement. In line with the general principles extracted from the Euratom social research, they rely on several instruments to allow the general public, local communities and other stakeholders to participate in RWM. The focus group shed more light on the actual use of procedural instruments for the involvement of local communities in the EU in relation to RWM decisions and activities. Participants confirmed that a wide range of instruments are used for the involvement of local stakeholders in RWM and, more broadly, nuclear issues across the EU. The instruments mentioned during the focus group fall in the inventory presented in chapter 5. Mayors have mentioned the use by governmental (regulatory and implementing) agencies of instruments aimed at the information (e.g., public events and information sessions), consultation (e.g., public meetings) and active participation of local communities.

We noticed that the NPs describe in more detail the use of instruments for information and consultation, while those enabling more active forms of public participation are somewhat less present across the EU (Figure 5.1). Instruments of active participation aim at developing closer collaborations between state and non-state actors by giving citizens more chances to influence public decisions (chapter 2). Collaborative arrangements for more active forms of involvement can take different organisational structures. The use of working groups, advisory bodies, national commissions and voluntary arrangements is crucial for the localities directly targeted by RWM project developments given that they (will) host a facility or are neighbouring a hosting community. These instruments embody the principles of partnering and voluntarism (chapter 4).

From the experiences reported by mayors, working groups are the most recurrent instrument for the active participation of local communities. Many variants of working groups exist across the EU; these liaison bodies can also take the form of local committees or associations of local entities (i.e. towns and municipalities) (see chapter 5). However, comparable features can be traced in the information shared by mayors from different countries with regard to their function, composition, institutionalisation and duration.

First, working groups – including local committees and associations – are established for the purpose of linking the national government (or its implementing agency) and the local communities that host or are candidate to host a RWM facility. The mayors present in the focus group confirmed that these bodies serve as platforms for communication, interaction and participation of stakeholders concerned by a facility. These bodies can have a specific focus on information (i.e. "local information committees") or safety ("local safety committees"). Not much was said, instead, about their active contribution to the preparation of strategic documents (e.g., NPs) or development of specific projects such as DGD.

Second, working groups involve a broad range of stakeholders – as also specified in the NPs. They can include national authorities, regulatory bodies, implementing agencies, operators, members of subnational parliaments, mayors, other representatives of the civil society and NGOs. The balanced representation of different interests determines to a large extent the legitimacy of any participatory effort (chapter 3). The presence and expression of multiple views is pivotal also for the credibility of working groups; hence, they tend to bring together many political, social and economic actors from the local level. However, the representation basis can be wider or narrower according to different national contexts. The representation basis also varies according to the geographical scope: it can be limited to the community hosting a RWM facility (in some MSs) or include also the neighbouring municipalities (in some other MSs).

Third, the level of institutionalisation of working groups varies considerably across countries. At the extreme of lowest institutionalisation, working groups are formed on a voluntary basis, do not meet often and have no public funding. In some MSs, working groups benefit, instead, from a higher level of institutionalisation in terms of appointment, operation and funding. In this case, their members are appointed by the central government (on the basis of proposals from the pertinent local community) and their meetings take place on a more regular basis than is the case for less institutionalised groups. With regard to funding, some institutionalised local committees depend entirely on the willingness and capacity of the local authorities, while others are funded by the central authorities. In particular, local safety committees are mostly financed directly by their national governments with the purpose of informing the general public on issues of safety and radiation protection. The existence of funds coming from the central government is crucial for the effectiveness of local committees.

Fourth, working groups can be established with a long-term perspective. This means that the working group lasts for a period of time that goes beyond the siting effort and, thus, continues during the development and operation of a RWM facility. However, even when such working groups have been intended for a long time, it is not certain that they will work in practice as permanent bodies that are able to maintain the public commitment over time. As discussed in chapter 3, mobilisation of the public over a long time is not an easy task. Citizens' attention and interest is very likely to decrease over extended time spans. We have indicated the stakeholders' fatigue as a major obstacle to protracted participatory decision-making processes. Once these processes become too long, it is increasingly difficult to mobilise citizens and keep them engaged. This aspect was also stressed by the mayors taking part in the focus group.

More stringent forms of local active participation rely on advisory and voluntary mechanisms which include the recognition of a veto power to the local communities involved in RWM, either formally (i.e. by law) or informally (through "gentlemen agreements"). However, the mayors in the focus group presented little evidence about these instruments of active participation. This confirms what we have argued in chapter 5: forms of active participation can certainly be strengthened and improved across the whole EU.

Therefore, more resources are needed by local communities. This is not only the case for resources such as knowledge (see previous section) and money, but also authority. The sharing of authority in favour of the local level through collaborative arrangements is still somewhat weak.

Identifying local participants: actors and geographical boundaries

Any participatory effort calls for careful reflection upon the actors who should participate in policy-making (chapter 2). This must be done with the purpose of ensuring a broad and balanced engagement of all stakeholders. The cautious definition of who constitutes a stakeholder and is, thus, entitled to participate in the decision-making about RWM has been indicated as a key issue across the

EU. The respondents to the survey presented in chapter 3 stressed the importance of involving a broad range of stakeholders, including local communities affected by a RWM decision or hosting a RWM facility and experts. This ensures fair representation and competent participation.

We have already discussed the role of expertise for RWM decision-making. With regard to the involvement of local communities, the focus group with mayors has provided further insights on the definition of who constitutes (or *should* constitute) legitimate and representative participants from the local level.

As explained in chapter 4, criteria for selecting the legitimate participants in a decision-making process may already be established by national laws or still await better and more transparent clarification in the case of practices that have developed more informally. As any other stakeholder, local communities, too, may be the object of formal or informal processes of public involvement in RWM. For instance, the public consultation of local communities is formalised and requested by law under EIA procedures. According to the mayors involved in the focus group, EIA consultations indeed constitute important opportunities for the public involvement of local communities. They are usually accompanied by precise rules that specify which actors, organisations and institutions should be consulted.

When actors are not formally identified, ensuring a genuine participation of all stakeholders from the local level presents several challenges. RWM and, more broadly, nuclear facilities are located in specific sites with geographical boundaries that delimit a community of local actors. Therefore, in the absence of formal rules that identify who is entitled to participate, two steps are crucial in the definition of local participants: identifying the actors and delimiting the community geographically.

First, in the specific geographical area affected by RWM, it is important that no actor is neglected in the identification of legitimate participants. For instance, a balanced representation of the local fabric is important to ensure the legitimacy of any partnership arrangement. This should include local elected representatives, local economic actors, trade unions, and community representatives from the public at large (chapter 4). However, for instruments of public involvement that have developed informally – i.e. out of the national legislative framework – the identification of relevant and legitimate stakeholders at the local level (and their representatives) is not always straightforward (Lee *et al.* 2013). In the focus group with mayors, diverging opinions emerged with regard to the precise identity of local stakeholders entitled to take part to RWM decisions. Views on who should participate at the local level tend to differ when there are no formal definitions of the concerned public in the national legislative and regulatory frameworks.

Second, the geographical area that needs to be involved in the decisions and development of a RWM facility has to be correctly identified. Identifying which areas should be involved in policy-making is a key responsibility, which gives great power to the ones responsible for this selection. For instance, the support or opposition to the siting of a given RWM project can be diluted (or strengthened) by changing the boundaries of a local community to actors with a different position in the debate. As explained by the NEA (2012b: 6), 'drawing boundaries is necessarily an artefact in the siting process, and contending participants in that process will have incentives to manipulate those boundaries in ways to advantage their own objectives'.

Indeed, the community hosting a RWM facility does not host it in isolation; the community is in relation with other neighbouring local communities. Furthermore, localities function in complex multi-layer governmental arrangements; hence, they are embedded in broader communities at the subnational level (NEA 2012b). Mayors taking part in the focus group indicated regional authorities as important actors that should be involved, particularly when a RWM project (such as DGD) will impact on the entire region for a very long time. The consequence is that the delimitation of community and, consequently, the definition of the participants who need to be involved become more complex as soon as other aspects are considered. As a mere example, once the transport of RW to the site is considered, then the set of legitimate participants broadens.[6]

Nevertheless, the opinions expressed in the focus group suggest that involvement decreases with the distance from the RWM facility. For example, the level of information is higher in communities situated closer to the facilities. An explanation can simply be that most citizens living closer to a RWM facility are likely to work in the facility. Another reason is the presence of information channels in the hosting communities such as local information committees (see above).

Dialogue and intergovernmental communication

Dialogue can clarify the reasons and motivations behind the diverging points of different stakeholders and often eases the development of constructive relationships among them (chapter 3). In particular, decisions around nuclear energy are complex and multifaceted, and often require a balance between policy priorities that are set at the national level and the needs of local stakeholders (see chapter 1). The relevance of both levels of government was confirmed by mayors intervening in the focus group. The complexity of policy-making around the wicked problem of RWM calls for an effective communication between central and local government.

The mayors expressed their opinion with regard to the quality and quantity of centre–local communication and the interactions between the local community and national decision-makers. An interesting distinction emerged from the focus group about the way intergovernmental communication is conducted in some EU countries. Some mayors distinguished between practices of "ordinary communication" and practices of "strategic communication". Ordinary communication is about everyday problems in the life cycle of a RWM facility and its interaction with its hosting community. Strategic communication has to do, instead, with strategic decisions taken by policy-makers at the national level.

In the case of ordinary communication between a facility and the community living nearby, several bodies have been established in MSs: working groups, associations of towns/municipalities and local committees (see above). Here, information is provided regularly through personal contacts between representatives of the local community and the WMO. In addition, citizens of the local community are informed through a regular newsletter for all inhabitants, websites, articles in the municipal monthly magazine, information campaigns, local events, information days, opinion polls, public debates, etc.

When it comes to key national decisions, communication between the centre (often through the national regulatory and implementing agencies) and municipalities reveals a more variegated landscape. Three scenarios emerge from the focus group. In some MSs, the local community is acknowledged an institutional role as interlocutor in this type of (strategic) communication and participatory arrangements are of a permanent nature. Communication is conducted, here, through channels that are more formal than the ones put in place for ordinary communication. In other MSs, the direct involvement of local communities in decision-making is acknowledged and possible in principle, but left to the initiative of the local community rather than formally required. Finally, in some other MSs, no special instruments are put in place for the interaction between national and local layers of government about key decisions. In other words, there are no institutionalised channels of active participation for local communities in national policy-making. In some cases, the lack of a formalised and stable centre–local relationship is due to the lack of a culture of local involvement in national policy-making.

Finally, dialogue and communication need trust (chapter 3). All mayors have expressed full trust in the work of national regulatory bodies. These bodies are commonly recognised as the experts' organisations responsible for ensuring the safety of nuclear and RWM facilities. The mayors stressed not only the important role of their national regulatory authorities but also the work conducted by international organisations such as the IAEA (see chapter 1) as independent bodies reviewing the work of both implementing agencies and operators.

The Euratom research has highlighted the importance of trust and the need to invest in the development or enhancement of trust among all stakeholders involved in RWM. How trust can be built where it is still lacking or rebuilt where it has been eroded constitutes the topic of the next chapter. This chapter concludes with some considerations on how principles for public involvement are experienced by local communities with regard to the emergent themes. The concluding section puts the results of the focus group in perspective with the formal information provided by MSs in their NPs.

Concluding remarks

The siting, construction and operation of facilities for the storage and disposal of RW clearly have significant impacts on local communities – for their environment, public health and economies – and have often solicited their strong reaction. Local opposition has for a long time been explained through selfish behaviour (or NIMBY syndrome), which has hidden a more complex set of motivations. Among these motivations, the need of local communities to be engaged in public decision-making seems particularly important. According to Weingart (2007), citizens not only have the right to contribute to RWM decisions that will affect them; they have a democratic duty to intervene in the policy-making process that will make things happen.

The focus group was aimed at collecting data from the perspective of local communities with RWM facilities (represented by their mayors) about their involvement in decision-making. The group of mayors who took part in the focus group has added important aspects to the ones stressed by national authorities in their NPs with regard to the themes explored in these chapters, namely public information, public participation, resources, participants, dialogue and trust, as reported in Table 6.1. The limited number of local communities that could be involved in the focus group must lead us to treat the generaliseability of such considerations with caution.

First, MSs reported on national legal frameworks and a wide array of instruments that ensure public involvement (chapter 5). The local communities seem to confirm that they can benefit from several instruments for public involvement available in their countries. In particular, they emphasise the importance and use of EIAs (for consultation) and working groups (for active participation) in addition to policy instruments for information (*Principle* 5).

Second, the provision and allocation of resources is often inadequate (*Principle* 6). Compared to what is reported in NPs (chapter 5), the mayors of the focus group feel that more knowledge is needed at the local level, particularly independent expertise. Financial resources are confirmed as a necessity if local communities are expected to embark seriously on activities of public involvement for several purposes. All instruments of information require funds. Consultations in practice can only be possible if money is available for organising consultation opportunities and ensuring adequate attendance. Likewise, active participation is not possible without sufficient resourcing. Finally, active participation cannot take place without the actual concession of authority from national public authorities to local counterparts and citizenry. In the absence of a real influence of the local level into national decisions, even centre–local partnership arrangements result in a figurative gathering of actors and organisations. The same weaknesses emerge from the analysis of the NPs (chapter 5) where we concluded that the governmental agencies have so far shared low decision-making authority with citizens and other stakeholders.

Third, MSs indicate in their NPs that roles and responsibilities for RWM are clear, particularly when it comes to the obligation of information provision or public consultation by the national regulatory authority and implementing agency (chapter 5). The role of other actors such as local communities varies, instead, depending on the level of institutionalisation of the participatory instrument used. According to the information exchanged among mayors, the specific role of local communities is formally acknowledged in the policy design only in some MSs and for some instruments (e.g., EIA or partnership

Table 6.1 Summary table (central and local perspectives)

Emergent theme	Policy design			Implementation process		
	General principles	*National practice*	*Local perspective*	*General principles*	*National practice*	*Local perspective*
Theme 1: Public information	**Principle 5** Foreseeing instruments for public involvement	MSs have legal frameworks in place to ensure public involvement and rely on several instruments for information, consultation and active participation in RWM.	The local communities benefit from several instruments for public involvement; EIAs and working groups are particulalry important for their formal consultation and active participation.			
Theme 2: Public participation				**Principle 8** Adopting a flexible process	Collaborative arrangements take different organisational structures, including consent-based processes that empower local communities at any critical step of the decision-making process.	(Missing information)
Theme 3: Resources	**Principle 6** Providing adequate resources	Several opportunities are created for the exchange of knowledge. The availability of financial resources is not sufficient in all MSs. The concession of the decision-making authority is weak.	Local communities need: more knowledge (particulalry as independent expertise); more financial resources (for their activities of public information and participation); and more authority (in public decisions).	**Principle 7** Promoting partnering and voluntarism	While the majority of MSs reported on the use of instruments for information and consultation, only almost half of MSs referred to instruments for active participation.	Local communities presented little evidence about instruments of active participation.
Theme 4: Participants	**Principle 4** Clarifying roles among organisations	Almost all MSs have clearly indicated the roles and responsibilities of the most relevant actors in the management of SF and RW and public involvement.	In MSs where there is no formal process of involvement specified in the national laws, the role of local communities is not well defined and grey areas are left to administrators' discretion.			
Theme 5: Dialogue and trust				**Principle 9** Building trust	(Missing information)	Although local communities have expressed trust in national regulators, dialogue and communication among the two levels of government remains confined to marginal decisions.

arrangements). In many MSs, particularly when there is no formal process specified in the national laws, the role of local communities is not well defined and grey areas are left to administrators' discretion (*Principle 4*).

Fourth, although on the basis of the focus group we cannot affirm that the current involvement of local communities in national decision-making on RWM is weak across the entire EU, opportunities for improvement exist. This is not so evident when we look at the provision of information, but it stands out once we consider the opportunities made available for active participation (*Principle 7*). These are somehow weak in several national contexts (as also discussed in chapter 5). More intergovernmental collaborative mechanisms are, thus, needed. This could be done on an informal basis – with no changes in the established policy design – or formally through reform to the legislative framework. One way is to foresee and conduct more informal interactions between central and local authorities. Another way to enhance intergovernmental coordination, formally, could be through local partnerships ensuring that national strategies are in line with local objectives (Lowry & Eichenberg 1986).

Finally, in the absence of a fair recognition of authority to local communities, dialogue and communication between the two levels of government also risk remaining confined to marginal decisions. Mayors have stressed their trust in national regulators. However, the call for increasing dialogue and rebuilding trust stressed by the Euratom research (chapter 4) constitutes an important reminder in the context described by local communities (*Principle 9*). Trust is discussed in detail in the next chapter.

Notes

1 Also called National Safety Authorities (NSAs).

2 Multiple levels of governance exist between the national and local level. Depending on the national constitutional framework, intermediate levels are regions, provinces, departments, etc. Although these other subnational levels are mentioned in some parts of this chapter, the emphasis is on the local level in an effort of simplifying the institutional complexity of the variegated EU-28.

3 The workshop took place in 2015 and brought together representatives of the European Commission (from the Joint Research Centre and the Directorate-General for Energy) and mayors from the Group of European Municipalities with Nuclear Facilities (GMF). I am particularly thankful to Mariano Vila d'Abadal for his help in organising the workshop and to Meritxell Martell for her role as moderator of the focus group. The GMF was established in 2000 with the purpose of enhancing governance in the nuclear field across the EU. It is an association of municipalities that host, are candidates to host, or are located near nuclear and RWM facilities. The GMF groups more than 120 municipalities from 14 European countries (Belgium, Bulgaria, Czech Republic, Finland, France, Germany, Hungary, Lithuania, Netherlands, Romania, Slovakia, Slovenia, Spain and Sweden). (For more information: http://www.gmfeurope.org/home; last access: 13.06.2016). The chapter attempts to report about the major insights emerging from the workshop; any misunderstanding is complete responsibility of the author.

4 For information on the Chatham House Rule, see https://www.chathamhouse.org/chatham-house-rule (last access: 27.04.2018).

5 The GMF has this objective as part of its organisational mission (see above).
6 Another important consideration is that the people who are located in a given space change over time (NEA 2012b). A local community is not a static entity: mobility, mortality and new births affect its composition. People leave the community and new ones join it over the years. We have seen that RWM projects develop and operate over several decades (chapter 1). The impact of these facilities spans, thus, across generations. It ends up concerning individuals who were not present at the time of decisions to express their opinion during the siting process.

References

Adams, P. W. and Hairtson, A. B. (1995) *Using Scientific Input in Policy and Decision Making*, Paper published by Oregon State University Extension Service, Oregon State University.

Aldrich, D. P. (2005) "Controversial Project Siting. State Policy Instruments and Flexibility", in *Comparative Politics*, Vol. 38, No. 1, pp. 103–123.

Armour, A. M. (1991) *The Siting of Locally Unwanted Land Uses: Towards a Cooperative Approach*, Pergamon Press, Oxford.

Asbury, J.-E. (1995) "Overview of Focus Group Research", in *Qualitative Health Research*, Vol. 5, No. 4, pp. 414–420.

Blomgren Bingham, L., Nabatchi. T. and O'Leary, R. (2005) "The New Governance: Practices and Processes for Stakeholder and Citizen Participation in the Work of Government", in *Public Administration Review*, Vol. 65, No. 5, pp. 547–558.

Bobbio, L. (2004) *A piu' voci – Amministrazioni pubbliche, imprese, associazioni e cittadini nei processi decisionali inclusivi*, Edizioni Scientifiche Italiane, Rome.

Boholm, A. and Löfstedt, R. E. (2004) "Introduction", in Boholm, A. and Löfstedt, R. E. (Eds) *Facility Siting. Risk, Power and Identity in Land Use Planning*, Earthscan, London.

Bollens, S. A. (1993) "Restructuring Land Use Governance", in *Journal of Planning Literature*, Vol. 7, No. 3, pp. 211–226.

Breukers, S. and Wolsink, M. (2007) "Wind Power Implementation in Changing Institutional Landscapes: An International Comparison", in *Energy Policy*, Vol. 35, pp. 2737–2750.

Cooper, T. L. (1984) "Citizenship and Professionalism in Public Administration", in *Public Administration Review*, Vol. 44, Special Issue March, pp. 143–151.

Di Nucci, M. R., Brunnengräber, A., Mez, L. and Schreurs, M. (2015) "Comparative Perspective on Nuclear Waste Governance", in Brunnengräber, A., Di Nucci, M. R., Isidoro Losada, A. M., Mez, L. and Schreurs, M. (Eds) *Nuclear Waste Governance – An International Comparison*, Springer, Berlin.

Frey, J. H. and Fontana, A. (1991) "The Group Interview in Social Research", in *The Social Science Journal*, Vol. 28, No. 2, pp. 175–187.

Gervers, J. H. (1987) "The Nimby Syndrome: Is it Inevitable?", in *Environment: Science and Policy for Sustainable Development*, Vol. 29, No. 8, pp. 18–43.

Hayden Lesbirel, S. (2005) "Transaction Costs and Institutional Change", in Hayden Lesbirel, S. and Shaw, D. (Eds) *Managing Conflict in Facility Siting*, Edward Elgar, Cheltenham and Northampton.

Hilson, G. (2002) "An Overview of Land Use Conflicts in Mining Communities", in *Land Use Policy*, Vol. 19, pp. 65–73.

Jobert, A., Laborgne, P. and Mimler, S. (2007) "Local Acceptance of Wind Energy: Factors of Success Identified in French and German Case Studies", in *Energy Policy*, Vol. 35, pp. 2751–2760.

Kahan, J. P. (2001) "Focus Groups as a Tool for Policy Analysis", in *Analysis of Social Issues and Public Policy*, pp. 129–146.

Klijn, E.-H. and Koppenjan, J. F. M. (2012) "Governance Network Theory: Past, Present and Future", in *Policy and Politics*, Vol. 40, No. 4, pp. 587–606.

Krueger, R. A. (1994) *Focus Groups. A Practical Guide for Applied Research*, Sage Publications, Newbury Park.

Kuhn, R. G. and Ballard, K. (1998) "Canadian Innovations in Siting Hazardous Waste Management Facilities", in *Environmental Management*, Vol. 22, No. 4, pp. 533–545.

Landström, C. and Bergmans, A. (2015) "Long-term Repository Governance: A Socio-technical Challenge", in *Journal of Risk Analysis*, Vol. 18, No. 3, pp. 378–391.

Lee, M., Armeni, C., de Cendra, J., Chaytor, S., Lock, S., Maslin, M., Redgwell, C. and Rydin, Y. (2013) "Public Participation and Climate Change Infrastructure", in *Journal of Environmental Law*, Vol. 25, No. 1, pp. 33–62.

Lowndes, V. and Sullivan, H. (2004) "Like a Horse and Carriage or a Fish on a Bicycle: How Well do Local Partnerships and Public Participation go Together?" in *Local Government Studies*, Vol. 30, No. 1, pp. 51–73.

Lowry, K. and Eichenberg, T. (1986) "Assessing Intergovernmental Coordination in Coastal Zone Management", in *Policy Studies Review*, Vol. 6, No. 2, pp. 321–329.

May, P. J. (2012) "Policy Design and Implementation", in Peters, B. G. and Pierre, J. (Eds) *The SAGE Handbook of Public Administration*, 2nd Edition, SAGE, Los Angeles and London.

McDaniels, T. L., Gregory, R. S. and Fields, D. (1999) "Democratizing Risk Management: Successful Public Involvement in Local Water Management Decisions", in *Risk Analysis*, Vol. 19, No. 3, pp. 497–510.

Morgan, D. L. (1997) *Focus Groups as Qualitative Research*, Sage Publications, Thousand Oaks, CA.

NEA (2012a) *Reflections on Siting Approaches for Radioactive Waste Facilities: Synthesising Principles Based on International Learning*, OECD, Paris.

NEA (2012b) *Clarity, Conflict and Pragmatism: Challenges in defining a willing host community*, OECD, Paris.

O'Hare, M. (1977) "Not On My Block You Don't: Facility Siting and the Strategic Importance of Compensation", in *Public Policy*, Vol. 25, pp. 407–458.

O'Toole, L. J. (2012), "Interorganizational Relations and Policy Implementation", in Peters, B. G. and Pierre, J. (Eds) *The SAGE Handbook of Public Administration*, SAGE, Los Angeles and London.

Page, E. C. (2010) "Bureaucrats and Expertise: Elucidating a Problematic Relationship in Three Tableaux and Six Jurisdictions", in *Sociologie du travail*, Vol. 52, pp. 255–273.

Popper, F. J. (1981) "Siting LULUs", in *Planning*, Vol. 47, No. 4, pp. 12–15.

Stoker, G. (1998) "Governance as Theory: Five Propositions", in *International Social Science Journal*, Vol. 50, No. 155, pp. 17–28.

Thomas, J. C. (2012) *Citizen, Customer, Partner: Engaging the Public in Public Management*, Routledge, Abingdon and New York.

Walker, G., Devine-Wright, P., Barnett, J., Burningham, K., Cass, N., Devine-Wright, H., Speller, G., Barton, J., Evans, B., Heath, Y., Infield, D., Parks, J. and Theobald, K. (2011) "Symmetries, Expectations, Dynamics and Contexts: A Framework for Understanding Public Engagement with Renewable Energy Projects", in Devine-Wright, P. (Ed.) *Renewable Energy and the Public – From NIMBY to Participation*, Earthscan, London and Washington DC.

Weingart, J. (2007) *Waste Is A Terrible Thing To Mind*, Rivergate Books, New Brunswick, NJ.

Wilsdon, J. and Willis, R. (2004) *See-through Science. Why Public Engagement Needs to Move Upstream*, Demos, London.

Winter, S. (2012b) "Implementation Perspectives: Status and Reconsideration", in Peters, B. G. and Pierre, J. (Eds) *The SAGE Handbook of Public Administration*, SAGE, Los Angeles and London.

Wolsink, M. (2000) "Wind Power and the NIMBY-Myth: Institutional Capacity and the Limited Significance of Public Support", in *Renewable Energy*, Vol. 21, pp. 49–64.

Yanev, Y. (2009) "Nuclear Knowledge Management", in *International Journal of Nuclear Knowledge Management*, Vol. 3, No. 2, pp. 115–124.

7 Public involvement, trust and social acceptance

The Euratom research has developed several principles to enhance public involvement in RWM and indicated building trust as pivotal for public involvement during the implementation process (see chapter 4, *Principle* 9). Stakeholders from the field (chapter 3), including local communities (chapter 6), have confirmed the importance of dialogue and trust, and stressed the need of public involvement to increase trust (see also chapter 2). The two aspects are so intertwined that any effort to understand public involvement in policy-making runs the risk of being incomplete if its relationship with trust is overlooked.

In the domain of RWM, a large number of useful insights on trust have been produced by the work of the Nuclear Energy Agency (NEA) of the OECD. The NEA established a Forum on Stakeholder Confidence in 2000 with the purpose of promoting a better understanding about dialogue among stakeholders and ways to develop trust, confidence and social acceptance of RWM solutions (NEA 2009). Government officials, regulators' and implementers' personnel, industry representatives, researchers and specialists take part in the FSC;[1] the EC is also a member (NEA 2014a; NEA 2014b). The chapter heavily relies on the lessons learnt from the NEA experience.[2]

The chapter clarifies the link between public involvement and trust. After defining trust in general, the chapter takes a closer look at trust in the domain of RWM and reviews the major works issued by the OECD's NEA. It explains which factors influence citizens' trust in the process of decision-making, the structure of roles and responsibilities, the actors and key organisations involved, and the facilities that all together constitute a national RWM system. Finally, the chapter touches upon the relationship between public involvement, trust and social acceptance, and its relevance for the nuclear energy field.

Public involvement and trust

Public involvement and trust are strictly interrelated: the establishment of trust eases the participation of citizens and all relevant stakeholders in policy-making; in turn, the engagement of stakeholders is likely to create more trust (Figure 7.1).

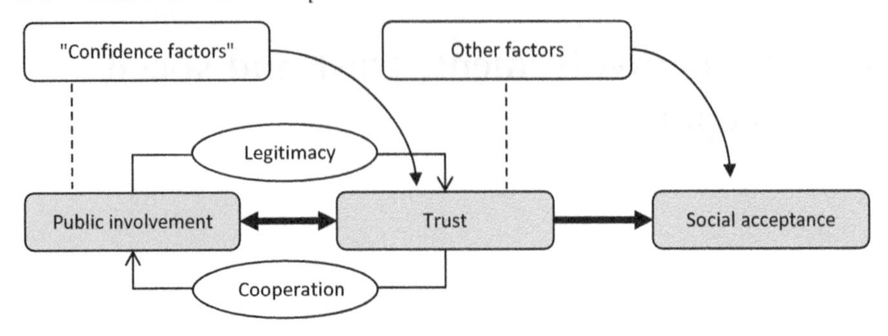

Figure 7.1 Public involvement, trust and social acceptance

The first relation (i.e. from trust to public involvement) rests on the fact that public involvement requires cooperation (chapter 2). However, no cooperation among actors can ever happen in the presence of mutual distrust (Bobbio 2004; Ellis & Ferraro 2016). This mechanism is also the reason why several Euratom projects investigating public involvement in RWM have highlighted the salience of building or rebuilding trust (chapter 4). Low levels of trust hamper any inter-organisational effort of collaboration (O'Toole 2012). For instance, all of the procedural implementation instruments (see chapter 5) presume that a certain amount of mutual trust exists among participants or that at least there is not a pre-existing distrust.

The second relation (i.e. from public involvement to trust) is based on the evidence that the interactions between individuals and organisations – that can take place, for instance, within policy networks – are likely to create trust (Greenberg 2014; Klijn 2007; Reed 2008). This link is the basis of the political rationale of public involvement (chapter 2). The OECD (2017: 112–113) explains that '[t]he importance of transparency to increasing citizen confidence and trust is borne out by data, which show that changes in the perceived transparency of policy-making are correlated with changes in trust'. Therefore, many countries are acting upon this proven link and are increasingly relying on practices of public involvement to (re)build citizens' trust in public institutions in many policy areas (OECD 2017).

The instrumental use of public involvement for building trust is particularly important in a sector like RWM and nuclear energy where citizens' trust has been eroded across time and scores still very low today (chapter 1). Any RWM strategy requires a sufficient level of confidence from the public to work successfully (NEA 2003).

However, while public involvement is a necessary condition for developing trust, it is not sufficient (OECD 2017). In other words, public involvement *per se* does not create (more) trust. Several sources of trust have been identified in the academic literature. In fact, such a rich body of research populates the field that it cannot be covered here in a comprehensive way. A comprehensive theory of trust, indeed, does not exist and the topic has been approached from varying disciplinary perspectives and dispersed analytical frameworks (Oomsels & Bouckaert 2012). The same definition of the concept is not easy since trust has been defined in many ways. Reasons of space and the goal of simplification impose narrowing down our research angle on trust as is explained in the following section.

The concept of trust

In the last twenty years, trust has increasingly been recognised as an important component in the relationships that emerge and develop within and among organisations operating both in the private and public sector. The growing importance attached to trust may be explained on the basis of the complexity of contemporary public problems that demand inter-organisational cooperation for their framing and solution (chapter 2). Therefore, trust has been acknowledged as crucial in many types of connections: in the relations of citizens with other citizens, business, political leaders and the governmental administration; in the interactions of public bodies with citizens; in the relationships between business and government; and in inter-organisational ties present within governments.

The OECD (2017) distinguishes between two major typologies of trust. The first type is "interpersonal trust", the one that is established in the social interactions among individuals. The second type is "institutional trust": it develops in the public and political interactions between citizens and their governments. Institutional trust has emerged as a significant component of public governance (Oomsels & Bouckaert 2012; 2014).[3] Braithwaite and Levi (1998) actually consider it a pillar of *good* governance. The recognition of the influence of institutional trust on public governance and policies has grown to the extent that trust constitutes nowadays both the means and the goal of effective administration in public institutions (Choudhury 2008; OECD 2017). This type of trust is particularly relevant for this book since institutional trust enables cooperation among networks of actors (Hardin 2006). Therefore, it lies at the basis of collaborative approaches to policy-making.

The general recognition of the salience of trust in inter-personal and inter-institutional relationships has been accompanied by an expanding attention from scholars (Hardin 2006). In particular, institutional trust has reached academic relevance in the disciplines of political science and public administration since the late 1990s (Oomsels & Bouckaert 2014). In the study of public administration, the importance of trust has been fully recognised not only in terms of trust of citizens for their government and the public sector. Trust of the government and public sector in citizens (understood as private sector, NGOs and society at large) has received attention, too. Likewise, (inter-organisational) trust within the government and the public sector has become an object of research (Bouckaert 2012). However, trust in the relation of the citizens towards their governments and public agencies has maintained its relevance (Braithwaite & Levi 1998).

The increased interest in trust has generated a growing literature on the topic (Hardin 2006) and a wide range of definitions and uses of the concept (see Oomsels & Bouckaert 2014 for a comprehensive overview). Confusion also increases because trust is often used interchangeably with other terms, namely "confidence". Both terms are taken as synonyms (Krouwel & Abts 2007), although nuanced differences exist between them. Confidence refers to the expectation that familiar things will remain stable (Luhmann 1988). Trust, instead, involves the belief that others will look after our interests and that they will not take advantage or harm us (Baier 1986). Trust implies an intentional suspension of vulnerability by an individual. We have trust when we accept giving up a certain measure of our control to another person (or organisation) on the basis of positive expectations about that person (or organisation) (NEA 2013c; Oomsels & Bouckaert 2014). In other words, trust consists of positive expectations about someone's conduct (Lewicki *et al.* 1998) and is linked with a good perception of the actions of an individual or organisation (OECD 2017).

Institutional trust has been eroded across time in many countries (chapter 1). Such loss is particularly problematic because of a general rule about trust: it is easily lost but regained with much struggle (Kasperson 2014). Gaining and regaining trust is, indeed, an incremental and very slow process where images built from past experiences have a long-term impact. In the domain of RWM and, more broadly, the field of nuclear energy, the lack of trust from citizens towards public agencies, as well as industry, is a recurrent concern for policy-makers (chapter 3) who are fully aware that human relationships are less about facts and more about emotions and perceptions.

In the presence of a general low level of citizens' trust in the nuclear energy field (see chapter 1), trust has become an important topic in the specific domain of RWM and has been debated in several fora in the recent past. Particularly, the NEA of the OECD has developed relevant insights with its work on the topic of trust (and confidence) in RWM over almost two decades.

Trust in radioactive waste management

A general low level of trust characterises the relations between citizens and the nuclear energy field. Despite national differences and changes over time (see Eurobarometer 2008), the Edelman Trust Barometer for the energy sector of 2015 shows that nuclear energy is the "least trusted" of all energy sub-sectors.[4] Several reasons have been presented in chapter 1 to explain such general mistrust towards nuclear energy, the safety of nuclear installations and the management of RW.

The NEA has extensively investigated how trust can be built (or rebuilt) for national RWM systems. The NEA (2008a; 2009; 2014b) argues that public involvement is essential to enhance trust in all the components that shape a national system for the management of RW. Any national RWM system can be understood as the combination of four components: a "process" of decision-making; a "structure" with roles and responsibilities; several "actors", i.e. the organisations involved in the management of RW; and a set of "facilities" that are planned, designed and operated in a country.

The relation between public involvement in RWM and trust is, nonetheless, *necessary* but not *sufficient*, similar to what is now commonly acknowledged for many policy fields (see above). Engaging the public is not enough in order to develop or restore trust: many more factors and causal mechanisms intervene to explain citizens' trust. In other words, it is the complementarity among public involvement and other factors that leads to (more) trust in the decision-making process, the structure of roles and responsibilities, the actors involved and the facilities built to manage a country's RW. These "confidence factors" – that include but are not limited to public involvement – are discussed in the following sections for each component of a national RWM system and summarised in Table 7.1.

Trust in the decision-making process for RWM

The core of any national RWM system consists of the decision-making process through which public administrators examine problems, assess possible choices and take decisions. It is in this component of a national RWM system that the trust of citizens for public institutions is crucial. In the absence of institutional trust at this level, trust must be built. In those contexts where trust existed but has been lost, public agencies will face the more difficult challenge of restoring it by adjusting the decision-making process and overcoming the legacy of past mistakes. Whether trust needs to be created (for the first time) or rebuilt (after losses), the adjustments needed in the decision-making must ensure public involvement, social learning, flexibility and accountability (NEA 2008b) (Table 7.1).

RWM is a wicked public problem (chapter 1); hence, RWM decisions are embedded in a complex set of interactions among multiple actors (or policy network) with diverging interests and values. In this context, agreed decisions can be taken only if all stakeholders agree to cooperate. The inclusion of a plurality of perspectives through collaborative arrangements in decision-

Table 7.1 RWM and trust: confidence factors

Trust in the process	*Trust in the structure*	*Trust in the actors*	*Trust in the facilities*
Decision-making	*Responsibilities*	*Organisations*	*Projects*
• Public involvement	• Clarity of roles	• Responsiveness	• Public involvement
• Social learning	• Public involvement	• Reliability	• Ownership
• Process flexibility	• Local participation	• Integrity	• Societal control
• Accountability		• Fairness	
		• Openness	

making is likely to result in more legitimacy for public decisions that are based on citizens' views. This will produce more trust of citizens for their government (see chapter 2).

Such an argument is confirmed by the work of the NEA: the decision-making process that allows public involvement seems to lead more easily to higher levels of trust of citizens for their national (and subnational) institutions (NEA 2008b). Public involvement helps regaining institutional trust too. Trust is largely influenced by the legacy of the past and many siting efforts take place in social contexts that have been polarised by earlier siting failures. Experience shows that participatory approaches are likely to facilitate decision-making also in the presence of distrust deriving from past experiences (Kasperson 2005).

The involvement of different stakeholders in decision-making tends to produce familiarity among the actors involved. The creation and repetition of contacts between state and non-state actors, central and local institutions, experts and non-experts in the field also facilitate social learning across different categories of stakeholders in the pursuit of an acceptable solution (NEA 2004a). Social learning happens when stakeholders interact, learn from each other, develop new (less adversarial) relationships, create alternative perspectives on societal issues and, collectively, enable change (O'Donnell *et al.* 2018; Reed 2008).

The result of more familiarity among actors and social learning through the exchange of views that are often polarised and conflictual may more easily lead to a common understanding of the issue at stake (NEA 2008b). Such common understanding overcomes the problem of conflictual issue-framing typical of wicked problems (chapter 1). For instance, all actors might end up converging on the idea that the current situation is no longer acceptable and that a solution needs to be found. In this context, trust relations between decision-makers and targeted publics, or industry and local communities can more easily develop.

For the purpose of building (and rebuilding) trust, decision-making in RWM should not only allow public involvement and, consequently, favour social learning; it should also be flexible. Indeed, decision-making should consist of an iterative process that adapts to contextual challenges that are constantly evolving (NEA 2004a). Such flexibility in the decision-making process can be achieved through the adoption of a so-called "stepwise approach", i.e. a way of proceeding per stages while taking public decisions. This recommendation of the NEA is in line with the insights developed by the Euratom research on public involvement in RWM (see chapter 4).

Proceeding per steps – for instance the different stages of a DGD (chapter 1) – means moving along small parts of a more complex and important decision. Each step is open to stakeholders' inputs. This facilitates citizens' understanding of RWM technologies, the adaptation of such technologies to social concerns, and interactions of local communities with RWM institutions. If necessary, certain steps may be revisited and adjusted (NEA 2008b). Overall, this approach to decision-making can help in the building of trust and, indirectly, lead to improvements in terms of social acceptance (NEA 2013c).

Finally, the decision-making process should allow for (more) accountability if public administrators want to increase citizens' trust in RWM decision-making. Decision-making can, indeed, be more easily trusted if it responds to citizens. In order to gain accountability, decisions need to be justified, well documented and clear for the public (NEA 2013c).

Trust in the RWM structure: roles and responsibilities

A second important component of a national RWM system consists of its structure as defined by the roles and responsibilities assigned to the different institutional actors by the national policy framework (NEA 2004a). Here, too, citizens' trust should be ensured by governments and their public agencies. According to the NEA (2004b; 2008a), trust in the structure of a national RWM system can be built by pursuing clarity and allowing engagement (Table 7.1).

First, we need a national policy framework that assigns roles and responsibilities to different actors in a clear way. The work of the NEA (2008a; 2009; 2013a) points out that trust can be built more easily if the roles, responsibilities and lines of authority that shape the structure of a RWM system are clearly defined in national policies and known by all actors with no room for ambiguity. In particular, the NEA stresses the important role played by the national Waste Management Organisation (or WMO): it has the full responsibility of steering the entire policy process around RWM. The aim of implementing agencies is to ensure that stable policies are developed and given prompt execution in spite of possible changes in the national political orientation. In the context of national politics that is too often volatile, the presence of a dedicated WMO is pivotal for the RWM structure (NEA 2004a).

Second, the national policy framework needs to allow public involvement and foresee that opportunities for participation are created through multiple instruments. In other words, the clear definition of roles and responsibilities among the actors involved in the national RWM system needs to be accompanied by the provision of opportunities for the involvement of a broad range of stakeholders who carry different interests, values, beliefs and worldviews. Multiple procedural implementation instruments can be adopted and used to open policy-making to the participation of citizens and other stakeholders (chapter 2), and many have been used by MSs for their management of RW (chapter 5). The NEA specifies that the choice of a specific instrument of public involvement needs to be made on the basis of several considerations: the purpose of public involvement (e.g., information, consultation or active participation); the level of decision (e.g., national policies or local projects); the phase in the policy- or decision-making process (e.g., policy formulation or implementation, project development or execution); the number and type of targeted stakeholders (e.g., national citizenry or local communities) (NEA 2004a; 2004b; 2015).

Moreover, the NEA (2015) highlights the importance of empowering stakeholders at the subnational level, whether regional or local, through instruments of public involvement. Indeed, the role of subnational stakeholders must be acknowledged in the RWM structure and their engagement needs to be made possible through sufficient space for debate. This space should aim at providing both hosting and neighbouring communities with valuable channels to express their concerns about a RWM facility. Local, as well as regional, stakeholders should have an active role in siting, planning, developing and overseeing RWM solutions with significant assistance from regulatory authorities and industry proponents (NEA 2009).

In particular, active participation (more than simple information and consultation) that is pursued through the application of principles of partnering and voluntarism seems to increase the trust of local communities in the RWM structure (NEA 2008a; 2010b; 2010d). These collaborative processes and interactions require, though, an important amount of time and resources so that all actors involved can understand and evaluate all possible options. The need for adequate resourcing is well known not only to local communities (chapter 6) but to all RWM stakeholders (chapter 3) and the scientific community that has investigated the social aspects of RWM (chapter 4).

The three elements needed for restoring trust in RWM structures – i.e. clarity of roles, instruments of public involvement and the active participation of local communities – echo some of the principles presented in chapter 4. This confirms the strong linkages that exist between public involvement and trust, and the virtuous circle leading from the former to the latter and back.

Trust in the RWM actors and organisations

We have looked at trust in the decision-making process and the structure of roles and responsibilities that compose a national RWM system. A third component of this system where citizens' trust is important is at the level of actors or, better, the public (or private) organisations responsible for RWM. Trust in those who are responsible for building and administering a RWM facility influences the willingness of a community to host that facility (Rosa & Short 2004). In fact, the failure of agents and institutions to perform responsibly and in the common interest lies behind much of the resistance to policy solutions genuinely based on scientific enquiry (Freudenburg 1993).

Multiple factors influence trust in organisations. They can be grouped under two main categories: organisational features (such as competence, capacity, independence, funding, etc.) and organisational behaviours (such as the presence of devoted staff, openness, transparency, consistency, willingness to involve others, etc.) (NEA 2004a; 2008a). The relevance of organisational features – mainly competences – and organisational behaviours – or values – as necessary conditions for trust has been stressed beyond the nuclear policy field by the OECD (2017) in a recent study on trust and public policy. Such insights on competences and values also apply to trust and public policy-making in the field of RWM, with its regulatory authorities, implementing agencies, and all relevant ministerial and non-state actors. They are useful to complement the work conducted by the NEA on trust in RWM (Table 7.1).

According to the OECD (2017), an actor, e.g. a public agency or a business organisation, cannot be trusted unless that actor proves to be competent. Being competent means that an organisation is able to deliver an output or a service according to expectations. For public administration, these expectations are that the government and its bodies listen to citizens and respond to their feedbacks. A first important competence to build trust is, thus, "responsiveness", which is in fact strictly linked to public involvement (e.g., through consultation efforts). A second competence relevant for trust towards (public) organisations is "reliability". Government institutions do not only need to respond; they have to do so effectively in order to anticipate emerging economic, social and political challenges and minimise uncertainties.

The importance of reliability is well known also in the scholarly literature that has dealt with risk and risk perception. Indeed, concerns about risks and inequities seem to be contained if the organisation in charge of a project can benefit from social trust. For instance, Armour stresses this point:

> Experts tend to focus on the properties of the risk per se (both quantitative and qualitative), whereas laypersons also include aspects of the context within which the risk is situated (most notably, the reliability and credibility of the proponent and regulatory bodies responsible for managing the risk).
>
> (Armour 1991: 29)

While competences have to do with the actual result of the action of a public or private organisation (in the form of output/service delivery), values relate to the behaviours of that organisation. Any organisation is worth trust only if it has integrity, fairness and openness as its core values. Integrity has to do with the way in which public administrations conduct themselves in safeguarding the public interest. Fairness refers to the distribution of costs and benefits among members of society and public organisations' pursuit of the benefit of the society as a whole. Finally, openness relates to public involvement and the engagement of citizens in the development and implementation of public policy (OECD 2017).

The factors stressed by the OECD (2017) as determinant for trust in organisations are confirmed by the academic literature. As a mere example, Kasperson (2005) argues that trust is usually higher for organisations that show competence, a past record of reliability, commitment and a caring attitude.

In conclusion, public involvement is pivotal for establishing and restoring trust in actors and organisations: it improves organisations' competence (e.g. through more responsiveness) and values (by ensuring openness). The relevance of public involvement for building trust needs, thus, to be acknowledged at the level of actors as well as process and structure. Public involvement is also needed to develop trust in the facilities, i.e. the RWM projects that so often heavily affect local communities.

Trust and RWM facility projects

A final, though, important component of a national RWM system consists of the set of concrete projects that are developed for the management of RW, i.e. the facilities sited, designed and operated for such purpose. Trust at this level seems to be determined by the degree of public involvement, and the allocation of ownership and societal control (Table 7.1).

The acceptance of the objective of a given project by the local community is an important prerequisite for its smooth development and execution. In general, a first cause of local opposition to hazardous facilities is that their need and utility is not always clearly communicated to the public and, more importantly, the local communities that are asked to host such facilities. It is, indeed, difficult for a community to accept the risks of a facility that it does not even perceive as a clear need. Therefore, societal need for a given facility and its utility for the general public interest must be the object of appropriate public information (NEA 2004).

However, a proper flow of communication in the single direction from public agencies and project developers to the public is not enough. If we want that RWM projects are trusted by the citizens more directly affected by these facilities, we need to ensure that they are sited, designed and operated in a way that takes into account the needs and aspirations of people, more precisely the local communities that either host the facility or are neighbours of the site (NEA 2004a). Therefore, adequate channels of feedback – from the public to public agencies and project developers – must be ensured (i.e. consultation).

Finally, any new project should be made an integral part of a local community through the active participation of local stakeholders at each step of the life of a facility. Only when a facility fits into a community and adds value to the local economic and social development, is it more likely to be durably "adopted" by the members of the hosting community. The NEA (2013c) argues that a shift is needed from the passive consent from a local community towards its active "ownership" of a facility. A local community feels ownership over a RWM project under the condition that it is involved in the siting, design, operation and oversight of the facility (NEA 2004a; 2008c).

Many factors shape our individual perceptions of safety and risk. It is evident that laymen and technical experts do not share the same level of knowledge, ideas and perceptions in matter of safety (see chapter 3). According to the NEA (2004a), people's familiarity with hazard and control over risk play an important role in risk perception. The position of the NEA is confirmed by the literature on risk. It is known that people feel less fear when they have more control on the source of possible hazard and are part of a related decision-making process (Weingart 2007). This justifies the use of voluntary approaches to RWM (chapter 4): our personal ability to decide upon, and thus influence, the risk we take contributes to weaken our perception of risk (Kasperson *et al.* 1988).

On these bases, the NEA (2013c) has invited governments, public agencies and the industry to give thoughtful consideration to the societal component of risk along the technical assessment of safety issues in RWM. Indeed, RWM must tackle not only technical and objective safety issues but also the subjective evaluation of these issues by different stakeholders. Often, technical experts argue that institutional control is key for the safety of a RWM facility and it must be exercised by a regulatory or safety authority (see also chapter 3). The NEA (2013a) counterargues that part of this control can be delegated to actors and organisations from the civil society. The NEA calls this partial delegation of control "societal control".

Ownership and societal control over a RWM facility will contribute to create familiarity of the local community with the facility and a feeling of safety (NEA 2013a). The NEA indicates also that societal control and familiarity can improve the technical component of safety because new viewpoints can be expressed and taken into due account. There is indeed both a technical and societal component of safety linked to, respectively, the actual and perceived risk of RWM.

In addition, the inclusion of local communities' concerns can also lead to policy designs that include financial instruments and tailored benefit packages for the host. Benefits of a socio-economic nature accompanying the development of a project for a new RWM facility are aimed at compensating the host communities for potential losses and externalities due to the presence of the facility (chapter 1). The NEA (2010b) stresses that community benefits should contribute to the sustainable development of the affected region.

In conclusion, the involvement of citizens that is determinant for building trust in RWM processes, structures and actors, also has an important role for the development of trust with regard to RWM facilities. Building or rebuilding trust at all these levels will ultimately have a positive impact on the whole national RWM system, in terms of institutional trust by the citizens.

Trust and social acceptance

Trust and public involvement are strictly intertwined. The chapter has shown that public participation is instrumental to build trust as a necessary (though not sufficient) condition. In turn, trust allows public involvement to take shape; the several instruments available for information, consultation or active participation in RWM (see chapter 5) require some amount of trust to be put in place and function. Trust is also important for social acceptance (Figure 7.1).

The definition of the concept of social acceptance is difficult (Williams & Mills 1986). The scholarly debate around it is populated by those who criticise the same concept for being too narrow to capture all the possible ways that people relate to new technologies and energy infrastructures (Ricci *et al.* 2008). This criticism points out the fact that many more nuances than the simple (or simplistic) dichotomy between acceptance and non-acceptance exist; they go from support to uncertainty, from resistance to apathy, etc. (Batel & Devine-Wright 2015).

Notwithstanding the oversimplification that the concept of social acceptance may bring with itself, no adequate alternative has been widely recognised. Several definitions of social acceptance are present in the literature and they tend to converge around the lack of opposition to a project (Cohen *et al.* 2014) – or, more broadly, any other initiative. A useful definition is offered by Upham *et al.* (2015) and used here. According to Upham *et al.* (2015), social acceptance is a favourable response (in attitude, behaviour and use) to a proposed technology or socio-technical system by the members of a social unit (be it a country, region, community, town, household or organisation).

Many uses of the land and technological developments face problems of social acceptance (Ellis & Ferraro 2016). The absence of a favourable response is often frequent at the local level, where it has usually – but not always correctly – been explained, though, through the NIMBY syndrome (see chapter 6). Trust seems to help the development of positive interactions among actors and support for a public decision/intervention (Breukers & Wolsink 2007; Jobert *et al.* 2007; Walker *et al.* 2011; Wolsink 2000).

In particular, the problem of social acceptance is a recurrent concern for policy-makers and the industry involved in the field of nuclear energy. The domain of nuclear energy has been for a long time dominated by low levels of acceptance as well as trust. Low levels of social acceptance are evident in many national debates on nuclear energy and in the reaction of local constituencies to many projects in the field – from the construction of new nuclear power plants (NPPs) to the siting of RWM facilities. RWM is an extremely controversial field with much polarised viewpoints; strong and very opposed positions exist in this domain.

The NEA (2010c; 2011a) has stressed the negative connotation often attached to the nuclear sector since its beginning (see also chapter 1). Nuclear energy and, consequently, RWM are commonly perceived as related to a policy context dominated by a powerful industry, lack of transparency and power imbalance between state and non-state actors. Therefore, it is not surprising that the NEA (2010b) has recommended openness, transparency, public involvement and citizens' participation as necessary conditions for the social acceptance of RWM policies, programmes and projects through the enhancement of trust.

In general, many factors – besides public involvement and trust – influence the social acceptance of facilities and technologies: trends and forecast in house prices, threat of increased traffic and noise, etc. An in-depth analysis of mechanisms of social acceptance was not the purpose of this final section. The main message that we want to reinforce here is that RWM must not only be technically feasible; it needs to be socially acceptable, too. But there cannot be social acceptance of RWM without trust and public involvement. For the purpose of building trust and improving social acceptance, public involvement needs to be actively pursued in national RWM systems in all its components: process, structure, actors and facilities.

Concluding remarks

RWM is 'a very volatile, emotional and difficult issue' (Weingart 2007: 91). In this field, techno-scientific analysis, as well as economic (cost-benefit) analysis, is not enough for decision-making. Public decisions are also determined by values and trust. In particular, the NEA experience suggests that, in addition to technical requirements, societal concerns about risk and safety need to be addressed in order for public trust and confidence to develop.

We have seen that trust, particularly institutional trust, is strictly linked to public involvement in RWM. On the one hand, trust will make it easier for decision-makers to involve their publics (OECD 2017). On the other hand, public involvement can improve public policies for RWM by making more and better information available to decision-makers, increasing the accountability of government agencies to citizens, allowing better conflict management and enhancing the understanding of decision-making and public decisions by laymen. This will ultimately improve the level of trust (NEA 2004b).

However, public involvement is not sufficient on its own to build trust. The NEA has investigated a set of elements that can elicit trust as shown in this chapter. The decision-making process, with related procedures and plans, should balance values that are often competing. The structure, with its roles and responsibilities, should rely on a clear national framework for RWM. Trustworthy RWM organisations have to be the committed driver of the policy process and demonstrate the willingness to listen to and involve all other actors. RWM facilities should bring an added value to the hosting and neighbouring local communities, and allow community oversight and stewardship.

Stakeholders' trust in RWM will remain on both political and research agendas still for some time. The work of the NEA has unveiled important insights about stakeholders' confidence and ways to develop institutional trust for the management of RW. However, some questions still remain open and beg for practical solutions. For example, to what extent do the different factors that have been identified play a role? What is the impact of specific local and national contexts? etc.

Other questions that call for an answer are the ones that have driven the research presented in this book (see Introduction). It is now time to answer those questions by drawing some conclusions from what we have learned so far. The next chapter presents answers and explain the key implications of our study on public involvement in RWM for policy action and academic research.

Notes

1 For more information on the work of the FSC, see https://www.oecd-nea.org/rwm/fsc (last access 22.05.2018).

2 A review of the NEA material was conducted in collaboration with the FSC for a report of the European Commission (Brans *et al.* 2015). I am particularly thankful to Marleen Brans and Jan van Damme for their support in the review of the FSC literature. The views expressed in this chapter about the NEA's insights on trust in RWM build on this report and are a personal re-elaboration on the major documents that the FSC has produced since 2000. Any responsibility for misinterpretation lies with the author.

3 The concept of trust has, indeed, become another "magic concept" (Pollitt & Hupe 2011) in the practice and study of public administration (see chapter 2).

4 Available at https://www.slideshare.net/EdelmanInsights/2015-edelman-trust-barometer-energy-sector-results (last access: 23.07.2017).

References

Armour, A. M. (1991) *The Siting of Locally Unwanted Land Uses: Towards a Cooperative Approach*, Pergamon Press, Oxford.

Baier, A. (1986) "Trust and Antitrust" in *Ethics*, Vol. 96, pp. 231–260.

Batel, S. and Devine-Wright, P. (2015), "A Critical and Empirical Analysis of the National–Local 'Gap' in Public Responses to Large-scale Energy Infrastructures", in *Journal of Environmental Planning and Management*, Vol. 58, No. 6, pp. 1076–1095.

Bergmans, A. (2006) (Ed.) *CARL – First Comparative Report: Towards a Typology of 'Stakeholders' in RWM*, University of Antwerp.

Bobbio, L. (2004) *A piu' voci – Amministrazioni pubbliche, imprese, associazioni e cittadini nei processi decisionali inclusivi*, Edizioni Scientifiche Italiane, Rome.

Bouckaert, G. (2012) "Trust and Public Administration", in *Administration*, Vol. 60, No. 1, pp. 91–115.

Braithwaite, V. and Levi, M. (1998) (Eds), *Trust and Governance*, Russell Sage Foundation, New York.

Brans, M., Ferraro, G. and Von Estorff, U. (2015) *The OECD Nuclear Energy Agency's Forum on Stakeholder Confidence, Radioactive Waste Management and Public Participation: A synthesis of its learnings and guiding principles*, Publications Office of the European Union, Luxembourg.

Breukers, S. and Wolsink, M. (2007) "Wind Power Implementation in Changing Institutional Landscapes: An International Comparison", in *Energy Policy*, Vol. 35, pp. 2737–2750.

Choudhury, E. (2008) "Trust in Administration: An Integrative Approach to Optimal Trust", in *Administration and Society*, Vol. 40, pp. 586–620.

Cohen, J. J., Reichl, J. and Schmidthaler, M. (2014), "Re-focussing Research Efforts on the Public Acceptance of Energy Infrastructure: A Critical Review", in *Energy*, Vol. 76, pp. 4–9.

Ellis, G. and Ferraro, G. (2016) *The Social Acceptance of Wind Energy: Where we stand and the path ahead*, Publications Office of the European Union, Luxembourg.

Eurobarometer (2008) *Attitudes Towards Radioactive Waste*, Special Eurobarometer 297, European Commission, Luxembourg.

Freudenburg, W. R. (1993) "Risk and Recreancy: Weber, the Division of Labor, and the Rationality of Risk Perceptions", in *Social Forces*, Vol. 71, No. 4, pp. 909–932.

Greenberg, M. (2014) "Energy Policy and Research: The Under-appreciation of Trust", *Energy Research and Social Science*, Vol. 1, pp. 152–160.

Hardin, R. (2006) *Trust*, Polity Press, Cambridge, UK.

Jobert, A., Laborgne, P. and Mimler, S. (2007) "Local Acceptance of Wind Energy: Factors of Success Identified in French and German Case Studies", in *Energy Policy*, Vol. 35, pp. 2751–2760.

Kasperson, R. E. (2005) "Siting Hazardous Facilities: Searching for Effective Institutions and Processes", in Hayden Lesbirel, S. and Shaw, D. (Eds) *Managing Conflict in Facility Siting*, Edward Elgar, Cheltenham and Northampton.

Kasperson, R. E. (2014) "Four Questions for Risk Communication", in *Journal of Risk Research*, Vol. 17, No. 10, pp. 1233–1239.

Kasperson, R. E., Renn, O., Slovic, P., Brown, H. S., Emel, J., Goble, R., Kasperson, J. X. and Ratick, S. (1988) "The Social Amplification of Risk: A Conceptual Framework", in *Risk Analysis*, Vol. 8, No. 2, pp. 177–187.

Klijn, E.-H. (2007) "Managing Complexity: Achieving the Impossible? Management between Complexity and Stability: A Network Perspective", in *Critical Policy Analysis*, Vol. 1, No. 3, pp. 252–277.

Krouwel, A. and Abts, K. (2007) "Varieties of Euroscepticism and Populist Mobilization: Transforming Attitudes from Mild Euroscepticism to Harsh Eurocynicism", in *Acta Politica*, Vol. 42, No. 2–3, pp. 252–270.

Lewicki, R. J., McAllister, D. J. and Bies, R. J. (1998), "Trust and Distrust: New Relationships and Realities", in *The Academy of Management Review*, Vol. 23, No. 3, pp. 438–458.

Luhmann, N. (1988) "Familiarity, Confidence, Trust: Problems and Alternatives", in Gambetta, D. (Ed.) *Trust: Making and Breaking Cooperative Relations*, Blackwell, New York.

NEA (2003) *Public Information, Consultation and Involvement in Radioactive Waste Management. An International Overview of Approaches and Experiences*, OECD, Paris.

NEA (2004a) *Learning and Adapting to Societal Requirements for Radioactive Waste Management. Key findings and Experience of the Forum on Stakeholder Confidence*, OECD, Paris.

NEA (2004b) *Stakeholder Involvement Techniques: Short Guide and Annotated Bibliography*, OECD, Paris.

NEA (2008a) *Decision-making for Radioactive Waste Management: Principles, Action Goals, Confidence Factors*, OECD, Paris.

NEA (2008b) *Stepwise approach to the long-term management of radioactive waste*, OECD, Paris.

NEA (2008c) *Towards waste management facilities that become a durable and attractive part of the fabric of local community – Relevant design features*, OECD, Paris.

NEA (2009) *About the Forum on Stakeholder Confidence*, OECD, Paris.

NEA (2010b) *From Information and Consultation to Citizen Influence and Power*, OECD, Paris.

NEA (2010c) *More Than Just Concrete Realities: The Symbolic Dimension of Radioactive Waste Management*, OECD, Paris.

NEA (2010d) *Partnering for Long-term Management of Radioactive Waste. Evolution and Current Practice in Thirteen Countries*, OECD, Paris.

NEA (2011a) *More Than Just Concrete Realities: The Symbolic Dimension of Radioactive Waste and Its Management*, OECD, Paris.

NEA (2012a) *Reflections on Siting Approaches for radioactive Waste Facilities: Synthesising Principles Based on International Learning*, OECD, Paris.

NEA (2013a) *Geological Disposal of Radioactive Wastes: National Commitment, Local and Regional Involvement*, OECD, Paris.

NEA (2013c) *Stakeholder Confidence in Radioactive Waste Management: An Annotated Glossary of Key Terms*, OECD, Paris.

NEA (2014a) *FSC national workshops*, OECD, Paris.

NEA (2014b) *Stakeholder confidence and transparency in radioactive waste management*, OECD, Paris.

NEA (2015) *Implementing Stakeholder Involvement Techniques*, OECD, Paris.

O'Donnell, E. C., Lamond, J. E. and Thorne, C. R. (2018) "Learning and Action Alliance Framework to Facilitate Stakeholder Collaboration and Social Learning in Urban Flood Risk Management", in *Environmental Science and Policy*, Vol. 80, pp. 1–8.

OECD (2017) *Trust and Public Policy – How Better Governance Can Help Rebuild Public Trust*, OECD, Paris.

Oomsels, P. and Bouckaert, G. (2012), "Managing Trust in Public Organisations: A Consolidated Approach and Its Contradictions", Paper presented at the XVI IRSPM Conference, 11–13 April, Rome.

Oomsels, P. and Bouckaert, G. (2014) "Studying Interorganizational Trust in Public Administration", in *Public Performance & Management Review*, Vol. 37, No. 4, pp. 577–604.

O'Toole, L. J. (2012), "Interorganizational Relations and Policy Implementation", in Peters, B. G. and Pierre, J. (Eds) *The SAGE Handbook of Public Administration*, SAGE, Los Angeles and London.

Pollitt, C. and Hupe, P. (2011) "Talking About Government. The Role of Magic Concepts", in *Public Management Review*, Vol. 13, No. 5, pp. 641–658.

Reed, M. S. (2008) "Stakeholder Participation for Environmental Management: A Literature Review", in *Biological Conservation*, Vol. 141, pp. 2417–2431.

Ricci, M., Bellaby, P. and Flynn, R. (2008), "What Do We Know About Public Perceptions and Acceptance of Hydrogen? A Critical Review and New Case Study Evidence", in *International Journal of Hydrogen Energy*, Vol. 33, No. 21, pp. 5868–5880.

Rosa, E. A. and Short, J. F. (2004) "The Importance of Context in Siting Controversies: The Case of High-Level Nuclear Waste Disposal in the US", in Boholm, A. and Löfstedt, R. E. (Eds) *Facility Siting. Risk, Power and Identity in Land Use Planning*, Earthscan, London.

Upham, P., Oltra, C. and Boso, À. (2015), "Towards a Cross-paradigmatic Framework of the Social Acceptance of Energy Systems", in *Energy Research and Social Science*, No. 8, pp. 100–112.

Walker, G., Devine-Wright, P., Barnett, J., Burningham, K., Cass, N., Devine-Wright, H., Speller, G., Barton, J., Evans, B., Heath, Y., Infield, D., Parks, J. and Theobald, K. (2011) "Symmetries, Expectations, Dynamics and Contexts: A Framework for Understanding Public Engagement with Renewable Energy Projects", in Devine-Wright, P. (Ed.) *Renewable Energy and the Public – From NIMBY to Participation*, Earthscan, London and Washington DC.

Weingart, J. (2007) *Waste Is A Terrible Thing To Mind*, Rivergate Books, New Brunswick (NJ).

Williams, R. and Mills, S. (1986) *Public Acceptance of New Technologies*, Routledge, London.

Wolsink, M. (2000) "Wind Power and the NIMBY-Myth: Institutional Capacity and the Limited Significance of Public Support", in *Renewable Energy*, Vol. 21, pp. 49–64.

8 Public involvement in RWM: answers and implications

Radioactive waste management (RWM) is a multifaceted problem. It faces technical, social and institutional challenges, and has multiple implications that are scientific, environmental, political, economic, etc. The book has focused on the institutional challenge and the interaction between the public and policy-making. We have looked at public involvement in policy-making, particularly during the implementation of national policies for RWM across the EU. We have seen that the implementation process entails multiple interactions among actors with competing interests and priorities that are not always aligned. The power distribution among these actors during the implementation process will determine who influences final decisions (chapter 2).

In the early 2000s, the NEA (2003) noticed that complex interactions between the institutions responsible for nuclear energy and civil society were emerging during decision-making at national, regional and local level. However, years later, Sundqvist and Elam (2010) argued that a "participatory turn" in nuclear energy policy, including RWM, was still more apparent than real. The authors also claimed that the same nature of public involvement in the field was somewhat obscure across the whole EU. Since then, a new Directive has been adopted in the EU (2011). The Waste Directive has recognised the importance of transparency, public information and participation for the responsible and safe management of spent fuel (SF) and radioactive waste (RW).

The chapter draws conclusions about public involvement in RWM in the EU. It starts by reflecting upon the findings of this research and answers the questions from where we started our investigation, i.e. the "why", "when", "how" and "who" of public involvement in RWM (see Introduction). It discusses the main achievements and open issues analysed in the previous chapters around these questions. Later, the chapter builds on these answers to indicate major implications for policy practice and policy research. It proposes policy recommendations for political actions by international, national and subnational institutions, and suggests indications for theoretical investigation by the academic world.

Why do we need public involvement in RWM?

The salience of public involvement in RWM is commonly acknowledged in the political and public debate. In practice, though, a strong commitment may still be lacking in some Members States (MSs). Therefore, it is important to stress at the conclusion of this work why participation initiatives are important for the field and the added valued that engaging the different publics may bring to the management of radioactive waste (RW).

In general, public involvement is motivated on the basis of a substantive, political and ethical rationale: it improves public policies, the process of policy-making and the democratic nature of a political system (chapter 2). In particular, public involvement is important during policy implementation, when administrative officials – who are not accountable electorally – have strong decision-making powers through the issuing of delegated legislation and high level of discretion on the operationalisation of public policies. Public involvement of those affected by the decisions and actions of national bureaucracies then becomes crucial for the accountability of unelected bureaucrats and the legitimacy of public agencies in a democratic political system.

In the specific domain of RWM, three additional reasons call for public involvement: the wicked nature of RWM as a public policy problem; people's concerns and misunderstandings related to actual risk and safety issues; and the atmosphere of distrust that characterises the nuclear energy field.

The complexity of the problem

We have defined RWM as a wicked problem due to the high level of complexity in both the framing of the issues at stake and the definition of possible solutions (chapter 1). RWM is, indeed, affected by contested facts and diverging values. The presence of polarised positions and strong disagreements about the management of RW makes collaborative arrangements fundamental in the policy-making around RWM. The recurrent policy failures across the EU in the recent past have shown the inadequacy of a technocratic approach to RWM.

Indeed, it has become clear that multiple societal concerns (as well as technical aspects) must be taken into account by RW managers. Public involvement can allow for a better balance of diverging views, facilitate mutual learning among stakeholders and, ultimately, transform confrontation into cooperation between different positions. In particular, we need to build and maintain across time a fruitful relationship between those legally responsible for RWM, the general public and the hosting communities.

However, public involvement calls for institutional changes, which presents national governments with new challenges. We have explained that a more participatory policy-making may require adaptations in the design of national RWM policies, and flexibility in both their development and execution (chapter 4). Changes such as the creation of opportunities for public involvement during the policy process and the adoption of a stepwise approach in decision-making will have costs in terms of financial resources and time.

Safety, risk and public perception

All locally unwanted land uses (LULUs) imply burdens that are concentrated on local communities (see Introduction). This also applies to RWM. Unlike other LULUs, though, RWM has to do with hazardous waste. The safety of managing, storing and disposing RW is a recurrent concern among all actors involved in the field (chapter 3). Public involvement makes sure that new channels of communication with the public are created, developed and, eventually, institutionalised.[1] This is pivotal if we want citizens to understand the actual risk of different types of RW and the adequacy of safety measures put in place for their management.

It could be argued that the public should not be involved in safety matters given the fact that safety falls under the responsibility of national regulators supported by technical experts, and must be based on factual data and scientific findings rather than feelings. However, the management of risk is 'a matter of both science *and* values' (Pidgeon 1998: 5, emphasis in original). The importance of emotional and socio-cultural factors in the perception of risk and safety in the domain of RWM has been stressed by the work of the NEA (chapter 7). In particular, the importance of creating a feeling of familiarity suggests the need to allow some form of societal control through collaborative arrangements between citizens and safety authorities.

Nuclear energy, trust and the legacy of the past

RWM is not only a wicked problem that entails contested land use. It also consists of managing the hazardous waste produced, in large amounts, by a controversial activity, i.e. the production of energy through nuclear power. RWM poses problems of social acceptance for the entire nuclear energy field; it also suffers from the general loss of trust that has characterised nuclear energy throughout its development (chapter 1). As we said above, RWM brings with itself concerns about safety as happens for other hazardous facilities. However, risk perception in RWM is amplified by the feeling of suspect and distrust that has grown in the nuclear field soon after the discovery of radioactivity and nuclear power.

Unmotivated fears can only be managed through the inclusion of the general public, targeted local communities and other stakeholders in political debate and policy-making. Public involvement is essential for regaining trust (chapter 7). In its turn, trust is likely to make public involvement in policy-making more effective by enabling a more constructive dialogue (chapter 4).

*

In conclusion, public involvement in RWM constitutes a priority for the field despite the additional costs it may imply for policy-making. Citizens should be adequately informed, consulted and engaged. Different levels of intensity are possible in public involvement; the final result would be that citizens know (information), say (consultation) and do things in collaboration with policy-makers and public administrators (active participation).

The book has opted for three degrees of public involvement (chapter 2). These levels are not rigidly defined in theory and additional intermediate degrees can be distinguished. For instance, consultation can be split into "listen" and "exchange". Likewise, in active participation, we could differentiate between collaborations and joint decision-making. Indeed, public involvement unveils along a continuum, but policy analysis requires that such continuum is made clear through the use of discontinuous analytical categories (Bardach 2012). The distinction used in the book has served the purpose of analysing national practices across the EU as presented in the National Programmes (NPs) (chapter 5); more refined typologies could have not been traced easily in the information provided therein.

Actual influence and authorship in the adopted decisions are particularly important for the publics who decide to participate. Nevertheless, we do not always need active participation. In some cases, consultation can be enough. In some other cases, information on its own solves any problem. We need a pragmatic approach that takes into account the benefit of public involvement without neglecting its costs. We do not need all degrees of public involvement at any time. According to the level of involvement needed or desired, different instruments are available (see below).

When can public involvement in RWM take place?

Public involvement can be foreseen and applied throughout the whole policy process, from the formulation of national policies to their execution. The book has focused on public involvement during policy implementation. However, we have explained that the implementation of national public policies cannot be understood in isolation from other components of policy-making.[2] Implementation tends to reflect and reinforce conflicts and ambiguities that are already present in the formulation of new policies and the content given to them (chapter 2). Therefore, public involvement should be foreseen and enabled during policy formulation and in the policy design as well as across the entire implementation process.

Policy formulation

Opening up the policy-making process to societal views at the stage of development of the national RWM policies allows the inclusion of citizens' values, concerns and ideas in the identification of possible courses of action (chapter 2). Such inclusion develops a more complete diagnosis of all existing constraints and potential obstacles to the course of action decided with the policies adopted. The action to be taken must be technically capable of correcting a problem, administratively feasible, and politically acceptable.

Research results from the Euratom experience recommend early involvement of the general public and local communities in the development of a national policy for RWM. It is important for the entire process of policy-making that the views of citizens, local communities and other stakeholders are brought in the discussions that populate policy formulation for the purpose of identifying viable policy options (chapter 4). Such discussions may even go beyond the remit of RWM and embrace the larger debate that goes over national energy production and consumption, and the role of nuclear energy in the country's energy mix (chapter 3).

Furthermore, trust in RWM solutions is far from being achieved. Therefore, it is vital that the many societal concerns that exist in the field (e.g., about the risk of RW and the safety of RWM solutions) are taken into account by policy-makers in the development of policy decisions. Citizens and local communities can bring into policy formulation ideas and knowledge that often differ from the insights given by experts. It follows that the bureaucratic agencies that develop contacts with a broad base of affected groups are likely to formulate better national RWM policies. In the EU, public consultation (in the form of informal debates or more formal arrangements) is conducted in some MSs for the amendment of existing legal frameworks for RWM (chapter 5).

Policy design

The content of RWM policies defined by national legal frameworks need to be grounded in technical research and scientific insights because of the highly techno-scientific nature of the issue (chapter 1). However, the Euratom research explains that considerations on the social implications of RWM should also inform the definition of policy objectives and policy tools, the designation of the responsible (governmental and non-governmental) organisations, and the allocation of resources for the different tasks (chapter 4). Public involvement needs to be given cautious consideration in the definition of all these components of policy design. Moreover, policy designs that acknowledge the relevance of societal values and, thus, foresee a role and resources for the participation of civil society in policy-making embody an important democratic principle (chapter 2).

The MSs of the EU ensure public involvement in their constitutional, legal or regulatory frameworks (chapter 5). Indeed, citizens' access to public information is foreseen in many national primary laws, either general ones or related to specific policy areas (environment, energy, nuclear energy, RWM and radiation protection).

National RWM policies across the EU define roles, responsibilities and participation of different stakeholders in a clear way (chapter 5). This is also important for the purpose of building or rebuilding trust and confidence in the RWM structure (chapter 7). Particularly, local communities should be recognised a key role, adequate responsibilities and appropriate ways to participate in RWM. Changes in policy design might be envisaged where the role of local communities remains weak and little defined (chapter 6).

Implementation process

Public involvement needs to be ensured in the set of interactions among multiple actors that constitutes the implementation process. Here, the power relationships between the national and local level are particularly important (chapter 6). Although, in some MSs, local communities have been empowered with a strong role (for instance through formal or informal veto power), the power balance seems to be still in favour of national authorities and national policy objectives.

According to research, public involvement at this stage should be pursued through the principles of partnering, voluntarism and flexibility (chapter 4). These principles seem to ease mutual learning among the actors involved and improve intergovernmental relations. Unfortunately, even when these principles are applied, collaborative inter-organisational and intergovernmental relations in RWM are difficult to develop in the absence of trust (see also chapter 7).

Public involvement is, nonetheless, expected to make implementation easier by means of conflict resolution among competing interests and veto avoidance (chapter 2). The involvement of the public in policy and administrative decisions increases, indeed, the legitimacy of such decisions in the eyes of citizens. Decisions recognised as legitimate by their targeted groups will, ultimately, face less opposition. In this context, trust in the government may eventually grow and, as a virtuous circle, make collaborative arrangements more viable.

How can the public be involved in RWM?

An important question about public involvement is how it can take place. The question was raised for RWM (chapter 3) but this aspect is relevant for the topic of citizens and stakeholders' engagement in general. Indeed, a wide variety of instruments of public involvement exists, and their use varies considerably across policy fields and countries (Aldrich 2005; OECD 2015). Although many typologies have been developed in the literature (e.g. Creighton 2005), Balla (2005: 62) argues that 'a systematic, large scale inventory of the use of forms of public involvement has not yet been taken'. Balla (2005) refers, in particular, to the phase of policy implementation, when stakeholders seek to participate in the making of rules and operationalisation of public policies.

We have explained that procedural implementation instruments are key to policy implementation because they allow governments to promote, create and institutionalise the inter-organisational interactions that shape the execution of national polices (Hanf & O'Toole 1992; Howlett 2000; 2011; Howlett *et al.* 2015). However, this type of policy instrument has not been fully studied. The book contributes to fill this gap through the assessment, inventory and classification of the procedural implementation instruments used for RWM across the EU.

A detailed inventory of the use and recurrence of the various ways public involvement takes place in RWM across the EU has been presented in chapter 5 on the basis of the official NPs. The multitude of possible tools has been arranged along information, consultation and active participation according to the degree of public involvement they pursue. These different levels of public involvement reflect different power positions among actors involved in policy-making – actors can be simply informed or consulted or directly engaged in decision-making. Local communities have confirmed the set of available instruments and added further information on their actual use (chapter 6).

In social sciences, inventories are often followed by the construction of classifications (Howlett 2011). We saw in chapter 2 that procedural implementation instruments can be distinguished according to the state resource on which they rely: knowledge, money, authority and organisation. Governments can manipulate policy networks to promote public involvement and open them to a broader presence of stakeholders through the use of these resources.

The instruments for public involvement in RWM can, thus, be classified on the basis of the resources used as well as the objectives pursued as shown in Figure 8.1. The classification proposed brings more analytical clarity in the study of 28 very different national contexts. Variations in the use of these instruments are possible: indeed, any instrument is adapted to the unique institutional and cultural settings that characterise each MS of the EU. Nevertheless, the analytical taxonomy presented in Figure 8.1 is helpful for practitioners who design and execute policies, and academics who study and assess policy processes.

Information provision and access

This first type of tools is procedural implementation instruments that alter the behaviour of policy networks through the use of knowledge at the disposal of governments. They rely on information disclosure and access to documents, and consist of communicating knowledge and information to target groups (chapter 2). Among the tools used by MSs in RWM, printed information, internet, media relations and public events fall in this category. Public meetings and workshops, citizen surveys and opinion polls aimed at communicating information and exchanging expertise are also included here (Figure 8.1).

The salience of knowledge – and more broadly, information, evidence and expertise – as a key resource is stressed by a number of RWM stakeholders (see chapter 3). Information has emerged as pivotal also in the intergovernmental relations between the centre and the local level, particularly when it comes to strategic decisions (chapter 6). In a field that is characterised by strong emotions, correct and unbiased information about RW, safety aspects and the related decision-making is very important. Some major challenges still remain with regard to information provision, though: a good balance between complete and simplified information; an adequate trade-off between transparency and security; and the acquisition of independent expertise by local communities.

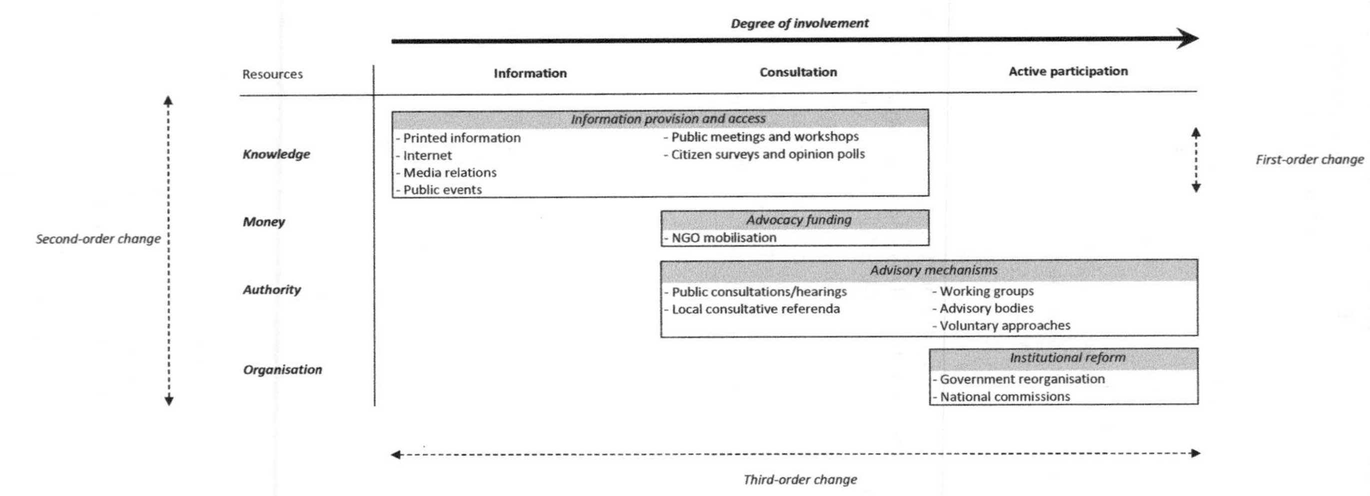

Figure 8.1 Public involvement: instruments, resources and objectives

Advocacy funding

Financial resources are extremely important for public involvement in RWM because they have a two-fold purpose. They are needed as funds to finance participation (information activities, actual engagement and capacity building – for instance by hiring independent experts at the local level) and as incentives (for the compensation of hosting communities and their local/regional development). The latter function of financial resources has been discussed in the framework of the need to balance the externalities borne by local communities in many uses of their land. However, this use of money does not constitute a procedural implementation instrument.

Procedural financial instruments are those aimed at altering the interactions that shape a policy process through the provision of money for the creation or mobilisation of interest groups (indeed, advocacy funding) (chapter 2). The availability of financial resources for public and local participation was raised as an important issue by RWM stakeholders (chapter 3), including local communities (chapter 6), and as pivotal for the actual empowerment of non-state actors according to the Euratom research (chapter 4). Although it is not common practice all over the EU, the funding of the participation of NGOs during public consultation is an example of the application of this instrument in the EU in the domain of RWM (chapter 5).

Advisory (and consent-based) mechanisms

Procedural authoritative instruments involve the exercise of government authority to mobilise specific actors in a policy process through the recognition of preferential access (chapter 2). These tools include diverse advisory processes, from public consultations and hearings to working groups and advisory bodies. In the view of the author, the recognition of a preferential status in decision-making also happens through local consultative referenda. Likewise, voluntary arrangements that, for their very nature, imply a partial share of government authority with local communities (for instance through formal or informal veto powers) can also be included among these instruments.

Advisory mechanisms have different level of institutionalisation (chapter 4). They vary from more informal and temporary working groups to more formal and permanent advisory bodies. Formal processes of public involvement rely on instruments that have an institutional and legal basis, i.e. they are included in national legislative frameworks. Informal processes are, instead, not institutionalised; in many cases, practices of public involvement have been introduced in MSs informally and without any change in the legislative framework (Ferraro & Martell 2015b; OECD 2015). MSs ensure opportunities for public consultation in RWM, both formally (e.g., in the framework of SEA and EIA procedures) and informally. MSs seem, instead, to make less use of advisory bodies for active participation (see chapter 5).

Institutional reform

Procedural organisational tools involve institutional reorganisation with the purpose of affecting policy processes through which governments perform their functions. Governments can, thus, create new agencies or reconfigure old ones (i.e. government reorganisation) to focus (or re-focus) interactions between state and non-state actors in a specific issue area. As an alternative, governments can create temporary task forces and national commissions within the existing political and administrative structure (chapter 2).

The creation of national commissions with the purpose of developing more collaborative decision-making arrangements with the public has been mentioned by a few MSs (chapter 5). In other cases, government reorganisation has taken place. However, the NPs and supporting documents do not contain enough level of details to let us understand the motivations behind such reorganisations. Indeed, these documents do not specify whether the creation of new agencies and reconfiguration of old ones was aimed at improving relationships with the public. More in-depth case studies on national administrative reforms would be needed to better investigate this type of instrument and understand the motivations lying behind national institutional reforms.

*

In conclusion, policy makers and public administrators have the chance to choose among a number of instruments for public involvement. They will have to decide which instrument(s) they need to use on the basis of the type and amount of resources they have available (i.e. knowledge, money, authority and organisation) and the intensity of public involvement they want to pursue (i.e. information, consultation and active participation).

We know from policy research, more precisely Hall (1993), that when changes to public policies consist of the introduction of new policy instruments (second-order change) or alteration of policy objectives (third-order change), such changes are more radical and challenging than simply varying the current use of a known instrument (first-order change) (Figure 8.1). Although the concept of order of change was elaborated for substantial policy instruments and objectives, we can stretch its utilisation to procedural implementation instruments and expect more difficulties and costs with higher orders of change pursued.

When we change the typology of instrument (i.e. second-order change) and move from informational and financial to authoritative and organisational instruments, the alteration of policy network changes from mild forms (based on voluntary responses from targeted organisations) to stronger government interventions that are more manipulative (Howlett *et al.* 2009).

With higher degrees of public involvement (third-order change), the complexity of the policy process will also increase and will demand larger amounts and different types of resources (Beierle & Cayford 2002; Gaventa & Valderrama 1999). In particular, the amount of decision-making authority that policy-makers and public administrators share with their publics also increases with this shift. Actors become more interested in influencing decisions than simply receiving information.

Who should be involved in RWM?

RW has traditionally been managed by national authorities and public administrators with the support of scientific experts (chapter 1). The change towards a new model of governance of RWM based on public involvement and the empowerment of civil society redefines who will participate in the political debate, policy formulation and implementation. In particular, who is included and given actual recognition and authority in the implementation process is crucial since, we have argued, policy implementation continues the competition for power among actors willing to influence a specific course of action (see chapter 2).

The definition of the stakeholders that should be included in policy-making remains an open issue in RWM (chapter 3). Such definition is not free from ambiguities – particularly in the presence of an informal process of participation – and national differences. The same meaning and understanding of public involvement have evolved from the simple participation of citizens to policy-making to a more variegated set of stakeholders that includes other non-state actors (e.g., industrial companies, trade associations, unions and environmental NGOs) interested in or affected by a collective decision, as well as governmental organisations (e.g., subnational governments) (chapter 2).

According to the evidence collected through stakeholders' insights from the field, social research on the topic, national programmes and the experience of local communities, we can conclude that public involvement in RWM should ensure a balanced representation through three key dimensions: citizens and government; central and local levels; experts and laymen.

Government and citizens

The relevance of both state and non-state actors in policy-making is now a *fait accompli* in most policy areas. The formulation and implementation of public policies has changed over the last decades. Public authorities on their own are no longer able to face the public problems of contemporary societies and the way to address such challenges is increasingly the result of a complex web of relations between public and private organisations. On the other side, 'the broadening of participatory opportunities can strengthen society by assuring that the actions of government are embedded in society, rather than imposed on society' (Thomas 1995: 7). This strong interaction between government and citizens, or more broadly societal interests, in the making of public policies is based on a mutual resource dependency and has been captured by scholars with the metaphor of policy networks.

Policy networks have redefined the relations between state and society: policy-makers and public administrators share power with the public. The public is – or should be – informed, consulted and actively engaged. All stakeholders from the RWM domain acknowledge this point; some scepticism emerges from the side of experts when public involvement also claims space on safety matters. The motivation that only facts, and not values, should lead safety is contested, though, by the same NEA that has invited regulators and other experts to welcome societal concerns and control (chapter 7).

Central and local levels

In the context of inter-organisational interaction in the formulation and implementation of public policies, relations between central and local institutions have a prominent role. This is particularly true when public policies concern uses of the land that are unwanted at the local level. LULUs always imply unbalances between costs and benefits, with the former mainly borne by local communities.

Therefore, the local communities hosting a RWM facility, candidate to host one or located in its vicinity are legitimate participants in RWM policies, programmes and projects. This makes intergovernmental relations crucial for RWM. Indeed, while we move through the phases of a RWM programme, from its adoption to its execution through localised projects, the potential and actual opposition moves from the national to the local level (chapter 6). It follows that while the national level is the predominant arena during policy/programme development and the initial stages of a siting process, it will have to interact with the local communities directly impacted as it becomes clear which communities are targeted by the development of siting. Even during operation and the following steps in the life of a RWM facility, the involvement of the local communities should continue. Ending any engagement after the siting has been completed would delegitimise the entire public involvement process.

Experts and laypeople

In very technical policy areas and wicked policy issues, we must ensure both inclusiveness and expertise. We have pointed out the need for a broad and balanced representation in public involvement that must guarantee that no interested actor is left out of the policy- and decision-making process. However, fair representation should not rule out competent participation. A high level of competence needs to be ensured in complex areas such as RWM. Therefore, the participants admitted to take part in the decision-making over RWM issues should not only be representatives of the relevant publics; a high-level of (independent) expertise needs to be present in participatory processes (on this point, see also OECD 2017b).

One of the major challenges that remain in a technical domain such as RWM is the need to improve communication from experts to non-experts. Laymen need complete and simplified information about the RWM issues on which they will have to be involved (chapter 2). It is the responsibility of the experts and scientists that sit in national public administrations, regulatory bodies, implementing agencies and industry to improve their communication strategies and practices, and reach out to a broader audience.

Recommendations for policy-making

The ultimate goal of policy research and analysis is to develop policy recommendations that specify how institutions and policy practices can be reformed to improve national policies (Bardach 2012; Hanf & O'Toole 1992). In the light of the insights gained on public involvement in RWM, the chapter wants to highlight key implications for policy practice with the purpose of improving the institutional arrangements that connect citizens and other stakeholders to the policy-making around RWM, from national policy decisions to individual local projects. Public involvement does not require simple changes in national policy frameworks; it needs to be incorporated into existing institutional structures and historical traditions of government–citizens relations as this section wants to show.

Reciprocal commitment vs. mutual disrespect

The success of any attempt of public involvement depends on the commitment of the government agency, the motivation of the public participating in the process, and the way the agency and the public interact and control the process (Beierle & Cayford 2002). We need, thus, reciprocal commitment to public information, public participation and dialogue, rather than the mutual disrespect and lack of trust that has often characterised state–society interactions in the nuclear energy and RWM fields.

There can be no public involvement without political will to include in policy-making all possible stakeholders and not only the usual suspects. However, we also need credible commitment from the side of societal actors towards constructive dialogue. This dialogue needs to be based on both facts and values, but must discard the deluge of fake news we experience in the current time. Moreover, we must acknowledge that RW exists and needs to be taken care of, regardless of our value systems about the future of nuclear power (chapter 1). The two discourses, i.e. about RWM and the use of nuclear energy, should possibly be decoupled in political and public debates. One debate should focus on the current need to ensure a safe and responsible management of RW that does not create burdens for future generations, in line with the core meaning of sustainable development. The second debate should cover the role of the nuclear option in the energy mix of a country for the future development of its economy and society.

Complementary of instruments vs. isolated techniques

Policy-makers and public administrators have the possibility of selecting among a "menu" of policy instruments for public involvement. A full inventory and a possible classification have been presented in the book. In fact, the action of policy-makers and public administrators will very likely rely on a combination of multiple instruments rather than a single one to pursue information, consultation and active participation. All procedural implementation instruments have shortcomings, as we tried to highlight (chapter 5). It follows that none of them, if taken alone, can be enough to ensure citizens' involvement in policy-making (Rowe & Frewer 2000). The pitfalls that exist for each instrument can be more easily overcome by relying on a mix of instruments rather than using a single participation method (Thomas 1995).

Therefore, an adequate strategy of public involvement consists of the combination of different instruments (Bobbio 2004), where each single tool becomes part of a "citizen's participatory toolbox" (Adams 2004). It is the complementary across different instruments that will solve the disadvantages existing for each one of them if used alone (Checkoway 1981; Kasymova & Schachter 2014). In the adoption of several instruments, the considerations on change and resources made in this chapter with regard to type of instrument and objective (Figure 8.1) can be taken into account. A gradual approach, based on different orders of change, could, for instance, be adopted.

Contextual adaptation vs. one-size-fits-all solutions

Decades of policy analysis have proven that policy solutions adopted and successful in one specific context at a given moment in time will not necessarily work in a different place or at a different moment. The same analytical framework that we adopted from Winter (1990; 2003; 2012a) takes into account the socio-economic context. Likewise, for the usage of policy instruments, a lot of their success will depend on place and time: an instrument useful here and now may lead to a failure in another place at another time.

Unlike principles (see chapter 4), practices cannot easily travel across space and time since they are context bound. As stated by Checkoway (1981: 578), participation practices 'operate in a political context and should be understood in this context'. On the same point, Rowe and Frewer (2000: 11) explain that 'the contextual/environmental factors will interact with method type, such that there will be no one universally effective method'. Therefore, the adaptation of the procedural implementation instruments discussed in the book to the cultural, social, political and economic features of a given national and local setting is an important pre-requisite for any effort of public involvement.

Formal power vs. informal influence

Public involvement needs to be enhanced at any degree, particularly as active participation of local communities (chapters 5 and 6). The legal recognition of the authority of local communities in RWM is not a common feature in all MSs. The principles of partnering and voluntarism have often been applied out of any legal reference, and based on the goodwill and discretionary power of national administrations. It is true that both formal and informal processes of public involvement have advantages and disadvantages (chapter 4). However, the absence of a legal reference for local communities' authority in RWM – for instance, in the form of a veto power in decision-making – represents an important concern for local communities (see Landström & Bergmans 2015).

Notwithstanding the validity of the argument that also channels of informal influence can benefit RWM, national policy design should integrate formal powers of local communities in the national laws ruling RWM. Without some degree of institutionalisation, the same use of the multiple instruments available can ensure better representativeness among publics, but does not guarantee *per se* that the local basis has a stronger impact on decision-making and public decisions. We have stressed that public involvement should not only be present in the process (of policy formulation and implementation) but also visible in the results (i.e. policy and administrative decisions).

Actual empowerment vs. rhetoric-reality gap

Public involvement suffers from a participation bias in favour of stronger interests (chapter 2). If citizens and local communities need to actively participate, their capacity must be built or strengthened with the help of national administrators. Not only opportunities for public involvement need to be foreseen in legislation or created out of legal frameworks. Adequate space and time must be provided in practice so that non-institutional stakeholders will be able to learn new roles in decision-making, build up their knowledge in RWM, examine possible choices and communicate with other constituencies. For instance, platforms for exchange could be developed both nationally and internationally with the aim of supporting social and local actors' capacity to participate in policy-making.

Furthermore, the capacity of the public and local communities needs to be enhanced through the use of multiple state resources (i.e. knowledge, money, authority and organisation). It is not sufficient to provide opportunities of being involved (written on paper). The formal acknowledgement of a social and local dimension in RWM needs to be followed by concrete actions and allocation of resources to empower public involvement in facts and rebalance the representation of weaker actors through multiple instruments. We defend a pragmatic approach to public involvement (chapter 2): we do not always need active participation since in some situations information and consultation are sufficient. However, in those cases where collaborative arrangements are the necessary solution, authority should be shared in favour of non-state actors and local communities to pursue a more balanced distribution of power. From the EU experience, it is not always evident that this shift of power has actually taken place and that collaborative arrangements are in place for key decisions.

Science–society communication vs. separated communities

The book has focused on the relations between policy-making and the multiple publics interested in or affected by RWM. Although it is not our focus, another type of relations is important when we want to elaborate policy recommendations in this domain. We have stressed the need for transparency in the formulation and implementation of national policies and suggested that regulators, implementers, operators and experts need to improve their communication. This leads to the broader problem of communication between science and society which has become crucial in a world where fake news is increasingly populating public and political debates.

Scientific and technological policy fields like nuclear energy have had problems in reaching out to laymen (chapter 1). The complexity of specific domains has to some extent motivated the use of a techno-scientific language that has ignored matters of content accessibility for the general public. The importance of conveying simple messages on complex contents has been touched upon in the book (chapter 3). The need for shortening the distances between nuclear science and the people deserves more emphasis and must be signalled as an important policy recommendation that is, actually, valid for many more sectors and for science as a whole. Science must engage with the public and clearly communicate its findings and their relevance. Any void left by science in society will be filled by irrational beliefs fed by false facts and fake news rather than factual evidence.

Indications for future research

Many aspects of public involvement in RWM have been investigated for the last two decades and the book has tried to bring together the insights developed by both scholarly research and practitioners' experience. A large amount of empirical material and analytical conceptualisations is available. Therefore, these indications for future research do not claim the need for further investigation on additional aspects of RWM and public involvement. They rather want to suggest alternative approaches to the study of the topic presented in this book and their utility to unveil specific features and dynamics.

The book has analysed the experience of public involvement in RWM across the 28 MSs that constitute the EU at the time of writing (2018). It has taken a regional perspective intentionally for the purpose of using a broad empirical basis without falling into national comparative assessments. Notwithstanding the validity of this regional approach, other research strategies can be taken to study public involvement in RWM the EU: single case studies, comparative analyses, longitudinal research, and investigation of unsuccessful cases.

The effects of procedural implementation instruments are largely impacted by the context where they are used. Therefore, it would be important to understand under which conditions a single instrument can be influential, rather than claiming that it is effective or not effective in general terms. Indeed, it is never a question of good or bad instrument but of when and how (Thomas 2012). As explained by Checkoway (1981: 578), '[r]esearch focusing on the quality of particular participation methods alone would contribute little without also analysing the larger context of which they are a part'.[3] National contexts and traditions cannot be neglected, and single case studies could investigate under which conditions a given policy instrument is effective (Rowe & Frewer 2000).

If we want to understand whether specific instruments work and under which conditions they do so, we could also rely on comparative research (Kasymova & Schachter 2014). Comparative studies could explore several independent variables in the attempt to answer important research questions, such as: Can the use of different procedural implementation instruments explain different processes and results across the EU? How can different structures of intergovernmental relations impact on implementation process and outcomes? Can the different status of implementing agencies (public bodies or industry-founded organisations) explain different processes and results?

Case studies could be conducted over a long time period. This would allow for longitudinal comparative analysis, which is particularly useful to understand institutional developments such as those happening in agency–community relations. Aldrich (2005) argues that political and policy research conducted on single cases over longer periods of time can lead to a more in-depth knowledge of the phenomenon under investigation. Particularly when public agencies rely on instruments to alter target groups' behaviours, the effect can become evident after years. Therefore, '[s]tudies investigating only a short period of time would overlook these important but often slow-moving processes of state–civil society interaction' (Aldrich 2005: 119).

Finally, single and comparative studies could focus on "bad" cases. According to Bardach (2012), practices should be studied both for why and how they succeed – i.e. "good (rather than best) practices" – and for what make them fail. More research in this direction would be useful for the study of public involvement in RWM.

Moving away from the disciplinary field of public policy and administration into the broader field of social sciences, it seems necessary to carry out research on the social and human dimensions of risk and safety in the nuclear energy field. Although this represents an important area of study, it is far from the political and institutional focus taken in the book.

Concluding remarks

With its focus on the institutional challenge of RWM, the book has investigated the topic of public involvement in this controversial area of policy-making. The regional perspective has unveiled to what extent the MSs of the EU are experiencing a shift from the government to the governance of RWM. Directive 2011/70/Euratom is relatively recent for any correct implementation analysis but, overall, RWM in the EU has experienced a radical change from its purely technical understanding to the inclusion of a social component in decision-making. National legal frameworks align with the call for transparency contained in the Waste Directive, and the right of public information and participation is generally acknowledged by the laws of MSs. Channels of information and consultation are available, although their institutionalisation varies across countries. Active participation lags, instead, somewhat behind when compared to lower degrees of public involvement; this weakens in particular the role of local communities in some national RWM systems.

It is important to understand how power is actually distributed or redistributed among the different actors involved in national RWM systems. International legal instruments such as the Aarhus Convention seem to empower civil society, local interests and NGOs to request the creation or enhancement of instruments of public information and participation. A salient point for the future of RWM is whether the Waste Directive will be able to play a similar role and steer MSs with such different policy-making traditions towards more public involvement. This will undoubtedly imply a redistribution of powers from state to non-state actors, and from national to local levels of governance, which will be more difficult in some national contexts than others. The contextual differences typical of the EU, under the common legal framework of the Directive on RWM, make it interesting to explore to what extent national differences and contextual factors influence RWM policy implementation and its opening to the involvement of societal and subnational actors.

Whether the Directive's framing of RWM will shape the potential for public participation in the EU's national systems remains to be seen. The importance of the social dimension and public involvement in RWM has been acknowledged quite recently and the risk of backlash cannot be completely excluded. Some MSs (e.g., Sweden, Finland and France) have selected a site for deep geological disposal (DGD) and are considered today as "leading countries" in RWM in Europe. In these countries that have succeeded with the biggest challenge of finding a site for repository of HLW, the interest in the social component of RWM and its governance might start to decrease. The danger is that the dominance of these leading countries no longer needing the social component may influence negatively other countries that are, though, far from having a site selected.

Notes

1 Institutionalisation is understood here as regular and formalised opportunities for public involvement (Thomas 1995).

2 I prefer to speak of components, rather than phases, of policy-making because policy design – unlike policy formulation and implementation – is not a phase in the policy cycle. In policy science, policy design is an "abstract concept" that is divorced from the actual process of policy-making (Howlett 2011). It is a combination of policy elements (as explained in chapter 2) and represents an important cluster of variables in the analytical framework adopted in this book.

3 It is important to retain here that the assessment of a specific process of involvement that may be the object of a case study needs to take into account the different views of the actors that have been involved in that specific process (Bobbio 2004).

References

Adams, B. (2004) "Public Meetings and the Democratic Process", in *Public Administration Review*, Vol. 64, No. 1, pp. 43–54.

Aldrich, D. P. (2005) "Controversial Project Siting. State Policy Instruments and Flexibility", in *Comparative Politics*, Vol. 38, No. 1, pp. 103–123.

Balla, S. J. (2005) "Between Commenting and Negotiation: The Contours of Public Participation in Agency Rulemaking", in *I/S: A Journal of Law and Policy*, Vol. 1, pp. 59–94.

Bardach, E. (2012) *A Practical Guide for Policy Analysis. The Eightfold Path to More Effective Problem Solving*, SAGE, London.

Beierle, T. C., and Cayford, J. (2002) *Democracy in Practice. Public Participation in Environmental Decisions*, Resources for the Future, Washington DC.

Bobbio, L. (2004) *A piu' voci – Amministrazioni pubbliche, imprese, associazioni e cittadini nei processi decisionali inclusivi*, Edizioni Scientifiche Italiane, Rome.

Checkoway, B. (1981) "The Politics of Public Hearings", in *The Journal of Applied Behavioural Science*, Vol. 17, No. 4, pp. 566–582.

Creighton, J. L. (2005) *The Public Participation Handbook. Making Better Decisions Through Citizen Involvement*, Jossey-Bass, San Francisco.

Ferraro, G. and Martell, M. (2015b) "Radioactive Waste Management and Public Participation in the EU. Lessons Learnt from the EURATOM Research Framework Programmes", in *International Journal of Nuclear Power*, Vol. 60, No. 12, pp. 708–713.

Gaventa, J. and Valderrama, C. (1999) "Participation, Citizenship and Local Governance", Background note prepared for a workshop on Strengthening Participation in Local Governance, 21–24 June, Institute of Development Studies.

Hall, P. (1993) "Policy Paradigms, Social Learning, and the State – The Case of Economic Policymaking in Britain", in *Comparative Politics*, Vol. 25, No. 3, pp. 275–296.

Hanf, K. and O'Toole, L. J. (1992) "Revisiting Old Friends: Networks, Implementation Structures and the Management of Inter-organizational Relations", in *European Journal of Political Research*, Vol. 21, pp. 163–180.

Howlett, M. (2000) "Managing the 'Hollow State': Procedural Policy Instruments and Modern Governance", in *Canadian Public Administration*, Vol. 43, No. 4, pp. 412–431.

Howlett, M. (2011) *Designing Public Policies. Principles and Instruments*, Routledge, Abingdon.

Howlett, M., Mukherjee, I. and Woo, J. J. (2015) "Thirty Years of Instrument Research: What Have We Learned and Where Are We Going", Paper Presented at the International Conference of Public Policy (ICPP), 3 July, Milan, Italy.

Howlett, M., Ramesh, M. and Perl, A. (2009). *Studying Public Policy – Policy Cycles and Policy Subsystems*, Oxford University Press, Oxford.

Kasymova, J. T. and Lauer Schachter, H. (2014) "Bringing Participatory Tools to a Different Level", in *Public Performance & Management Review*, Vol. 37, No. 3, pp. 441–464.

Landström, C. and Bergmans, A. (2015) "Long-term Repository Governance: A Socio-technical Challenge", in *Journal of Risk Analysis*, Vol. 18, No. 3, pp. 378–391.

NEA (2003) *Public Information, Consultation and Involvement in Radioactive Waste Management. An International Overview of Approaches and Experiences*, OECD, Paris.

OECD (2015) *Stakeholder Engagement for Inclusive Water Governance*, OECD, Paris.

OECD (2017b) *Policy Advisory Systems – Supporting Good Governance and Sound Public Decision Making*, OECD, Paris.

Pidgeon, N. (1998) "Risk Assessment, Risk Values and the Social Science Programme: Why We Do Need Risk Perception Research", in *Reliability Engineering and System Safety*, Vol. 59, pp. 5–15.

Rowe, G. and Frewer, L. J. (2000), "Public Participation Methods: A Framework for Evaluation", in *Science, Technology, & Human Values*, Vol. 25, No. 1, pp. 3–29.

Sundqvist, G. and Elam, M. (2010) "Public Involvement Designed to Circumvent Public Concern? The 'Participatory Turn' in European Nuclear Activities", in *Risk, Hazards & Crisis in Public Policy*, Vol. 1, No. 4, pp. 203–229.

Thomas, J. C. (1995) *Public Participation in Public Decisions: New Skills and Strategies for Public Managers*, Jossey-Bass, San Francisco.

Thomas, J. C. (2012) *Citizen, Customer, Partner: Engaging the Public in Public Management*, Routledge, Abingdon and New York.

UNECE (1998) *Convention on Access to Information, Public Participation in Decision-Making and Access to Justice in Environmental Matters*, Aarhus

Winter, S. (1990) "Integrating Implementation Research", in Palumbo, D. J. and Calista, D. (Eds) *Implementation and the Policy Process – Opening Up the Black Box*, Greenwood Press, New York, Westport, CT and London.

Winter, S. (2003) "Introduction", in Peters, B. G. and Pierre, J. (Eds) *Handbook of Public Administration*, SAGE Publications, London, Thousand Oaks and Delhi.

Winter, S. (2012a), "Implementation", in Peters, B. G. and Pierre, J. (Eds), *Handbook of Public Policy*, Sage Publications, London.

Conclusions

The growing complexity of public problems has increasingly demanded for the engagement of societal interests in government decisions and administrative actions. Contemporary public policies have become, thus, the result of interactions between public authorities and citizens. This general trend presents, though, some variation across countries, policy areas and issues. The book has tried to shed some light on the topic of public involvement (mainly during policy implementation) by looking at the management of radioactive waste (RW) in the European Union (EU).

The book concludes with some reflections on the major findings of this research and their validity beyond the domain of RWM, nuclear energy and energy policy. The nuclear field has sectoral specificities, which we have thoroughly discussed (e.g., the hazardous nature of waste, a polarised socio-political context around the use of nuclear energy and the endeavour of deep geological disposal). However, nuclear energy policy is strongly linked with land use, namely for power plant siting and RWM: '[r]esistance to nuclear siting decisions is part of a larger public resistance to locational decisions about a wide variety of noxious facilities' (Pasqualetti & Pijawka 1996: 63). Therefore, some of the insights developed about RWM can be generalised to other hazardous facilities and – more broadly – to contested infrastructures and controversial land uses that a society may need but local communities are reluctant to host (Weingart 2007). Conflictual situations and the consequent salience of public involvement extend even beyond the use of the land to the use of the sea, the governance of water and many more environmental matters (Bollens 1993).

The chapter generalises insights on public involvement derived from the field of RWM to other land uses and environmental matters. It takes a final look at public involvement and emphasises its strong ties with politics, particularly when it takes place during policy implementation. Public involvement interrelates, indeed, with aspects that are at the core of politics, namely the resolution of conflicts, the distribution of power, and democracy.

Public involvement and conflict resolution

Environmental decision-making triggers demands from several fronts that are often competing over objectives, interests and values (Reed 2008). It also struggles between including scientific knowledge and technical expertise, on the one hand, and engaging citizens, on the other. Finally, it is often affected by clashes between national policy objectives, and local priorities and concerns. These competing perspectives that enter environmental decision-making often result in an escalation of conflicts over governmental decisions (Senecah 2004). The management of these conflicts remains a central problem of politics (Schattschneider 1960); indeed, politics is made of conflicts, either manifest and explicit, or potential and hidden (Bobbio 2004).

Public involvement has emerged as a possible way to solve conflictual situations among the actors concerned by a policy issue. Because environmental decisions impact on a broad spectrum of interests, multiple actors should be included in policy-making on environmental matters. In particular, controversial land uses (such as the ones for contested infrastructures) can only be realised if the complex set of interests affected is involved in the definition of the problem and the search for a *socio-technical* solution. The book has presented a set of complementary policy instruments for developing and enhancing public involvement. We still need more efforts, though, to understand which instrument or, rather, combination of instruments better suit a specific policy issue in a particular context at a given time (on this point see also Irvin & Stansbury 2004).

The book has also stressed that the use of these instruments can improve the inter-organisational relations that shape the implementation process because a strong connection exists between public involvement, trust and social acceptance. Beyond the domain of RWM, national laws ruling land uses and, more broadly, the environmental field have increasingly tried to rebuild trust in governments through the inclusion of requirements for public involvement in policy design (Weingart 2007). Indeed, rebuilding trust is not only important for RWM. It has been identified as a need common to many policy areas and constitutes an important variable for all those controversial uses of the land that have a long history of distrust and social opposition towards project developers and regulators (Lehtonen 2014).

Similarly to what we have seen for RWM, feelings of familiarity and control with hazardous facilities (deriving from public involvement) are also likely to improve people's perception of risk. Therefore, new institutional approaches to hazardous facilities (and, more broadly, other contested infrastructures and controversial uses of the land) need to take a collaborative nature. This will allow decision-making to take into account the "strong intermingling of social and technical issues" that exists, for instance, in facility siting (Kasperson 2005). Collaborative arrangements must integrate scientific and technical considerations, on the one hand, and societal concerns and public engagement, on the other. The resulting policy-making will, thus, be able to develop public policies that are both informed and participated; this is crucial in environmental matters and in decisions that deal with risk (Creighton 2005).

Among the categories of stakeholders involved in policy implementation, the book has stressed the salience of local communities. The local dimension of governmental decisions and actions is particularly important not only in RWM but also in land use and environmental governance in general (Bollens 1993).

Indeed, local opposition to unwanted land uses has caused policy failures, particularly when national policies imply locational decisions such as those taken for siting and developing RWM facilities and other contested infrastructures. The engagement of local communities in the formulation and, more importantly, in the implementation of public policies – when conflicts become more manifest – is pivotal for many national policies entailing contested infrastructures and hazardous facilities. The assumption of a selfish behaviour (under the NIMBY syndrome) is not enough and not always adequate to explain local opposition.

In intergovernmental relations, what counts is the distribution, balance and change over time of the power between central policy- and decision-makers, and local governments. How the power balance (or unbalance) between the central and local level is pursued and realised through the engagement of local communities strongly influences citizens' acceptance of policies, programmes and projects (Bollens 1993).

Public involvement and power (re)distribution

Governments face a growing amount of complex public issues that call for new allocation of responsibilities among state and non-state actors, and higher degrees of engagement of citizens and other stakeholders. Citizens' engagement in policy-making has been debated for long time in the Western world. Both practitioners – from multiple policy areas at different levels of government – and scholars – particularly from the discipline of political science and public administration – have promoted public involvement. However, the general call for a shift away from the decide–announce–defend (DAD) approach to decision-making (see Introduction) has not been fully put into practice in many environmental policy decisions. Many countries, even within the EU, still need to take important steps towards a new paradigm in policy-making based on interaction, cooperation and engagement. As put by Aldrich (2005: 118),

> Bureaucracies often adopted the language of transparency, deliberative democracy, and popular sovereignty in public relations campaigns but generally did not live up to these lofty concepts. Despite their rhetoric, state agencies have not ceded procedural control to citizens, but rather often seek to mollify concerns about their "nondemocratic procedures" through symbolic gestures toward accountability and improved public participation.

It often remains unclear how to design institutional and legal frameworks that actually allow for citizens' and other stakeholders' input in policy-making. In particular, more clarity is needed with regard to why, when, how, and with whom to engage (Adams 2004; Blomgren Bingham *et al.* 2005; McDaniels *et al.* 1999; Rowe & Frewer 2000). Without these clarifications, the call for public involvement may remain purely rhetorical and nothing more than a "commitment in principle" (Lee *et al.* 2013). The book has tried to provide answers to these questions by looking at public involvement in RWM in the EU (see chapter 8). These answers also provide suggestions for creating actual opportunities of information and participation for the concerned citizens and other stakeholders. In particular, we have argued that formal authority needs to be shared to a greater extent.

Policy-making involves and reflects power relations that are present in society; these relations shape public policies. In practice, power no longer lies in one state actor only, but is increasingly dispersed; the result is that even non-state actors can obstruct a policy intervention (Börzel 1997; Lehtonen 2015). This actual reallocation of authority, though, still needs to be acknowledged in the policy design of many national environmental policies through a formal recognition of more power to societal and local interests (Reed 2008). The institutionalisation of public involvement would, thus, formalise changes in the distribution of power among the state and non-state actors that have already taken place in real political life. In the absence of such changes in policy design, a "participation gap" in environmental policy-making will continue to exist, i.e. 'a gap between citizen expectations and their actual ability to contribute to decisions' (Fiorino 1996, quoted in Duffield Hamilton 2004: 60).

To sum up, multiple procedural implementation instruments are available for state organisations willing to involve more publics. In particular, policy instruments for active participation imply a redistribution of authority between state and non-state actors at a central and local level. The decision-making power remains in the hands of the authority designated by national laws, but it is exercised by taking into account the input coming from stakeholders (Bobbio 2004). However, public involvement can easily confirm existing patterns of power relations rather than changing them through the exclusion of some publics to the advantage of those who usually dominate public debates (Reed 2008). What remains to be seen is whether active participation implies a new formal division of roles as well as an actual change in the exercise of power between policy-makers and citizens (Michels & De Graaf 2010).

Public involvement and democracy

The topic of public involvement links to a broader debate about the relationship between representative democracy and participative democracy. Representative democracy has its core moment in elections and lies on a more vertical accountability structure where the elected representatives decide. This type of democracy has been questioned in recent years; indeed a general malaise afflicts representative democracy in the Western world (Wilson 1999). The decreasing voter turnout at national and local elections, the increasing electoral volatility and the consequent decline of the representation function of political parties have started a vivid debate on the legitimacy of representative democracy. In the context of growing apathy of the electorate to party politics, the right to vote in general elections (on which representative democracies are based) can no longer be considered the only expression of democratic life (Wilson 1999).

Additional forms of citizens' participation have, thus, been demanded, particularly when important decisions are taken by public agencies that are not elected (see chapter 2). As claimed by Wilson (1999: 247), '[r]epresentative democracy [...] needs to be supplemented by participatory democracy'. Participative democracy takes place through policy networks (and a governance turn) that include stakeholders in policy-making (Michels & De Graaf 2010; Klijn & Koppenjan 2012). However, public involvement does not *per se* change any power relationship unless several conditions (e.g., commitment, resources and institutionalisation) are ensured (see chapter 8). Moreover, we have argued, public involvement is an important instrument in contemporary society and essential in public policy-making, 'though neither for all matters nor always to the same extent' (Thomas 1995: 2).

Indeed, public involvement is not free from costs and difficulties that can jeopardise its usefulness. The idea (or hope) that public involvement would make the world a better place has proven to be "a little naïve and unreflective" (Lee et al. 2013). Public involvement is certainly beneficial, but its advantages might take some time to be visible. By contrast, its costs are certain and immediate (for instance in terms of money and time). Public involvement implies a series of trade-offs that need to be taken into account when policy-making is opened up to the participation of citizens and other stakeholders: majority rule vs. minority rights (particularly when minorities are vociferous), state power vs. local autonomy, expeditious decision-making vs. responsive citizen participation, economic efficiency vs. broader social responsibilities, etc. (Armour 1991).

Notwithstanding the costs and trade-offs that public involvement brings along, its importance is generally acknowledged as this book has attempted to show. The interface between the two types of democratic forms, where participative decision-making takes place inside the system of representative democracy, should be the topic for further investigation (Klijn 2006; Klijn & Koppenjan 2012). Participative democracy does not represent an alternative to representative democracy, but can play an important complementary role: both, together, can enhance democracy.

References

Adams, B. (2004) "Public Meetings and the Democratic Process", in *Public Administration Review*, Vol. 64, No. 1, pp. 43–54.

Aldrich, D. P. (2005) "Controversial Project Siting. State Policy Instruments and Flexibility", in *Comparative Politics*, Vol. 38, No. 1, pp. 103–123.

Armour, A. M. (1991) *The Siting of Locally Unwanted Land Uses: Towards a Cooperative Approach*, Pergamon Press, Oxford.

Blomgren Bingham, L., Nabatchi. T. and O'Leary, R. (2005) "The New Governance: Practices and Processes for Stakeholder and Citizen Participation in the Work of Government", in *Public Administration Review*, Vol. 65, No. 5, pp. 547–558.

Bobbio, L. (2004) *A piu' voci – Amministrazioni pubbliche, imprese, associazioni e cittadini nei processi decisionali inclusivi*, Edizioni Scientifiche Italiane, Rome.

Bollens, S. A. (1993) "Restructuring Land Use Governance", in *Journal of Planning Literature*, Vol. 7, No. 3, pp. 211–226.

Börzel, T. A. (1997) "What's So Special About Policy Networks? – An Exploration of the Concept and Its Usefulness in Studying European Governance", in *European Integration Online Papers*, Vol. 1, No. 16.

Creighton, J. L. (2005) *The Public Participation Handbook. Making Better Decisions Through Citizen Involvement*, Jossey-Bass, San Francisco.

Duffield Hamilton, J. (2004) "Competing and Converging Values of Public Participation: A Case Study of Participant Views in Department of Energy Nuclear Weapons Cleanup", in Depoe, S. P., Delicath, J. W. and Aepli Elsenbeer, M.-F. (Eds.) *Communication and Public Participation in Environmental Decision Making*, State University of New York Press, New York.

Irvin, R. A. and Stansbury, J. (2004) "Citizen Participation in Decision Making: Is It Worth the Effort?", in *Public Administration Review*, Vol. 64, No. 1, pp. 55–65.

Kasperson, R. E. (2005) "Siting Hazardous Facilities: searching for Effective Institutions and Processes", in Hayden Lesbirel, S. and Shaw, D. (Eds.) *Managing Conflict in Facility Siting*, Cheltenham and Northampton: Edward Elgar.

Klijn, E.-H. (2006) "Managing Stakeholder Involvement in Decision-Making. A Comparative Analysis of Six Interactive Processes in The Netherlands", Paper presented at the Conference on Governance and Performance: Organizational Status, Management Capacity and Public Service, 15–16 March, Birmingham.

Klijn, E.-H. and Koppenjan, J. F. M. (2012) "Governance Network Theory: Past, Present and Future", in *Policy and Politics*, Vol. 40, No. 4, pp. 587–606.

Lee, M., Armeni, C., de Cendra, J., Chaytor, S., Lock, S., Maslin, M., Redgwell, C. and Rydin, Y. (2013) "Public Participation and Climate Change Infrastructure", in *Journal of Environmental Law*, Vol. 25, No. 1, pp. 33–62.

Lehtonen, M. (2014) "Evaluating Megaprojects: From the 'Iron Triangle' to Network Mapping", in *Evaluation*, Vol. 20, No. 3, pp. 278–295.

Lehtonen, M. (2015), "Megaproject Underway. Governance of Nuclear Waste Management in France", in Brunnengräber, A., Di Nucci. M. R., Isidoro Losada, A. M., Mez, L. and Schreurs, M. (Eds) *Nuclear Waste Governance – An International Comparison*, Springer.

McDaniels, T. L., Gregory, R. S. and Fields, D. (1999) "Democratizing Risk Management: Successful Public Involvement in Local Water Management Decisions", in *Risk Analysis*, Vol. 19, No. 3, pp. 497–510.

Michels, A. and De Graaf, L. (2010) "Examining Citizen Participation: Local Participatory Policy Making and Democracy", in *Local Government Studies*, Vol. 36, No. 4, pp. 477–491.

Pasqualetti, M. J. and Pijawka, K. D. (1996) "Unsiting Nuclear Power Plants: Decommissioning Risks and Their Land Use Context", in *Professional Geographer*, 48(1): 57–69.

Reed, M. S. (2008) "Stakeholder Participation for Environmental Management: A Literature Review", in *Biological Conservation*, Vol. 141, pp. 2417–2431.

Rowe, G. and Frewer, L. J. (2000), "Public Participation Methods: A Framework for Evaluation", in *Science, Technology, & Human Values*, Vol. 25 No. 1, pp. 3–29.

Schattschneider, S. S. (1960) *The Semi-Sovereign People: A Realist's View of Democracy*, Holt, Rinehart and Winston, New York.

Senecah, S. L. (2004) "The Trinity of Voice: The Role of Practical Theory in Planning and Evaluating the Effectiveness of Environmental Participatory Processes", in Depoe, S. P., Delicath, J. W. and Aepli Elsenbeer, M.-F. (eds.) *Communication and Public*

Participation in Environmental Decision Making, State University of New York Press, New York.

Thomas, J. C. (1995) *Public Participation in Public Decisions: New Skills and Strategies for Public Managers*, Jossey-Bass, San Francisco.

Weingart, J. (2007) *Waste Is A Terrible Thing To Mind*, Rivergate Books, New Brunswick, NJ.

Wilson, D. (1999) "Exploring the Limits of Public Participation in Local Government", in *Parliamentary Affairs*, Vol. 52, No. 2, pp. 246–259.

Index

Aarhus Convention 6–7, 32, 42, 98–100, 170
access to information *see* information
accountability 48, 105, 141–3, 149, 154, 175–6
active participation 42–3, 88–9, 109–10, 115, 126, 144
administrative decision–making 2, 47–8; *see also* policy implementation
advisory body 52, 111, 115, 126, 161
associations: of civil society 59, 66, 119, 163; of local communities 110, 126, 130
authority: as regulatory body *see* regulatory authority; as resource 50–2, 88, 93, 127, 161, 176; *see also* resources

citizens 21, 41–3, 82, 122, 139–40, 163
civil society 59, 63–6, 86–7, 147, 157, 163
collaborative arrangements *see* active participation
communication 21–2, 64, 129–30, 155, 164–5, 168; *see also* dialogue
community benefits 87–8, 147
complexity 1–2, 28, 31, 81, 154, 168
confidence 63, 140; *see also* trust
conflicts 4–5, 28–9, 45, 81, 120–1, 142, 173–5
consultation: as degree of public involvement 5–8, 42–4, 105–9, 126, 131, 146; *see also* public consultation

decommissioning 2, 25
Deep Geological Disposal 26–8, 110, 120, 126, 129, 170
delegated legislation 2, 47–8, 154
democracy 1, 45, 109, 122, 154, 176–7
dialogue 70–2, 85–6, 88–91, 129–31, 165; *see also* communication
disposal (of radioactive waste) 25–6, 29, 62

energy mix 24, 66, 157, 165
environmental governance 3, 6, 174; *see also* governance
Environmental Impact Assessment 7–8, 69, 107–8, 115, 128, 131
environmental policy 1–3, 6, 175–6
Espoo Convention 6–8, 108
Euratom Treaty 32, 77
European Union 2, 5–7, 11, 20–1, 23–5, 30–3, 101–2
experts 5–6, 30, 45, 62–4, 70–2, 124–5, 145–7, 163–5

facilities: hazardous 4–5, 62–3, 87, 121, 146, 174–5; for radioactive waste management 29, 62, 68, 102, 120, 146–9
facility siting 89, 112, 120, 128–9, 164, 173–5
flexibility *see* stepwise approach
funds *see* money

governance 1, 39, 50–1, 122, 139, 169

hazard 14n4
hazardous facilities *see* facilities

Joint Convention 31

knowledge 45, 51–2, 86, 115, 124–5, 146, 159

IAEA 19, 31, 130

implementation process 49–53, 87–8, 113, 118–9, 158; *see also* policy implementation
implementing agency (or implementer) 59–60, 82, 88–9, 102, 119, 143
information: as degree of public involvement 32, 42–4, 61–4, 92, 101–2, 123–5; as right of (access to) 7, 52, 99–102, 157, 159, 169; as resource *see* knowledge; *see also* resources
infrastructures, contested 121, 174–5; *see also* locally unwanted land uses
instruments *see* policy instruments
interest groups 41, 45, 66, 107
intergovernmental relations 51, 112, 122, 129–30, 164, 175
inter–organisational relations 49–51, 87, 121, 139, 158, 164

legitimacy 45, 48, 51, 88, 111, 128
local committee 110, 115, 126–7
local community 4–5, 29–30, 86–9, 112, 118–122, 164
local level *see* local community
Locally Unwanted Land Uses (LULUs) 4–5, 121, 155, 164
local partnership *see* partnering

media 22–3, 104
money 46, 51–2, 67–8, 86–7, 115, 131, 159–161; *see also* resources

national legislation 47, 85, 99–100
National Programme 98, 103, 107–8, 110, 113, 126
NEA 137
NGOs 40–1, 60, 67, 108, 119, 161
NIMBY syndrome 120–1
nuclear energy 18–21, 23–4, 29, 82, 155, 165

openness *see* transparency
opposition *see* conflicts
order of change 162
organisation (as resource) 52, 86, 162; *see also* resources
ownership 146–7

partnering 43, 88–9, 109–10, 115, 126, 58, 166
partnership approach *see* partnering
perception (of risk) 92, 121, 174; *see also* risk
policy design 49–51, 83–4, 113, 133, 157, 167, 176
policy formulation 49–50, 80–1, 113, 156–7, 167, 176
policy implementation 1, 47–51, 53, 87, 93, 158
policy instruments (or tools) 51–2, 85, 157–8, 165–6
policy networks 50–2, 90–1, 119, 159, 163–4, 177
politics 53
power 50–1, 86–8, 93, 161, 166–7, 175–6
procedural implementation instruments *see* policy instruments
public consultation: 7–8, 107–8, 128, 161; *see also* consultation
public hearing 107–9
public involvement: 1–3, 30, 39–41; benefits of 44–6; costs of 46–7
public participation *see* public involvement
public policy 1, 39–40, 47–8, 50, 173–4
public, the 41, 43, 164

radiation 18–9, 22, 25, 29, 63
radiation protection 77, 99–101, 115, 117
radioactive waste 2, 20–2, 24–5, 29
radioactive waste management 2, 5–6, 28–9, 32–3, 77
radioactivity 18–9, 62–3, 71, 155
regulator *see* regulatory authority
regulatory authority (or body) 27–8, 33, 59–60, 72, 102, 130–1
repository *see* disposal
representation 46, 67, 69–70, 88, 126–8, 163–4, 176
resources 67, 81, 86, 115, 131
right of (access to) information *see* information
risk 4–5, 14n4, 22, 27–9, 61–4, 82, 145–7, 155–7

safety: nuclear 19–24, 31–2, 61–3, 77, 82, 146–7, 155
science *see* experts
security: energy 20, 23–4; nuclear 26, 33, 64, 77, 102, 159
siting *see* facility siting
social acceptance 4, 24, 27, 45, 120, 147–8, 155
social learning 141–2
societal control 89, 146–7, 155
spent fuel 2, 24–5, 31, 98, 102–3, 115

stakeholders 41, 59–61, 69–70, 119, 127–8, 163
stepwise approach 27, 89, 142, 154
storage (of radioactive waste) 25, 62, 120
Strategic Environmental Assessment 6–8, 107, 115, 162

time 46, 67–9, 90, 127
transparency 31–3, 40–1, 64, 98–100, 138, 175; *see also* public involvement
trust 21–2, 45, 70–2, 90–1, 130, 139–40, 155; *see also* confidence

uncertainty 2, 28, 70–71

values: in society 3, 29–30, 40–1, 44–6, 63, 70, 81–2, 154–7; organisational 144–5
veto power: 30, 89, 112, 127, 158, 161, 167
voluntarism 5, 88–9, 109, 112, 126–7, 146
voluntary approach *see* voluntarism

Waste Directive 2, 24, 32, 98, 113, 153, 169–70
Waste Management Organisation *see* implementing agency
wicked problem 28–31, 121, 129, 142, 154

For Product Safety Concerns and Information please contact our EU representative GPSR@taylorandfrancis.com Taylor & Francis Verlag GmbH, Kaufingerstraße 24, 80331 München, Germany

Printed and bound by CPI Group (UK) Ltd, Croydon, CR0 4YY
01/05/2025
01858430-0001